TAOISM

TAOISM

*The Parting
of the Way*

Revised Edition

BY HOLMES WELCH

Frontispiece: Ta Ssu-ming, the Great Director of Destinies, who is the oldest Taoist divinity and is still worshipped under the name of the Kitchen God. Originally attributed to Chao Meng-fu, but more recent studies indicate that it is Ming.

First published by the Beacon Press in 1957
First published as a Beacon Paperback in February 1966
Beacon Press books are published under the auspices
of the Unitarian Universalist Association
Printed in the United States of America

International Standard Book Number: 0–8070–5973–0

19   18   17   16   15   14   13   12   11

Contents

Acknowledgements

Permission was kindly given by the publishers to quote from the following:

George Allen & Unwin Ltd.
  Arthur Waley, *The Way and Its Power*, 1933
Cambridge University Press
  Joseph Needham, *Science and Civilisation in China*, 1956
Harper & Brothers
  Kirsopp Lake, *Introduction to the New Testament*, 1937
  Aldous Huxley, *Doors of Perception*, 1954
Houghton Mifflin Company
  Henry Adams, *The Education of Henry Adams*, 1918
  Ruth Benedict, *Patterns of Culture*, 1934
The Macmillan Company
  F. C. S. Northrop, *Meeting of East and West*, 1946
The *New Yorker*
  New Yorker, November 14, 1953
Princeton University Press
  Fung Yu-lan, *A History of Chinese Philosophy*, 1937, 1953
Arthur Probathain
  J. J. L. Duyvendak, *The Book of Lord Shang*, 1928
Random House
  Lin Yutang, *The Wisdom of China and India*, 1942
Routledge & Kegan Paul
  Arthur Waley, *Travels of an Alchemist*, 1931
Simon & Schuster
  Edward R. Murrow, *This I Believe*, 1952
  William H. Whyte, *Is Anybody Listening?*, 1952
The University of Chicago Press
  H. G. Creel, *Chinese Thought*, 1953

Foreword

This book is not intended to be a contribution to Sinology, but to public understanding of the Chinese point of view, one component of which is Taoism. It is written in four parts. The first explains a fact which some translators have concealed from their readers: that neither they nor anyone else can be sure what Lao Tzu was talking about. Part Two explains what *I* think he was talking about. Part Three takes up the vast and curious movement which claimed him as its founder. Part Four tests his teachings on the problems of today. The third part — on the Taoist movement — must be read with particular caution. The subject is infinitely complicated; the information is difficult to get at; and mistakes are easy to make.

The reader may be disappointed to find that this volume does not include a complete translation of Lao Tzu. Since we already have thirty-six in English, it hardly seemed necessary. The fact is that no translation can be satisfactory in itself because no translation can be as ambiguous as the Chinese original. However, because I have taken an analytical approach, I owe an apology to Lao Tzu. He believed that many of his most important ideas could not be put into words. That is why he so often sounds ambiguous. I shall attempt to express them unequivocally and directly, which is at best presumptuous. Lao Tzu's teaching methods were intuitive. He put a low price on system and formal logic. I shall attempt to give his philosophy a logical and systematic form, demonstrating that I have not learned one of the lessons Lao Tzu teaches, that "the good man does not prove by argument."

I want to thank the following persons for the help they have given me in preparing this book: Chang Hsin-pao, Henry D. Burnham, Mrs. Arland Parsons, William Hung, James R. Hightower, Kenneth Ch'en, Ch'ü T'ung-tsu, and Arthur Waley.

Stowe, Vermont   HOLMES WELCH
March, 1957

Foreword to This Edition

Since there is still no convenient synopsis of the various aspects of Taoism written in English, the present volume is being reissued. I have not attempted to update or revise it completely, but only to make changes that seemed important and typographically possible and to eliminate certain superfluities.

HOLMES WELCH

Cambridge, Massachusetts
December, 1965

TAOISM

Part One: THE PROBLEM OF LAO TZU

As to the Sage, no one will know whether he existed or not.—LAO TZU

There is a legend that on the fourteenth of September, 604 B.C., in the village of Ch'ü Jen in the county of K'u and the Kingdom of Ch'u, a woman, leaning against a plum tree, gave birth to a child. Since this child was to be a great man—a god, no less—the circumstances of his birth were out of the ordinary. He had been conceived some sixty-two years before when his mother had admired a falling star, and after so many years in the womb, he was able to speak as soon as he was born. Pointing to the plum tree, he announced: "I take my surname from this tree." To Plum (Li) he prefixed Ear (Erh)—his being large—and so became Li Erh. However, since his hair was already snow-white, most people called him Lao Tzu, or Old Boy. After he died they called him Lao Tan, "Tan" meaning "long-lobed."

About his youth little is told. We learn, however, that he spent his later years in the Chinese Imperial capital at Loyang, first as Palace Secretary and then as Keeper of the Archives for the Court of Chou. Evidently he married, for he had a son, Tsung, who became a successful soldier under the Wei and through whom later generations, like the T'ang emperors, traced their descent from Lao Tzu.

Though he made no effort to start a school, people came of their own accord to become his disciples. Confucius, who was some fifty-three years his junior, had one or perhaps several meetings with him and does not appear to have given too good an account of himself. In 517 B.C. Lao Tzu closed their meeting by saying: "I have heard it said that a clever merchant, though possessed of great hoards of wealth, will act as though his coffers were empty: and that the princely man, though of perfect moral excellence, maintains the air of a simpleton. Abandon your arrogant ways and countless desires, your suave demeanour and unbridled ambition, for they do not promote your welfare. That is all I have to say to you." At which Confucius went away, shaking his head, and said to his disciples: "I understand how birds can fly, how fishes can swim, and how four-footed beasts can run. Those than run can be snared, those that swim may be caught with

1

hook and line, those that fly may be shot with arrows. But when it comes to the dragon, I am unable to conceive how he can soar into the sky riding upon the wind and clouds. Today I have seen Lao Tzu and can only liken him to a dragon."

At the age of 160 Lao Tzu grew disgusted with the decay of the Chou dynasty[1] and resolved to pursue virtue in a more congenial atmosphere. Riding in a chariot drawn by a black ox, he left the Middle Kingdom through the Han-ku Pass which leads westward from Loyang. The Keeper of the Pass, Yin Hsi, who, from the state of the weather, had expected a sage, addressed him as follows: "You are about to withdraw yourself from sight. I pray you to compose a book for me." Lao Tzu thereupon wrote the 5,000 characters which we call the *Tao Te Ching*.[2] After completing the book, he departed for the west. We do not know when or where he died. But a last glimpse is given us in a late source, influenced by Buddhism, which describes his first three nights in the mountains beyond the pass. Lying under a mulberry tree he was tempted by the Evil One and by beautiful women. Lao Tzu did not find it hard to resist temptation, however, since to him the beautiful women were only "so many skin-bags full of blood."

The biography I have just given does not represent a consensus of all our sources. Actually, there can be no such consensus because different sources tell different stories. Possibly Lao Tzu was born not in 604 B.C., but in 571 B.C.; not in Ch'u, but in Ch'en. He may have spent not 62, but 81 years in his mother's womb and departed for the west at the age of 200, not 160. Possibly he was not even a contemporary of Confucius, but identical with Lao Tan, a Keeper of the Archives who we know held office at the court of Chou about 374 B.C.; or, on the other hand, he may be identical with one Lao Lai Tzu who figures in stories about Confucius and wrote a book (which has not survived) in

---

[1] See Appendix II for table of dynasties.

[2] *Tao* (pronounced *dow* as in dowel) means "way"; *te* (pronounced *dir* as in dirty) means "virtue" in the sense of "power"; *ching* (pronounced *jing* as in "jingo") means "classic." *Tao Te Ching* means, therefore, "The Classic of the Way and the Power." As to the pronunciation of Lao Tzu, the *lou* in louse is close to "Lao." To approximate "Tzu," say *adz* without the "a," and prolong the resulting buzzing sound enough to make it a separate syllable. In the Wade-Giles system of transliteration from Chinese to English, consonants are unaspirated unless they are followed by an apostrophe. Thus "ta" is pronounced *da*, but "t'a" *ta*; "ching" is pronounced *jing*, but "ch'ing" *ching*.

fifteen chapters on the practices of the Taoist schools. Finally, it is possible that Lao Tzu never existed at all and that both the *Tao Te Ching* and its putative author are composites of various teachings and teachers. This is the opinion of some contemporary scholars.

It is my own opinion that, except for a few interpolations, the book was written by one man.[3] But I would agree that we know nothing about him. All we have are legends, most of which may have been incorrectly attached to his name, while his name may have been incorrectly attached to the book which bears it. The great historian, Ssu-ma Ch'ien, who attempted the first biographical sketch of Lao Tzu about 100 B.C., ends it by throwing up his hands in despair. His source material was certainly more complete and 2,000 years fresher than what we have to work with today. I do not think we shall ever succeed where Ssu-ma Ch'ien failed, unless, of course, archaeology provides new data. We shall never, that is, be able to write a life of the author of the *Tao Te Ching*.

Is this a great loss? I think not. The important thing about the book is not its author, but its ideas. One of its ideas is the value of anonymity, which is expressed in the line (somewhat freely translated) that heads this chapter. The book really had to be anonymous. That may be why it mentions no dates, no places, no persons, no events.

Though Sinologists cannot say who wrote the book, they have more to go on when it comes to deciding when it was written. Arthur Waley assigns it to about 240 B.C., on the basis of its vocabulary, grammar, and rhyme structure and because he believes that the ideas which it attacks were not current until this period. Mr. Waley is joined by many contemporary scholars. On the other hand Bernard Karlgren and Henri Maspero place it towards the beginning of the fourth century, while Hu Shih and Lin Yutang adhere to the traditional sixth-century date. Lin Yutang decries the textual critics who are "merely aping a fashion that has by now become very tiresome."

Authorship in China is obscured by the fact that the earlier the traditional author, the later the book may have been written. In China the man with a new idea knew that it had little chance of being accepted if he presented it under his own name. So he or his disciples would "discover" a book about it by some ancient worthy. As time

[3] See Appendix I.

passed, the more historical of the ancient worthies began to be used up and innovators had to draw on names increasingly legendary. This explains why a man of the sixth century B.C. could be the author of a book belonging to the fourth or third.

One thing we know: we have a book. Some person or persons wrote it. It is convenient to call that person or persons Lao Tzu, and in the following pages I shall do so. Furthermore, in using the words "Taoist" and "Taoism" I shall refer to the doctrines of the *Tao Te Ching* alone, not to those of Chuang Tzu or Lieh Tzu, who also taught what they considered Taoism, and certainly not to the doctrines of the later Taoist movement. These will be treated in a separate chapter.

No other book except the Bible has been translated into English as often as Lao Tzu's. Here is a list of translations, with the cities and years in which they were first published:

John Chalmers, London, 1868
Frederick Henry Balfour, London, 1884 (in his *Taoist Texts*)
James Legge, London, 1891
Walter R. Old, Madras, 1894
Gen. G. G. Alexander, 1895 (no place of publication indicated)
Paul Carus, Chicago, 1898
Thomas W. Kingsmill, Shanghai, 1899
L. W. Heysinger, Philadelphia, 1903
Walter Gorn Old, Philadelphia, 1904
Lionel Giles, London, 1905
E. H. Parker, London, 1905 (in his *China and Religion*)
G. Evans, 1905
C. Spurgeon Medhurst, Chicago, 1905
Isabella Mears, Glasgow, 1916
Dwight Goddard, New York, 1919
Shrine of Wisdom, Fintry, Brook (near Godalming), Surrey, 1924
Wu-wu-tzu (i.e., Dryden Linsley Phelps & Shei Ching-shan), Cheng-tu, 1926
Theosophical Press, Chicago, 1926
Arthur Waley, London, 1934
Bhikshu Wai Tao and Dwight Goddard, Santa Barbara, California, 1935
A. L. Kitelsman II, Palo Alto, California, 1936
Hu Tse-ling, Cheng-tu, 1936
Dirk Bodde, Peiping, 1937 (incomplete: in his translation of Fung Yu-lan's *History of Chinese Philosophy*)

Ch'u Ta-kao, London, 1937

Sum Nung Au-Young, New York, 1938

John C. H. Wu, 1939-40 (in *T'ien Hsia Monthly,* Vol. 9-10)

F. R. Hughes, London, 1942 (incomplete: in his *Chinese Philosophy in Classi-cal Times*)

Lin Yutang, New York, 1942

Witter Bynner, New York, 1944

Hermon Ould, London, 1946

Orde Poynton, Adelaide, Australia, 1949

Cheng Lin, Shanghai, 1949

Eduard Erkes, Ascona, 1950 (with Ho Shang-kung's commentary)

J. J. L. Duyvendak, London, 1954

R. S. Blakney, New York, 1955

Why have there been so many translations? Certainly one reason is that the book is short. Its brevity appeals not only to the translator, but also to the reader with broad interests who cannot resist an important slender volume reasonably priced, tempting him by its very slenderness to do a little serious reading.

A more significant reason for so many Western versions lies perhaps in the parallels between the *Tao Te Ching* and the New Testament. Some examples follow. The Chinese is in Lin Yutang's popular translation,[4] which has not been altered to press the point.

New Testament	Tao Te Ching
Do good to them which hate you (Luke 6:27)	Requite hatred with virtue (Chapter 63)
Resist not evil (Mat. 5:39)	It is because the [sage] does not contend that no one in the world can contend against him (22)
They that take the sword shall perish with the sword (Mat. 26:52)	The violent man shall die a violent death (42)
Except ye become as little children, ye shall not enter into the kingdom of heaven (Mat. 18:3)	In controlling your vital force to achieve gentleness, can you become like the newborn child? (10)

[4] Lin Yutang, *The Wisdom of China and India,* pp. 583-624. Two examples are from Mr. Waley's.

New Testament	*Tao Te Ching*
Behold the Lamb of God which beareth the sin of the world (John 1:29)	Who bears himself the sins of the world is the king of the world (78)
If anyone would be first, he must be last of all (Mk. 9:35)	The Sage puts himself last and finds himself in the foremost place (7)
For whosoever will save his life shall lose it (Mat. 16:25)	He who aims at life achieves death (50W)
Lay not up for yourselves treasures upon earth . . . where thieves break through and steal (Mat. 6:19)	When gold and jade fill your hall, you will not be able to keep them safe (9)
For what is a man profited if he shall gain the whole world and lose his own soul? (Mat. 16:26)	One's own self or material goods, which has more worth? (44)
Whosoever shall exalt himself shall be abased (Mat. 23:12)	He who is to be laid low must first be exalted to power (36)
Parable of the lost sheep (Mat. 18:12)	Did [the Ancients] not say, "to search for the guilty ones and pardon them"? (62)
Consider the lilies of the field, how they grow; they toil not neither do they spin (Mat. 6:28)	[Tao] clothes and feeds the myriad things (34)
[A sparrow] shall not fall on the ground without your Father (Mat. 10:29)	Heaven's net is broad and wide, with big meshes, yet letting nothing slip through (73)
Ask and it shall be given you, seek and ye shall find (Mat. 7:7)	Work it and more comes out . . . draw upon it as you will, it never runs dry (5 & 6W)
My yoke is easy and my burden is light (Mat. 11:30)	My teachings are very easy to understand and very easy to practice (70)

In these examples the similarity of ideas and even of phraseology is impressive. In amazement the reader may exclaim: "To think that those words were written 500 years before Christ in a wild mountain pass in China!" It is not hard to understand the readiness of early scholars to assert that the doctrine of the Trinity was revealed in the *Tao Te Ching* and that its fourteenth chapter contains the syllables of "Yahveh." Even today, though these errors have been recognized for more than a century, the general notion that Lao Tzu was Christ's forerunner has lost none of its romantic appeal. It is a false notion, as we shall see. Though it is true that in certain situations the two teachings would recommend to a man the same course of action, they would do so on different grounds.

The *Tao Te Ching* is much translated for still another reason, namely, that it is very hard to decide what it means. It is a famous puzzle which everyone would like to feel he had solved. Certainly few other books have managed to achieve such obscurity as that which we find in its first ten lines:

> The Way that can be told of is not an Unvarying Way;
> The names that can be named are not unvarying names.
> It was from the Nameless that Heaven and Earth sprang;
> The named is but the mother that rears the ten thousand
>   creatures, each after its kind.
> Truly, "Only he that rids himself forever of desire can see
>   the Secret Essences";
> He that has never rid himself of desire can see only the
>   Outcomes.
> These two things issued from the same mould, but never-
>   theless are different in name.
> This "same mould" we can but call the Mystery,
> Or rather the "Darker than any Mystery",
> The Doorway whence issued all Secret Essences (1W).[5]

Then consider Chapter 6.

> The Valley Spirit never dies.
> It is named the Mysterious Female.
> And the Doorway of the Mysterious Female
> Is the base from which Heaven and Earth sprang.

[5] From here forward some readers, aware of the importance of context, may wish to refer to a complete translation. If so, let it be Arthur Waley's, *The Way and Its Power*, which I have generally followed in supplying the quotations for this book. Quotations with a "W" after the chapter number are from Mr. Waley's translation, and even those not so marked may contain elements of his phraseology.

> It is there within us all the while;
> Draw upon it as you will, it never runs dry (6W).

Here Lao Tzu is expounding his metaphysics—always a difficult topic. One might expect that his views on the practical problems of ethics would be easier to grasp. On the contrary, many of them are stated so paradoxically that the reader begins to wonder whether he or Lao Tzu views the world standing on his head.

> When the six family relationships have disintegrated
> You have filial piety and parental love (18).

> Banish human kindness, discard morality
> And the people will be dutiful and compassionate (19W).

> The truthful man I believe, but the liar I also believe,
> And thus he gets truthfulness (49W).

> To remain whole, be twisted.
> To become straight, let yourself be bent.
> To become full, be hollow (22W).

"Straight words," as Lao Tzu innocently remarks, "seem crooked" (78W).

The esoteric paradox has been a working tool of many religious teachers. It is a species of pun, stating a simple truth in a cryptic form. This makes the truth easier to remember, for the listener does not forget his initial bewilderment and the flash of understanding that followed it. He will remember the truth, and he will prize it because its secret is known only to him and a few other special people. Also, a paradox may express not a simple, but a complex truth and do so more succinctly than logical exposition, just as Picasso, rather than painting two profiles with one eye, paints one with two.

Succinctness in the *Tao Te Ching* is not confined to paradox and here is another reason for the book's obscurity. The *style* is one of extraordinary compression. Volumes seem reduced to chapters and chapters to hints. The style is more than compressed: it jounces the reader violently from subject to subject. The train of thought is an express on a bad roadbed; like Zen Buddhism, it seems to be trying to shake sense into us. Here is an example.

Tao gave birth to the One; the One gave birth successively to two things, three things, up to ten thousand. These ten thousand creatures cannot turn their backs to the shade without having the sun on their bellies, and it is on this blending of the breaths that their harmony depends. To be orphaned, needy, ill-provided is what men most hate; yet princes and dukes style themselves so. Truly, "things are often increased by seeking to diminish them and diminished by seeking to increase them." The maxims that others use in their teaching I too will use in mine. Show me a man of violence that came to a good end, and I will take him for my teacher (42W).

Evidently Lao Tzu subscribed to the rule of Confucius: "If, when I give the student one corner of the subject, he cannot find the other three for himself, I do not repeat my lesson." And yet one becomes accustomed to his style. The structure is regular. A chapter will begin with three or four applications of the principle that seems to be its subject. Then Lao Tzu jumps across an abyss of *non sequitur,* and if the reader can jump after him, he finds himself in an unexpected vantage point, able to see the original principle with new contours. Often the chapter will end with an injunction or warning designed to drive home the importance of the lesson.

The main reason, however, for the obscurity of the *Tao Te Ching* is not its succinct and paradoxical style, but the inherent difficulty of Archaic Chinese itself. If the reader has not tried his hand at Archaic Chinese, he will find its difficulty hard to imagine. But, if he cannot imagine it, he will be unable to appreciate what kind of book is being discussed in the ensuing pages. Therefore a digression is in order.

Archaic Chinese—and this is true of the modern literary language for that matter—has no active or passive, no singular or plural, no case, no person, no tense, no mood. Almost any word can be used as almost any part of speech—I have seen "manure," for instance, used as an adverb. And there are no inviolable rules: indeed, as soon as one makes a statement about the language, he is confronted with an exception— and this applies to the statements just made. Sometimes the segment of a Chinese ideogram called its "radical" is omitted in writing it, a little as though we were to put down "ization" for "civilization." Since the practice was more common at the time the *Tao Te Ching* was written, and since we do not have the original manuscript, sometimes we cannot be sure whether a copyist has not supplied the wrong radical; that is, he may have written in *barbar*ization where Lao Tzu intended *civil*ization.

Connecting words in Archaic Chinese are reduced to a minimum, and often below it. If the author possibly can, he leaves out the subject of the sentence. There is no punctuation whatever: one must decide for oneself where a sentence ends, and naturally there are many cases where moving a period reverses the meaning. Last, but not least, most of the texts we have are corrupt. Sometimes copyists have merely been careless, mixing, for instance, the commentary into the text. Sometimes they have deliberately introduced material to launch their own ideas.

All these points have been emphasized by Western Sinologists in explaining the difficulty of Archaic Chinese. But another point, which they have not emphasized often enough perhaps, is that these things make the language more than difficult: they make it vague. And it can be vague without being difficult. Let us take an example from the book we are about to examine. *Tao Te Ching,* Chapter 49, contains the grammatically very simple line: "Good persons, I good them. Not good persons, I good them too." "Good" (*shan*) as an adjective is like the English "good," but here it is a verb. We can understand either "I consider that they are good," "I treat them with goodness," or "I make them good." Which is it? There is no way of telling. Furthermore, it could mean all three. This is an alternative that I think translators have too seldom adopted, because, of course, it is so difficult to translate. Lao Tzu used ambiguity to save words.

The quotation just given is at the lowest level of vagueness. When we go on to the two words that immediately follow it, we strike something knottier. These two words are *te shan. Shan,* as before, is "good." *Te* is the power or virtue that comes from following Tao. What can "power good" mean? One possibility is "(Thus my) power (stems from) good (ing people)" (cf. Blakney's translation). A second possibility is "(This is the) goodness (of) Power" (cf. Lin Yu-tang's translation). But there is another word, also pronounced *te,* which means "to get," and it is sometimes written with the character for *te,* "power." Substituting it we have "gets goodness." Who gets goodness? Mr. Waley says that the not-good person gets goodness. James Legge says that everyone gets goodness. Who can tell?

At least we know that Lao Tzu is telling us something about goodness, and that it is somehow connected with the words that preceded it. But in the last lines of this chapter, we find a third level of vagueness. Mr. Waley renders them:

"The Hundred Families all the time strain their eyes and ears
The Sage all the time *sees and hears no more than an infant sees and hears*" (49W)

The words in italics are literally "grandchilds it (or them)." What on earth can that mean? Here is what some other translators think:

"He deals with them all as his children" (Legge)

"They are all the children of the self-controlled man" (Mears)

"While people in general strain their eyes and ears, the Sage wishes to have them sealed" (Cheng Lin)

"For wise men see and hear as little as children do" (Blakney)

All this from "grandchilds it"! The reason for the differing interpretations is a grammatical one. The word "it" (*chih*) is sometimes used to verbalize a noun that precedes it. In that case we would have here "to be like (or play the role of) a grandson, an infant." The other use of *chih* is pronominal. In that case we would have "he treats *them* as grandchildren, infants." These two interpretations have so little connection with each other that I do not think Lao Tzu could have intended both, but no one in the world can tell us with certainty which he did intend. If a translator is emphasizing the mystical side of Lao Tzu, he chooses the first: if he is emphasizing the ethical side, he chooses the second.

I have discussed these examples in such detail because I fear it is the only way of making the reader understand the problems confronting the serious student of Lao Tzu, or of any of the classics. And there are other kinds of difficulty. There is, for instance, the use of allusions. Because most literate Chinese knew several thousand pages of text by heart, they could use and enjoy allusions a lot more freely than we do. Some poems are little more than a patchwork of earlier literature, meaningless unless we recognize the sources. But even if we recognize the sources, we still cannot be sure what is meant. Perhaps the allusion is not to the content of its source, but to an event in the life of the man who wrote it, or to the place in which it was written; or perhaps, as sometimes happens, an attractive phrase has simply been appropriated without regard to its setting. By now it should be easy to see how, with most of Chinese poetry and much of Chinese prose, we have to decide for ourselves what is meant, within more or less broad limits set by the text. To read is an act of creation.

No one, not even the Chinese, could be comfortable with a literature so much of whose meaning was uncertain. Hence there arose the institution of the commentary. When a Westerner decides to read the Gospel according to St. Mark, he opens the Bible and reads. If he meets an occasional expression that is obscure, he turns to a footnote; often he can afford to ignore it. But until this century no Chinese, if he decided to read the *Analects* of Confucius, would ignore the Commentary. He would turn to it after reading every clause—if he had not already learnt it by heart. Written hundreds or many hundreds of years after the original text, the Commentary explained what each clause meant, sometimes each word in each clause, even where the meaning was already clear. After consulting it our Chinese reader might have to turn to the Subcommentary. This was a higher stratum of trot, written hundreds or many hundreds of years after the Commentary. It explained what the Commentary had failed to explain in the text, or what was clear in the text and had been garbled by the Commentary, or difficulties not in the text but raised by the Commentary itself. All this could only work like compound interest: it has left a vast accumulation. On every one of the major classics hundreds of commentaries and subcommentaries have been written, often running to several times the length of the classic itself. This extraordinary system was necessary, let us note again, not merely because the classics were difficult, but because they were vague. Not only was there the possibility that the reader would not understand, but that he would misunderstand. He might choose the wrong meaning and take the first step down the road to heresy.

This may give us a clearer idea of what we have in our hands when we open the translation of a Chinese classic like the *Tao Te Ching*. It is not a translation as we usually understand the word, but a spelling out in English of what is not spelled out in Chinese. If it follows an orthodox commentator—in the case of the *Tao Te Ching*

that would be Wang Pi—it represents his selection of the many possible meanings in the original text. If it follows several commentators,
it represents the translator's selection of their selection. If the translator has put commentaries aside and started from scratch, it represents
his concept of Chou Dynasty life and thought. The Chinese classics are
deep waters indeed, and I think we must recognize at the outset that
of all of them the *Tao Te Ching* is the one least susceptible of a defini-
tive translation. We cannot be certain of what it means. We never
will be. While some texts are more corrupt, some more archaic, and
some more esoteric, no text—certainly none of comparable importance
—so nicely combines vagueness with all these difficulties.

We have already noted how this combination is to be seen in Lao
Tzu's metaphysics, in his paradoxes, and in his style. We have also
noted that the *Tao Te Ching* is tied down by no references to specific
persons, places, or events. There is an important consequence to such
uncertainty. A critic of Shakespeare has pointed out that each era finds
its own image in his plays; its values, sentiments, and preoccupations.
How easily we can find our own image in the *Tao Te Ching*! It is a
magic mirror, always found to reflect our concept of the truth. That
may be the reason so much of all religious literature is obscure. When,
for example, St. John of the Cross writes, "To arrive at being everything, desire to be nothing," each of us, revolving the precept in his
mind and observing life, can find situations to fit it. Then we say that
we have found the precept is true, whereas actually we have only found
in what sense it is true. From person to person the sense changes, but
the truthfulness remains. This Protean quality, this readiness to furnish whatever the reader needs, gives the *Tao Te Ching* an immense
advantage over books written so clearly that they have only one meaning.

It is an advantage which has not appealed to all students and
translators, especially those of the Victorian era. At Cambridge
H. A. Giles wrote that Chapter 8 should "seal the fate of this book
with readers who claim at least a minimum of sense from an old-
world classic." [6] At Oxford James Legge called the *Tao Te Ching*
"extraordinarily obscure" and pronounced the following judgement:
"There has been a tendency to overestimate rather than to underestimate
its value as a scheme of thought and a discipline for the individual and

[6] H. A. Giles, *History of Chinese Literature*, p. 59.

society. . . . We must judge of Lao Tzse that, with all his power of thought, he was only a dreamer."[7] It was probably a disagreeable experience for a Sinologist as eminent as Legge to find that he could often extract little meaning from his own translation. He shared this experience with Victorian and post-Victorian colleagues. For that matter, in China itself the *Tao Te Ching* has baffled and irritated orthodox minds. One such was Yüan Ku, who in the second century B.C. was asked by the Dowager Empress Tou for his opinion of the writings of Lao Tzu. He replied that such trashy books were more suitable for the baggage of maidservants than for a royal court. This infuriated the Empress, an ardent Taoist, who thereupon had him thrown to the pigs. This was an early chapter in the long feud between the Taoists, on the one hand, and the Confucians who found their theories so baffling.

The same kind of bafflement may help explain the fact that after an initial deluge from 1895 to 1905, English translations were appearing at the rate of only one in six years until 1934. Since 1934 there has been one every sixteen months. This is the date of Arthur Waley's excellent book *The Way and Its Power*. However, I do not think that he can be considered solely responsible for the revival of activity. In the last two decades the West has seen a growing interest in Buddhism, especially in Zen, which owes much to Taoism. New tools have been developed, such as semantics, psychoanalysis, and parapsychology, all of them, possible approaches to a reappraisal of the *Tao Te Ching*. Lao Tzu is in tune with our relativism.[8] He wrote in a time of troubles not unlike our own. For all these reasons it is natural that the book should again attract translators and attention.

This is not to say that there is much more general agreement about its meaning than there was fifty years ago. Those who study it still come to many a parting of the way.

As backdrop for the chapters that follow, let us now take a brief sam-

---

[7] See the article on "Lao Tsze" in the Encyclopaedia Britannica, 11th edition.

[8] Lin Yutang's version of Chapter 25 can be interpreted as a reference to the curvature of space:

Being great implies reaching out into space.
Reaching out into space implies far-reaching.
Far-reaching implies reversion to the original point.

I doubt that this is a premonition of Einsteinian physics; it is, rather, an example of the perils of translation.

pling of recent interpretation. The reader must not expect to find it easy to follow unless he has already studied Lao Tzu. But what he will be able to see, perhaps, is how far apart—and how close—several interpretations can be.

Mr. Waley, like Duyvendak, approaches the *Tao Te Ching* not to find out what it means to Chinese readers today, but what it meant to the contemporaries of its author. He believes that it was written by a practitioner of *tso-wang,* the early Chinese equivalent of yoga. But it was not intended as a manual on the various breathing exercises which induced trance, though it alludes to them. Rather, it was intended to show how to use the Power that such trance states gave over the material world and also how such trance states could be the basis for a metaphysic. The book is primarily addressed to the ruler of a country. Just as in earlier days the medium at great feasts prepared himself by *abstinence* to receive the ancestral spirits, so the Taoist ruler must become *desireless* if he is to achieve trance and the Power that it gives. How does this Power work? In trance the ruler returns to the roots of his nature, perceives the Unity of the Universe, the non-existence of absolutes, the non-existence of contraries. What does this Power do? It makes it possible to act without action, to bring things about without interfering, to act through by-passing the contraries of every dilemma. Those who try to rule by other means—by morality or fear—only spoil what they do as fast as they do it. Waley's interpretation, then, is mystical.

F. C. S. Northrop reduces the mystical to metaphysics.[9] His interest in the *Tao Te Ching* is to illustrate his thesis that all oriental doctrines—from Hinduism to Zen—are grounded on the "aesthetic component" of mental function. Reality is directly sensed, not theorized about as in the West. It is an "aesthetic continuum," whose differentiations provide the transitory objects of the external world. But the Taoist can perceive this "aesthetic continuum" without differentiations. For him the aesthetic self and the aesthetic object become one, which, for one thing, permits him to paint the object from the inside. For another thing, being one with this timeless continuum, he is immortal. (This is a far cry from the very physical immortality of the later Taoists, as we shall see.) Such metaphysics have an ethical consequence. If we are one with another person or thing, we must feel

[9] F. C. S. Northrop, *The Meeting of East and West,* pp. 329-346.

their suffering as we do our own. The Taoist, therefore, like the Confucian, is motivated by compassion. Here Mr. Northrop stops. He barely mentions the doctrine of inaction. As for returning to the root of one's nature, he equates it with the Confucian objective of a society's return to the morals of the golden age.

Lin Yutang is the translator whose quotations were used above to illustrate the ease of parallells between Christianity and Taoism. He is an enthusiast for the *Tao Te Ching,* regarding it as "the one book in the whole of oriental literature which one should read above all others." [10] In particular he believes it is the answer to the Western scientist in search of religion. This is because it "does not presume to tell us about God," but only how we may approach God, or Nature. This approach is mystical, intuitive. Lin Yutang finds Ralph Waldo Emerson expressing clearly the Taoist doctrines of the unity, the relativity, and the cyclical pattern of reality. These, he feels, provide a rational basis for the doctrine of inaction. For what is the use of trying to bring a thing about when it will happen anyway in a turn of the cycle? Or of desiring what the cycle will destroy? What is the use of resisting evil when it is the same as good? What, for that matter, is the use of anything except recognizing the unity to which all things revert? Although Lin Yutang acknowledges his debt to Mr. Waley, he is impatient with the latter's philological-historical approach. Waley's *power* is for Lin Yutang *character* in the Sunday-sermon sense. Waley's *breath-control* (for trance) becomes *self-control* (for gentleness). Waley's *fixed staring* becomes *enduring vision.* Lin Yutang, perhaps, does not want the *Tao Te Ching* to sound so *outré* to our Western ears that we will fail to share his enthusiasm.

Fung Yu-lan, the great historian of Chinese philosophy, offers, like Northrop, a careful analysis of the metaphysics of Tao. [11] But then, unlike Northrop, he goes on to relate the metaphysical to the ethical. Indeed, he maintains that Lao Tzu is primarily "concerned with how one should respond to the world." As to metaphysics, Tao is Non-Being, "the all-embracing first principle for all things." Tao's most important manifestation in the world around us is the cyclical pattern of change. This is central to Fung's interpretation, even more so than

[10] Lin Yutang, *op. cit.* p. 579.
[11] Fung Yu-lan, *A History of Chinese Philosophy,* Vol. I, Chap. 8; *A Short History of Chinese Philosophy,* Chap. 9.

to Lin Yutang's. Unvaryingly the wheel turns; what goes up must come down. Victories lead in the end to defeat, force to weakness, laws to lawlessness, good to evil—all because, as Fung puts it, "if any one thing moves to an extreme in one direction, a change must bring the opposite result." He does not tell us why this is so, but from it he deduces Lao Tzu's humility and doctrine of inaction. He mentions Hegel's theory of history as a parallel. Because of the cyclical pattern, our desires can only get us into trouble. Therefore, according to Fung, Lao Tzu urges upon us not an absence of desires, but a reduction of them. That is why we must learn how to unlearn. If we do not know about the objects of desire, we cannot desire them. In his later work, Fung also points out that only when we unlearn the difference between high and low, right and wrong, can we abide in the Undifferentiated One (cf. Northrop). But he has little or nothing to say about yoga and trance as avenues to the One.

By now the reader may feel not only confused, but little inclined to devote further attention to the *Tao Te Ching*. What can it be but a waste of time to study a book without an author, without a date, and with little meaning that those who study it can agree upon? That is a hard question to answer. There will be many of us who, as one Sinologist put it, "prefer to work with things that are more tangible."

But there are motives for the study of Lao Tzu. One is curiosity. What can it be that has fascinated such a variety of people for so long? How is it possible to contrive a book in which everyone finds what he needs? Can nothing be done to determine its meaning once and for all? There *must* be a way. (It is curiosity about this last question that has even led to "translations" not from Chinese to English, but from English to English[12] and caused Duyvendak, the Dutch Sinologist, to cry in despair, "The *Tao Te Ching* has become the victim of the worst dilettantism." [13])

One can mention other motives for the study of Lao Tzu—like the need to understand our Chinese neighbours, or the importance of assigning the *Tao Te Ching* its proper place in the history of thought, or even the search for wisdom—but I think that the soundest motive is curiosity.

[12] W. R. Old, Bynner, and Ould based the texts they published on existing English versions, not on the Chinese original, "aided," as Old put it, "by such intuitions as have arisen from familiarity with theosophical and mystical speculations."

[13] J. J. L. Duyvendak, *Tao Te Ching* (Wisdom of the East Series), p. 1.

Part Two: THE *TAO TE CHING*

1. *Inaction*

I have said that Lao Tzu wrote his book in a time of troubles, very much like our own. This time of troubles began in 771 B.C. when the Chou Dynasty was pushed out of its capital by barbarians from the north-west and then re-established itself 200 miles eastward in Loyang. The decay of the Eastern Chou, as the dynasty thereafter was called, lasted 522 years. From feudal monarchs able to control their vassals, the rulers of Chou sank slowly to the level of impotent figureheads, privileged only to carry out certain ceremonials, like the ploughing of the Sacred Field in spring. Concurrently their vassals began to make war, not, as propriety required, upon the barbarians at their outer borders, but upon one another. At first these civil wars were characterized by a certain orderliness. They were fought according to *li,* the Rites. The Rites in China covered not only the religious ceremonials which kept Heaven and Earth in order, making rain fall, crops grow, and livestock fertile, but also the whole gamut of human behaviour from tipping one's hat to dying for one's honour. Whatever the act, there was a correct, ritual way of doing it, and the purpose of war at this time was more to display one's mastery of the Rites—one's chivalry—than to conquer and pillage. Battles often centered on personal combat between champions dressed in armour, who, the evening before, might have drunk together and exchanged weapons and who now shouted "haughty compliments" to one another across the battlefield. If the vanquished showed courage and courtesy, they were spared, and it was better to be vanquished than to violate the chivalric code. That was why the Duke of Sung, for instance, refused to attack the armies of Ch'u when they were fording a river. When they were across the river but had not yet regrouped for battle, he still refused, and gave the order to attack only after the enemy was ready, so that his own forces were disastrously defeated. Afterwards he said: "The Sage does not crush the feeble, nor does he order the attack before the enemy have formed their ranks." This is an example of *li,* the Rites.

In 681 B.C. the larger feudal states had united in a league for mutual

18

defense, which did not prevent wars, but helped give them to some extent the orderly character I have mentioned. However, two centuries later this league collapsed and the decay of the Chou Dynasty began its acute and final phase. One cannot point to a particular year as the beginning, but it is an interesting coincidence that 479 B.C., the year which saw the annihilation of the first major feudal state and the "discontinuance of its sacrifices," was also the year of the death of Confucius, whose life had been devoted to imposing on China a moral system which would have made such an event impossible. From the fifth century onwards there ensued a ruthless struggle for power, which ended only in 221 B.C. with the recognition of the first emperor of China. During this period the purpose of the warring prince was no longer a show of chivalry, but to weaken and annex his neighbors. Now war ceased to be a noble exercise. The vanquished were killed, not spared. The soldiers of one state, in fact, were paid off only when they presented the paymaster with severed heads of the enemy. Atrocity answered atrocity. Whole cities were put to the sword; some chiefs boiled up the bodies of those they had defeated into a soup which they drank "to increase their prestige."

Among the three to seven principal contenders for supremacy, leagues and alliances formed and dissolved; war led to war; treachery to treachery; and, as armies marched to and fro over the land, "thorns and brambles grew." This came to be called the "Period of the Fighting States." China seemed to be spinning down a whirlpool of ruin. To the people of the fighting states, as to some people today, it appeared that the world—the known world—must finish as a wasteland.

These were the times in which Lao Tzu lived. Though we cannot know how his philosophy developed, I think the times were a determining factor. He looked about, beheld reprisal following reprisal, and asked the question: *Can this ever be stopped?* If such a question was not in fact the point of departure for his philosophy, it is a good point of departure for understanding it.

Lao Tzu rejected the Confucian answer. Indeed, he probably believed that Confucius was the person who had triggered China's decline by preaching morality. Lao Tzu's answer was the doctrine of inaction, or, in Chinese, *wu wei* (literally, "not doing"). In his opinion the best method of coping with pillage, tyranny, and slaughter

was to do nothing about them. Now, as in his own days, those who
hear this doctrine for the first time are surprised, even exasperated. It
sounds harebrained; worse than that, dangerous. What would happen
to the world if none of us did anything about evil?

Lao Tzu means that we should "do nothing" in a rather special
sense. The inaction he recommends is abstruse and difficult to practice.
It will take a good many pages to explain. Let us begin by considering
four statements from the *Tao Te Ching*.

"Such things [weapons of war] are wont to rebound" (30W).

"The more laws you make, the more thieves there will be" (57).

"The Sage does not boast, therefore is given credit" (22).

"He who acts harms, he who grabs lets slip" (64W).

What is the principle that underlies these four statements? It is
a simple one: In human relations force defeats itself. Every action
produces a reaction, every challenge a response. This accounts for the
rhythm discernible in life by which "the man who is to be laid low
must first be exalted to power" (36) (pride goeth before a fall) and
"whatever has a time of vigour also has a time of decay" (30).

Some readers may be reminded of Toynbee's theory of history.
This is natural. Toynbee finds in history the same pattern that Lao
Tzu finds in politics, personal relations, indeed, in all of life. How
does this pattern arise? It arises out of the inertia of existence, the
tendency of every existing object or arrangement to continue to be
what it is. Interfere with its existence and it resists, as a stone resists
crushing. If it is a living creature it resists actively, as a wasp being
crushed will sting. But the kind of resistance offered by living creatures is unique: it grows stronger as interference grows stronger up
to the point where the creature's capacity for resistance is destroyed.
Evolution might be thought of as a march towards ever more highly
articulated and effective capacity for resistance. Humans and human
societies are thus highly responsive to challenge. So when anyone, ruler
or subject, tries to *act* upon humans individually or collectively, the
ultimate result is the opposite of what he is aiming at. He has invoked
what we might call the Law of Aggression.

Many writers on Lao Tzu have noted his concept of the cyclical
pattern of life. The wheel turns: what rises must fall. But to conceive

of the cycle in these terms is to miss the reason why it is there. It is not a cycle governed by time, but by cause and effect. The wheel, revolving unvaryingly and inescapably, is a poor analogy. Actually, no mechanical analogy can be satisfactory because the operation of cause and effect in human affairs is too complex. In its vast complexity we discern certain causal chains of challenge and response which represent the functioning of the Law of Aggression. It is this law, not the mere passage of time, which is the reason for the cyclical pattern of life.

We might note in passing that in evaluating "challenge and response" Toynbee and Lao Tzu come to apparently opposite conclusions. Toynbee believes that a society decays when it faces no challenge and perishes when it makes no response. Lao Tzu believes that challenges are to be ignored and that to cope with them by responding is the greatest of mistakes.

In Lao Tzu's opinion no one can achieve his aims by action. How then can he achieve his aims? The answer was *wu wei*. "To yield is to be preserved whole. . . . Because the wise man does not contend no one can contend against him" (22).

Is this the same doctrine as our Christian Quietism, in which we turn the other cheek? It is not. A Christian returns good for evil in a spirit of self-abnegation, as a holy duty, and as an expression of his love for God and fellow man. Ostensibly, Lao Tzu would have us return good for evil, or, as he puts it, "requite hatred with virtue (*te*)" (63), because that is the most effective technique of getting people to do what we want.

"The soft overcomes the hard and the weak the strong" (36W). Of the many similes Lao Tzu uses, his favourite is water, "which is of all things most yielding and can overwhelm [rock] which is of all things most hard" (43).

The Westerner today might admit the attractiveness of the simile, but would question its validity in practice. It is all very well, he would feel, to talk about "actionless activity" and "doing nothing, yet achieving everything." He would acknowledge that positive measures frequently boomerang. But how can inaction succeed?

It succeeds by being rather than doing, by attitude rather than act, by attraction rather than compulsion. What is meant by "attraction"? First, we must understand the Taoist ideal of *tz'u*—love in the sense of compassion or pity. It has only a brief mention in the *Tao Te Ching:* "Here are my Three Treasures: guard and keep them. The first is compassion . . ." (67); "Compassion cannot fight without conquering or guard without saving. Heaven arms with compassion those whom it would not see destroyed" (67). For the Christian love is the mainspring of action: for the Taoist it is ostensibly what makes inaction effective. It has a practical rather than a theological justification. It must be coupled with humility. Without humility a man will boast; thus he will not only lose credit for what he has done, but those for whom his boasting is a challenge will try to undo it. "The wise man puts himself in the background" (7); "The greatest skill seems like clumsiness, the greatest eloquence like stuttering" (45W). Humility and compassion together, if they come from our original nature, make it possible to act upon others passively, to obtain ends without the use of means. Like water, where the lowest stream is "King" of the upper streams, *the Taoist causes others to want what he wants.* Humility and compassion work like gravity between man and man. They bring into play the power of example, so that the Taoist "becomes the model for the world" (22 and 28). Lao Tzu recognized that we intuitively sense one another's feelings, and that my attitude, rather than my acts, is the determining factor in your attitude and your acts.

Lao Tzu, as I have presented his doctrine so far, appears to be a forerunner of Dale Carnegie. I do not think that is contrary to his intent. Ostensibly, he comes to us with a technique of human relations which, according to him, works, and that is why we should adopt it. This technique "is called the power (*te*) that comes of not contending, is called the capacity to use men" (68W). All of us would like to use men. Richard Nixon once said to his brothers about their father: "Just don't argue with him: you'll have a better chance of getting what you want out of him in the long run." [1] Similarly, Lao Tzu tells us that in using men the Sage "achieves his aim" (2W). All of us would like to achieve our aims. "In that case," Lao Tzu seems to be saying, "you had better listen to me."

I have outlined his technique for causing others to act. How would he prevent them from acting? By absorbing hostile aggression. Again the determining factor is other people's intuitive sensing of our

[1] Quoted in *Life*, Dec. 14, 1953.

attitudes. If they realize that we oppose what they are determined to do, even the most conspicuous yielding on our part will only redouble their determination. On the other hand, genuine yielding can be like a masochist red flag to a sadist bull. What, then, is the correct point of departure for the compassion and humility that absorb aggression? It is a complete relativism. The Taoist "has no set opinions and feelings, but takes the people's as his own. He approves of the good man and also of the bad man: thus the bad becomes good" (49). How can he do so without hypocrisy or total confusion? By realizing that good creates evil. Lao Tzu would say not that two wrongs make a right, but that two wrongs make two rights.

> It is because everyone under Heaven recognizes beauty as beauty that the idea of ugliness exists. And, equally, if everyone recognized virtue as virtue, this would merely create fresh concepts of wickedness. For truly Being and Not-Being grow out of one another. . . . Therefore the Sage relies on actionless activity (2W).

"Therefore" in the last sentence has three implications. First, the Sage never tries to do good, because this requires having a concept of good, which leads to having a concept of evil, which leads to combatting evil, which only makes evil stronger. Second, the Sage never tries to do good, because "every straight is doubled by a crooked, every good by an ill" (58W). Human affairs are complex: good done to one person may be evil to another. Reward the deserving man with a prize and we plant envy in the hearts of the undeserving. "Therefore the Sage squares without cutting" (58W). Third, our attention is being called not merely to the *fact* that the Sage relies on actionless activity, but to the *basis* on which he is capable of doing so— the point of departure for his effective compassion and humility. Good and evil being subjective, he can consider another man's criteria as valid as his own. Thus he can take the next step of "believing the truthful man and also believing the liar. Thus all become truthful" (49). Now this is in one sense a solipsist trick—if he believes it, it is true—but it is also a psychological fact. For "it is by not believing people that you turn them in liars" (17W). Distrust spreads in a vicious circle. If, for instance, our neighbours distrust us, what is the use of telling them the truth? They deserve to be lied to. And when we lie to them, they will lie to us in return.

It is to avoid this vicious circle that the Sage makes his radical approach to the problem of what is true and what is not. He has a double standard. "In his own words he chooses to be truthful . . . because he prefers what does not lead to strife and therefore cannot go amiss" (8). But he considers it as impossible for anyone to tell him the truth as it is for them to tell him a lie. To tell the truth is impossible because of the semantic problem. When the Southerner says to the Eskimo, "Yesterday was a chilly evening," the words "chilly" and "evening" mean different things to each. All of us are in some degree Southerners and Eskimos to one another. On the other hand, to tell a *lie* is impossible because every statement has a reason. That reason is the truth of the statement. Ask two forty-year-old women their age. The first may answer: "I am forty." She answers this because, in fact, she is forty. The other may answer: "I am thirty-five." The reason she answers this is because she is afraid to lose her looks. From her lips "I am thirty-five" means "I fear old age." The listener who understands the Tao of human nature catches this meaning. Her use of symbols was oblique, but to him she has told the truth. To him meaning is problematical and can be determined neither with certainty nor out of the context of gestures, facial expression, and history.

Now this indifference to our concept of "truth" helps the Sage in practicing his technique of human relations. Because he knows that everyone is telling him the truth—if he can only understand it—he never becomes angry at their lies and he never finds it necessary to correct them. He does not commit aggression because of a difference of opinion—that great first cause of human misery. He understands the connection between truth and consequences. He stays out of trouble. It reminds me a little of the wise observation by John Hughes, a New York taxi driver who contributed to Edward Murrow's book, *This I Believe*. Mr. Hughes wrote: "In all my years of driving a taxicab I have never had any trouble with the public, not even drunks. Even if they get a little headstrong once in a while, I just agree with them and then they behave themselves."

Or it might be said that Lao Tzu understood the usefulness of being able to keep our thoughts in separate compartments. He would have us consider that any deed is both right and wrong. For only by considering it right are we in a position to cope with its wrongness.

There is another element to the technique of inaction or *wu wei*: "To deal with the hard while it is still easy, with the great while it is still small" (63W); "In actions [the wise man values] timeliness" (8W). If one has understood Tao, i.e., the way the universe works, one can detect things at an exceedingly early stage in their development. Indeed, one can "deal with a thing before it is there" (64), while if one waits until it is full grown, one will face a much more difficult—perhaps impossible—undertaking for inaction. That is why one must understand the importance of "stopping in time" (9, 44) and why one must "requite hatred with *te*" (63)[2] at the beginning of what might otherwise turn out to be a vicious circle of aggression.

This brings up another difference between Taoist and Christian doctrine: the former is less opposed to the use of force. If, as some pacifists are often asked to imagine, a madman entered the Taoist's house and began to chop up his children, he would not respond by passively interposing himself, because that would be ineffective. He would use force, but he would use it as a *regrettable necessity*. The regret which legitimizes the use of force is a cardinal point of Taoism. As we have noted, the *Tao Te Ching* was written when China was in the "Period of Fighting States." Lao Tzu comments on good generalship as follows: "The good [general] effects his purpose and then stops. . . . He does not glory in what he has done. . . . He fulfills his purpose, but only as a step that could not be avoided" (30W); "He who delights in the slaughter of men will never get what he looks for out of those that dwell under Heaven" (31W). In other words, when force does become necessary, what we do is less important than the attitude with which we do it. If our attitude is bloodthirsty and destructive, the conflict will go on until the vicious circle of aggression results in mutual ruin. If our attitude is compassionate and sad, the enemy will sense that his hostility has not aroused a response and so, gradually, his hostility will atrophy. Only thus can the vicious circle of aggression be broken. Therefore, "he that has conquered in battle is received [home] with rites of mourning" (31W). Such an attitude makes a war of conquest impossible for the Taoist. "He who by Tao purposes to help a ruler of men will oppose all conquest by force of arms;

[2] The meaning of this famous phrase, often translated "return good for evil," will become clear in the next chapter.

for such things are wont to rebound. Where armies are, thorns and brambles grow. The raising of a great host is followed by a year of dearth" (30W).

It is to rulers in particular that the *Tao Te Ching* directs its message. Lao Tzu tells them, just as Mencius did, that if they will follow his way, they can have kingdoms for the asking. "If kings and barons would but possess themselves of it, the world would yield to them of its own accord: Heaven and Earth would conspire to send sweet dew" (32). Sweet dew, which tastes like barley sugar or honey, falls only when a kingdom is at complete peace.

Lao Tzu classifies rulers as follows:

> As to the best, the people only know that they exist. The next best they draw near to and praise. The next they fear and despise. . . . When the best [ruler's] work is done, throughout the country people say "we have done it ourselves" (17).

Thus Lao Tzu recommends government by non-interference. Governments must by-pass the dilemma of action, recognizing in particular the futility of trying to control so complex a thing as a nation.

> Some go in front, some follow; some are blowing hot, while others are blowing cold. Some are vigorous when others are worn out. Some are loading when others are unloading. . . . The empire is like a holy vessel, dangerous to tamper with. Those who tamper with it harm it. Those who grab at it lose it (29, transposed).

Government controls defeat themselves, for "they may allay the main discontent, but only in a manner which produces further discontents" (79). Therefore, "rule a big country as you would fry small fish" (60), i.e., do not keep stirring them or they will turn into a paste.

Government controls—and these include laws—defeat themselves for another reason. They are a form of aggression on the nature of man. The idea of man's original nature will be discussed later; but we must note here Chapter 57: "The more laws you make, the more thieves there will be." This is like the American Indian dictum: "In the old days there were no fights about hunting grounds and fishing territories. There were no laws then, so everyone did what was right." [3] Lao Tzu believes that man's original nature was kind and mild, and that

[3] Ruth Benedict, *Patterns of Culture*, p. 233.

it has become aggressive as a reaction to the force of legal and moral codes. This is the basis for some of the surprising statements quoted in the first chapter. "Banish human kindness, discard morality, and the people will become dutiful and compassionate" (19W); "It was when the great Tao declined that human kindness and morality arose. . . . It was after the six family relationships disintegrated, there was 'filial piety' and 'parental love.' Not until the country fell into chaos and misrule did we hear of 'loyal ministers'" (18). Thus Lao Tzu reverses the causal relationship which most of us would read into such events. It was not that people began preaching about "loyal ministers" because ministers were no longer loyal: rather, ministers were no longer loyal because of the preaching, i.e., because society was trying to *make* them loyal.

The wise ruler does not try to *make* his people anything. He "carries on a wordless teaching" (2W) because he knows that "he who proves by argument is not good" (81W). Some of us may recall reading about the occasion when President Adams took his grandson Henry to school. Henry was six years old, and had decided that to avoid going to school he would have a tantrum. In the midst of it old Mr. Adams emerged from the library, took the boy's hand, and led him down the road right to his schoolroom desk. Curiously enough, Henry felt no resentment. This was because his grandfather "had shown no temper, no irritation, no personal feeling, and had made no display of force. Above all, he had held his tongue. During their long walk he had said nothing; he had uttered no syllable of revolting cant about the duty of obedience and the wickedness of resistance to law; he had shown no concern in the matter; hardly even a consciousness of the boy's existence." [4] Lao Tzu would agree, I think, that on this occasion President Adams showed he understood the Tao of ruling.

The *Tao Te Ching* would have the people act on the ruler, not the ruler on the people—a democratic ideal less novel today than it was in 300 B.C. That is why he "takes the people's opinions and feelings as his own" (49) as though, in effect, he counted their votes. His role is to be "heavier" and "lower" than the people, attracting them by what he is, not compelling them by what he does. "In this way everything under Heaven will be glad to be pushed by him and will not find his guidance irksome" (66W). He must "rear them, feed them;

_____
[4] *The Education of Henry Adams,* p. 13.

rear them, but not lay claim upon them; control them but never lean upon them; be chief among them, but not manage them" (10W). Furthermore, the ruler "must not mind if the people are not intimidated by his authority. A Mightier Authority will deal with them in the end. . . . For the very reason that he does not harass them, they cease to turn from him" (72W).

Lao Tzu specifically opposes capital punishment. "He who handles the hatchet for the Master Carpenter is lucky if he does not cut his hand" (74). In any case, when the government finds it necessary to use capital punishment, it is its own fault. The people's lives must have been made intolerable by taxes and interference. With life hardly worth living, the death penalty becomes necessary and by the same token it becomes useless. "The people attach no importance to death because those above them are too grossly absorbed in the pursuit of life" (75W). "The people are not afraid of death: how can they be intimidated by the death penalty" (74). (This was the passage which struck a fourteenth-century emperor of China when he first picked up the *Tao Te Ching*. He reflected that while every morning in the capital ten men were executed, by evening there were a hundred others who had committed the same crimes. Therefore he withdrew the death penalty and soon "his heart was relieved.")

Rulers who flout Lao Tzu's warnings about the use of force and governmental interference will come to a bad end. "The man of violence does not die a natural death: I take this as my basic doctrine" (42). Lao Tzu is wrong about it, of course. Violent men usually die unnatural deaths, but not always. In our day the dictatorial score is two to one—assuming Stalin was not done in by his doctors. On the other hand, we might agree with Lao Tzu if he had said merely that the chain reactions of violence ignited by a violent ruler will always bring unnatural death to *someone*. Stalin's associates have found this to be true. It was true in Chinese history. There was Wu Ch'i, for example, an early Chinese general, who once murdered his wife to prove his loyalty to the state and was in the end murdered himself. There was Han Fei, who preached ruthless government and was executed by his comrade, Li Ssu. There was Li Ssu himself, who practiced ruthless government and was tortured to death by his collaborator, Chao Kao. All these men were connected with the Legalists, or School of Force. Because this school had certain similarities with

Taoism and because the life of its founder provides such an extraordinary instance of violence recoiling upon itself, I would like to tell his story. Though it has been told before, it will be new to some readers.

During the "Period of the Fighting States," in 361 B.C. a certain Kung-sun Yang reached the court of Ch'in, a poor state in the western wilds to the throne of which a new duke had just succeeded. In a series of conversations Yang explored the ambitions of this duke. At first he talked moralistically, but then, when he found the duke cared for power, not morality, he opened his heart to him. Yang had a scheme which, he guaranteed, would make the dukedom of Ch'in a great power. The duke appointed him chancellor. Thereupon, Yang established a fascist state, the first in China's history and completely at variance with the Confucian and chivalric traditions. It was based on a legal system of rewards and punishments. Ssu-ma Ch'ien, the historian, wrote about it as follows:

> He ordered the people to be organized into cells of fives and tens mutually to control one another and to share one another's punishments. Whoever did not denounce a culprit would be cut in two: whoever denounced a culprit would receive the same reward as he who decapitated an enemy. . . . People who had two males or more [in the family], without dividing the household, had to pay double taxes [this was to encourage early marriage and breed soldiers]. Those who had military merit all received titles from the ruler according to a hierarchic ladder. . . . Great and small had to occupy themselves, with united force, with the fundamental occupations of tilling and weaving and those who produced a large quantity of grain and silk were exempted from forced labour. Those who occupied themselves with secondary sources of profit and those who were poor through laziness were taken on as slaves.[5]

These laws proved to be a complete success. Under their stimulus Ch'in became the great military power of China, and a century later in 221 B.C. its duke, after a series of campaigns in just one of which, according to the histories, 400,000 prisoners were decapitated, was recognized as the First Emperor of China—an event which he celebrated in 213 by burning all the books in his empire except those on divination, medicine, and agriculture.

[5] Translated by J. J. L. Duyvendak, *The Book of Lord Shang*, pp. 14 ff.

To return to Yang, he soon led a military expedition against his home state of Wei, which he defeated after murdering its prince at a friendly dinner party. For this he was given the title of Lord Shang. He was still unpopular. He would venture into public only with a heavy escort of his secret police. Also, he had alienated the Heir Apparent by having his tutor's nose cut off—to show that none were above the law, including the Heir for whose crime it was payment. Therefore his prosperity depended on the life of the old duke, his master. At last the latter died, and Yang fled. He stopped at an inn for lodging, but did not dare to identify himself. The innkeeper said: "According to the law of the Lord Shang whoever shall receive at his inn guests who cannot be identified will be punished." Yang sighed and went on. He managed to reach home in Wei. There the people, who remembered his murder of their prince, said: "The Lord of Shang is a rebel of Ch'in; as Ch'in is a powerful country, when its rebels come to Wei, we have no choice but to send them back." This they did. Finally Yang returned to his seigniory in Ch'in, raised an army, was defeated and slain. But the young duke was not finished with him. He had Yang's body torn to pieces by war chariots and, according to the new laws, his whole family exterminated.

We might suppose that Yang's politics were in all respects the antithesis of the *Tao Te Ching*. This is not the case. Lao Tzu and Lord Shang both believed in "keeping the people ignorant" (65), though for a different reason and in a somewhat different way. In the *Tao Te Ching* we read: "The more knowledge people have, the harder they are to rule. Those who seek to rule by giving knowledge are like bandits preying on the land" (65W). What can Lao Tzu mean by this? Does he simply refer to the political fact that a people who are ignorant of how miserably oppressed they are, as well as of how to organize against their oppressors, will be unlikely to revolt? He refers partly to this. Lao Tzu liked the violence of revolution no better than any other kind of violence. But revolution is not his chief concern here. Rather, it is the damage to man's character which results from ambition and greed and which we shall discuss at greater length in the next chapter. What he wants to keep the people ignorant of is "rare, valuable goods" that will give them "sleepless nights" and cause them to "feed life too grossly." He wants to keep them ignorant of the thrill of power, which will tempt them to violent struggle for high position. He wants to keep them ignorant of "favour and disgrace," both of which will drive them out of their senses. Finally, and perhaps most important of all, he wants to keep them ignorant of Confucian morality, with its 3,300 rules of etiquette, such as the right occasions for using *wei* and *o* (formal and informal words for "yes"). This makes hypocrites of men who were once simple-hearted, for they outwardly conform while they inwardly rebel. "Banish learning," says Lao Tzu, "and there will be no more grieving. Between *wei* and *o* what after all is the difference?" (20W). Conformism can only lead to aggression: "He who is best versed in the Rites does not merely act, but if the people fail to respond he will roll up his sleeves and advance upon them. . . . The Rites are the mere husk of loyalty and promise-keeping and are indeed the first step towards brawling" (38).

The fundamental difference between the popular ignorance espoused by Lao Tzu and that espoused by Lord Shang is a difference of purpose. Unlike Lord Shang, the purpose of Lao Tzu's ruler is not to oppress the people. On the contrary, he expects *them* to oppress *him*. "Only he who takes upon himself the evils of the country can be its King" (78). This quotation has several facets. One translator, as we have seen, renders it: "He who bears himself the sins of the world is King of the world." But the Taoist is not the Lamb of God. Rather, the Taoist, when a ruler, must in clear-sighted humility accept the blame for whatever is amiss in his country, realizing that he is ultimately responsible and that it is within his power to absorb the feelings of aggression that are multiplying themselves throughout the land. The attitude of the ruler will directly determine the attitude of his people.

This is not quite so theoretical as it may sound. We can find an up-to-date illustration of it in William Whyte's excellent book *Is Anybody Listening?* Some may remember his story about the Marine Corps officer in the last war. He begins,

> One of the worst hurdles a staff man faces is the vale of distrust that exists between echelons of command. . . . To meet this one of the Marine Corps' finest divisional staff officers developed a remarkably simple antidote: the most important thing he ever did, he told subordinates, was to listen. Late at night, he went on to explain, he would be bothered time and again as some regimental or battalion officer called him up to complain of this or that or make some impossible request. "Most of the time it was a matter

for G-1 or G-2 or G-4, and sometimes the way they talked I should have told them to go to hell. But I didn't. And after a while the real trouble would come out. They were uneasy—the troops were itchy, maybe the outfit was low on rations—and it seemed to them there wasn't anyone else in the world who understood." And so he listened, and whenever he handed down an operation order, there was none of the usual what-the-hell-have-those-goldbrickers-up-in-the-division-done-to-us-now. Instead an almost instantaneous acceptance.

Lao Tzu would have commended this Sage of the Marine Corps.

I have frequently alluded to the interplay of attitudes. It is a cornerstone of my interpretation of the *Tao Te Ching*. However, between *groups* of men this interplay is more complex and less reliable than between individuals. One nation, for instance, cannot practice *wu wei* upon another with the assurance that, within a predictable time, the policy will be successful. That is why the *Tao Te Ching* sanctions the use of force as a regrettable necessity. On the other hand, Lao Tzu does not except international relations from Tao. He considers inaction always the correct approach, though it may have to be temporized with self-defense.

> A large kingdom must be like the low ground towards which all streams flow down. It must be a point towards which all things under heaven converge. Its part must be that of the female in its dealings with all things under heaven. The female by quiescence conquers the male: by quiescence gets underneath. If a large kingdom can in the same way succeed in getting underneath a small kingdom, then it will win the adherence of the small kingdom (61W).

Lao Tzu asks of any situation: is hate breeding a vicious circle of hate, or, by a compassionate response, is the original challenge losing its vigour? The troubles in Kenya and Cyprus offered good examples of the vicious circle of hate. In particular I recall the incident in which a British officer had some Mau Maus tied up with thongs around their necks, the soles of their feet whipped, and their eardrums burned with a lighted cigarette. This officer was arrested and brought to trial. The British judge, giving him a light sentence, said: "It is easy to work oneself up into a state of pious horror over these offenses, but they must be considered against their background. All of the accused were en-

gaged in seeking out inhuman monsters and savages of the lowest order." [6] In this British judge we see exemplified the antithesis of Lao
Tzu's formula for inaction. Lao Tzu said: "The good man I approve:
the bad man I also approve: thus the bad becomes good" (49). But
the judge was guilty of an error more serious than intolerance. He did
not regard the Mau Maus as human. When one person does not regard another as human, Tao will not "lend its power" to either of
them.

We have finished for the moment with the doctrine of inaction,
or *wu wei*. Let us summarize. *Wu wei* does not mean to avoid all
action, but rather all hostile, aggressive action. Many kinds of action
are innocent. Eating and drinking, making love, ploughing a wheat-
field, running a lathe—these *may* be aggressive acts, but generally they
are not. Conversely, acts which are generally aggressive, like the use
of military force, may be committed with such an attitude that they
perfectly exemplify *wu wei*. The Taoist understands the Law of Aggression and the indirect ways that it can operate. He knows that vir-
tuousness or non-conformity can be as aggressive as insults or silence.
He knows that even to be non-aggressive can be aggression, if by one's
non-aggressiveness one makes others feel inferior. It is to make another
person feel inferior that is the essence of aggression.

It is because of this Law that the Taoist practices *wu wei*. He
sees spreading all about him the vicious circles of lying, hatred, and
violence. His aim is not merely to avoid starting new circles, but to
interrupt those that have already been started. Through his peculiar
behaviour he hopes to save the world.

The Taoist well understands that *wu wei* is ineffectual if his compassion and humility are worn like a hat. These attitudes, to have their
effect, must come from the roots of his nature. It is not easy for him to
find these roots, as we shall see.

Now this may seem fairly close to another interpretation of the
doctrine of inaction, perhaps the most common of all. As H. G. Creel
puts it, *wu wei* means "doing nothing that is not natural or spontaneous." In effect that is true. The man who practices *wu wei* does
nothing which is unnatural, for, as I have just said, he has had to
return to the roots of his nature in order to practice it. But *wu wei* in
itself does not mean avoiding the unnatural; it means avoiding the

[6] Reported in *Time*, Dec. 7, 1953.

aggressive. If we fail to appreciate this, we end up with a complete misunderstanding of Lao Tzu. Mr. Creel, for instance, goes on to write:

> The enlightened Taoist is beyond good and evil; for him these are merely words used by the ignorant and foolish. If it suits his whim, he may destroy a city and massacre its inhabitants with the concentrated fury of a typhoon, and feel no more qualms of conscience than the majestic sun that shines upon the scene of desolation after the storm. After all, both life and death, begetting and destruction, are parts of the harmonious order of the universe, which is good because it exists and because it is itself. In this conception of the Taoist sage, Taoism released upon humanity what may truly be called a monster. By any human standards, he is unreachable and immovable; he cannot be influenced by love or hate, fear or hope of gain, pity or admiration.[7]

I think we have already seen enough of Lao Tzu's insistence on compassion and humility to know that *his* Sage—unlike that of some of his successors, perhaps—could never be such a monster. Mr. Creel prefaced his statement by quoting Lao Tzu's words, "The Sage is ruthless . . ." (5). Those words are indeed a puzzle. We shall study them closely in the next section.

[7] H. G. Creel, *Chinese Thought,* pp. 112-113.

2. The Uncarved Block

In exploring the doctrine of inaction we have met the most common symbols in the *Tao Te Ching:* water, which, though unresisting, cuts the most resistant materials; which "is content with the [low] places all men disdain"; towards which, when it has reached the lowest place (the Valley) all else flows; which in its lowliness and non-resistance "benefits the Ten Thousand Things"; and the symbol of the Female, who, like the Valley, is *yin,* the passive receiver of *yang;* who conquers the male by attraction rather than force; and who without action causes the male to act.

Lao Tzu makes use of symbols in expounding another basic doctrine—the return to our original nature. He speaks of the Uncarved Block (*p'u*), Raw Silk (*su*), and the Newborn Child (*ying erh*). *P'u* and *su* today mean "plain," but originally *p'u* was wood as it came from the tree before man had dressed it, while *su* was silk that man had never dyed or painted. The last of the three symbols, the Newborn Child, is man himself, naturally simple and good before Society forces him into its mold.

Lao Tzu believed that the evolution of the individual parallels the evolution of the race. In his opinion, the earliest man did not belong to a complex social organization. He lived in small settlements, of perhaps no more than a single family, and his desires were few: "to be contented with his food, pleased with his clothing, satisfied with his home, taking pleasure in his rustic tasks" (80W). There was a minimum of culture and technology. Instead of writing, he used knotted cords. Instead of labour-saving devices, he used "strong bones" (3). Since there was no society, there could be no aggression by society upon the individual: no morality, no duties to the community, no punishments. And so the individual was not driven to commit aggresson in return. He did not make war. He killed, but only animals, and he killed to eat them, not to prove his power over them. In eating, satisfying his physical needs, he "filled his belly and weakened his ambition" (3). For him money and power, wisdom and reputation did not even exist.

He was so unambitious, in fact, that though "the neighbouring settlement might be so near he could hear the cocks crowing and the dogs
barking, he would grow old and die without ever having been there"
(80). It is this Eden, this indifference to good and evil, that Lao Tzu
would have humanity recapture.

Even as our ancestors were untouched by society, so is each child
at birth. The child too fills his belly and lacks ambition (when he
fusses, we give him his bottle). In Lao Tzu's opinion, his nature—his
original nature—is free from hostility and aggressiveness. But society
mars this nature—and here Lao Tzu would seem to align himself
with the extremists in progressive education. From the first parental
whack to the last deathbed prayer, man is kneaded and pummelled,
either by those who want to make him "good" or those who want to
use or destroy him. He becomes a reservoir of aggression on which
society can draw to produce its goods competitively, fight its wars
fiercely, and raise children more aggressive than himself.

Such a man will find it hard to practice inaction. Inaction, as we
have seen, depends on attitude, and his attitude—whatever he may
believe or pretend—has become inwardly aggressive, deeply disturbed.
He is too much on guard for compassion, too much on edge for the patience of good timing. In a word, he does not hold the Uncarved
Block.

If I had to name the point in Lao Tzu's philosophy which I find
least convincing, it would be the premise mentioned just above, that
the Uncarved Block, or man's original nature, is free from hostility
and aggressiveness. I suppose it is not a question that can be settled
until behavioural scientists succeed in bringing up children in a to-
tally neutral environment. There is this much to be said for Lao Tzu,
however. In some human societies the aggressive, competitive modes
of behaviour simply do not exist. It is interesting that the most perfect
example of this is probably the most primitive of all societies, and
hence the one nearest to what Lao Tzu would call man in his natural
state. I refer to the Semang of Malaya, a remnant tribe of Negritos
who have no social organization, who have refused to accept machines
or any other "clever devices" from their civilized neighbours, and to
whom war and competition are unknown. To some extent the same
is true of the Eskimos, one of whom, describing his childhood to an
American observer, echoed the reasoning of Lao Tzu's radical theories

on education. "Eskimo parents," he said, "do not approve of striking a child because then the child will feel ugly. He will want to strike someone himself. In our family we were encouraged to be good—not scolded. We could feel we were being loved and that made us love right back."

Competition is almost unknown to other primitive tribes like the Zunis, the Arapesh, and to Polynesians like the Typees, among whom Herman Melville spent six months after jumping ship in the Marquesas. The Typees made Melville an enthusiastic convert to their way of life. It does appear that their long-range plan was to convert him into a stew, but he escaped in time to forgive their cannibalism and praise them in such passages as the following.

> Here you would see a parcel of children frolicking together the live-long day, and no quarrelling, no contention, among them. The same number in our own land could not have played together for the space of an hour without biting or scratching one another. There you might have seen a throng of young females, not filled with envyings of each other's charms, nor displaying the ridiculous affectations of gentility, nor yet moving in whalebone corsets, like so many automatons, but free, inartificially happy, and unconstrained. . . . With the young men there seemed almost always some matter of diversion or business on hand that afforded a constant variety of enjoyment. But whether fishing, or carving canoes, or polishing their ornaments, never was there exhibited the least sign of strife or contention among them. . . . In short, there were no legal provisions whatever for the well-being and conservation of society, the enlightened end of civilised legislation. And yet everything went on in the valley with a harmony and smoothness unparalleled, I will venture to assert, in the most select, refined, and pious associations of mortals in Christendom. . . . I do not conceive that they could support a debating society for a single night: there would be nothing to dispute about. . . . But the continual happiness which so far as I was able to judge appeared to prevail in the valley, sprung principally from that all-pervading sensation which Rousseau has told us he at one time experienced, the mere buoyant sense of a healthful physical existence.[1]

It would be hard to find a better vignette of Lao Tzu's escapist anarchy.

Now in contrast to these happy savages, I cannot help thinking

[1] Herman Melville, *Typee,* pp. 184-185, 293, 298.

of a neighbour of mine, a Vermont dairy farmer, who is always having trouble with his hired man. Lao Tzu's theories would not be much help to him, I am afraid. He might agree that there was something to them (laissez-faire being an accepted principle in Vermont) but the next time his hired man smashes a side-rake or strips a cow with milk fever, my neighbour is going to lose his temper—and his hired man—again. How can he do otherwise? Milk prices are down; the farmer next door has just put up a new silo while his own has started to lean; his wife is boss; he drinks and is disapproved of.

If this neighbour of mine asked us how his fits of temper could be avoided, what should we answer? Should we say: "It is morally wrong to abuse a hired man the way you do. Remember that, and learn a little self-control"? Lao Tzu, if he could overhear us, would shake his head. To use *that kind* of self-control, he would say, is to do violence to one's own nature, already violated by others: the feelings "controlled" will only grow stronger.

Should we say to the farmer then: "Understand the Tao of human relations. When you see with perfect clarity that each of your fits of anger only rebounds on you, you will cease to be angry. No man knowingly harms himself"? Again Lao Tzu would shake his head. He would say that while *that kind* of understanding was a step forward, it was not enough. On the contrary, men do harm themselves, knowing quite well how they do it, though not why.

If we then addressed ourselves to Lao Tzu and asked what *his* prescription would be for the farmer, he would answer: "Give him Raw Silk to look at, the Uncarved Block to hold, give him selflessness and fewness of desires" (19). "Favour and disgrace," he would add, "drive men out of their minds" (13). If we passed this formula on to the farmer, I am afraid he would not feel we had helped him much. It is a little too Chinese. But I think it can be made understandable to us if not to the farmer.

First, what does Lao Tzu mean by "fewness of desires"? We might suppose he meant asceticism because, in our Judaeo-Christian tradition, it is the desires of the flesh that are considered the primary enemy of spiritual progress. But Lao Tzu is not talking about the desires of the flesh. The desires that he would make few are those fostered in us by human society—the desires for money, power, and importance. We must reduce them not merely because "wealth, importance and pride bring their own downfall" (9), but also because they turn us away from self-cultivation: they distract us from the search for *p'u*, the Uncarved Block of our original nature.

"Fame or one's own self, which matters to one most?
One's own self or riches, which should count most?" (44)

And again:

"Riches, hard to obtain, get in the way of their owner" (12).

The desires for money and power lead to aggression, sometimes in the form of physical violence, more often in the form of economic competition. Competition is the seed and the fruit of the greatest social evils. How ominously Lao Tzu hammers out his warning!

No lure is greater than to possess what others want
No disaster greater than not to be content with what one has
No presage of evil greater than that men should be wanting
        to get more (46W).

Whereas the "social" desires lead to aggression, the desires of the flesh do not. We cannot commit aggression on our belly. Quite the contrary, when, like the early man and the child, we fill it, our attention may be diverted from aggression that we would otherwise undertake.

On the other hand, Lao Tzu, though not an ascetic, warns us against satisfying our bodily desires beyond the body's natural capacity for satisfaction. If we do so, satisfaction defeats itself.

The five colours blind the eye,
The five sounds deafen the ear,
The five tastes spoil the palate,
Excess of hunting and chasing makes minds go mad (12).

Furthermore, overindulgence is offensive. People who feel that we eat too well, drink too deeply, or live too hard, take it as a challenge—"to fill life to the brim is to invite omens" (55W)—just as they will seek revenge on us if we enjoy our food not because it is good, but because it is better than theirs.

This is what Lao Tzu means, then, by "fewness of desires." While we must *moderate* sensuality, we must *annihilate* ambition. Ambition, whether for money or power, endangers the whole community, for it spreads like the plague. Even today we can observe this, at a fashion show, at an auction, in a nursery school. My two daughters were recently by my desk. They like to explore for "treasures" in the wastebasket. After the elder finished, the younger began. She discovered a calendar in which her sister had shown no interest whatever. But as soon as she decided she wanted it, her sister wanted it too, and so there was a crisis. Lao Tzu says: "If we did not prize rare valuable goods, there would be no more thieves" (3).

We should note that Lao Tzu plays a trick on us. He lures us on with promises of power. "Apply [Tao] to an empire and the empire shall thereby be extended" (54W). "Possess the Uncarved Block and the world will yield to you of its own accord" (32). This has an intriguing sound to it as though the Uncarved Block were a kind of magic lamp by which every one of our desires could be satisfied. It is like Lao Tzu's statement, referred to in the last chapter, that inaction gives us "the capacity to use men." But in accepting these doctrines, we must reject the very rewards that have attracted us to them. We cannot practice inaction or hold the Uncarved Block unless we cease to care whether the world yields to us or not; and for that very reason it will yield. "It is because the Sage does not strive for any personal end that all his personal ends are fulfilled" (7). Here is the paradox of Taoism, a good trap for bad men: the quiet, all-potent means cannot be means to aggressive ends. And so we must amend our earlier comparison of Lao Tzu to Dale Carnegie. He is not really offering us a human-relations technique. If we adopt it as such, we shall not in fact be adopting it. Compassion is much more than a means of making inaction effective. If we adopt it as such, we shall not in fact be compassionate. And to return good for evil is simply beyond the reach of the man who does it, as the last chapter suggested, to get what he wants. Lao Tzu having trapped his disciples with the lure of power, teaches them indifference to power. Such traps are not uncommon in mysticism. The objective of mystical teachers is, after all, to attract those who need their teaching, not those who have already renounced the world. Westerners have been attracted to Yoga because they wanted to exercise supernormal powers, a motive that will always prevent them from succeeding. In Christ's ministry, as Kirsopp Lake put it, "the crowd and possibly some of his disciples thought that he was the Davidic Messiah." [2] They were attracted to him because he promised the Kingdom: by the time they realized that he was not speaking of a Davidic Kingdom on earth, they cared only for the Kingdom of Heaven.

After "fewness of desires," the second part of Lao Tzu's prescription for getting hold of the Uncarved Block is the rejection of public opinion, or of "other-directedness" as some call it today. "Favour and disgrace drive men out of their minds. When a ruler's subjects get it [favour, praise], they turn distraught. When they lose it, they turn distraught" (13W). Favour can lead a man to infatuation. Disgrace can lead him to seek revenge upon those who have disgraced him or in whose eyes he has been disgraced. Even favour can lead a man to seek revenge, for it puts him in the position of being patronized. In either case, once he submits himself to the goads of public opinion, he will find it hard to keep his balance and even harder to continue the search for his original nature.

If we are to return to our original nature, or help others to, we must discard what everyone under Heaven accepts: not only ambition, but morality, law, duty, knowledge of right and wrong. That is why "everyone under Heaven says that our Way is greatly like folly" (67W). That is why Lao Tzu in his own book never urges his views on us as "right" or "good" but only on the basis that if we do not follow them, we invite disaster. We saw in the last chapter how futile he believes it is for the ruler to attempt making his people just, compassionate, or wise. Now we see the converse: that the people, for their part, should ignore his attempts to make them such. Let them understand the relativity of good and evil; let them do nothing and believe nothing merely because they have been told it is "right"; let them not be intimidated by scholars and critics or read a book because it is Great; let them "prize no sustenance that comes not from the Mother's breast" (20W). Thus they will never permit violence to be done to their inner natures and their inner natures will never cause them to do violence in return. "Banish wisdom, discard knowledge, and the people will be benefited a hundred fold: banish human kindness, discard morality, and the people will be dutiful and compassionate" (19W).

---

[2] Kirsopp and Silvia Lake, *Introduction to the New Testament*, p. 233. Cf. Acts 1:6. Even after the Resurrection the Apostles looked to Jesus for a restoration of the Kingdom.

But until morality is discarded by everyone, there will be the dilemma of conformance. Those who conform are full of resentment against those who do not: those who do not conform are a challenge to those who do. Therefore the Taoist conceals his non-conformance. He does not flaunt the Uncarved Block. He does not make a morality of amorality, for that would be committing the error he set out to avoid. He does not insist on strange clothes, strange food, or strange words, no matter how strange his ideas may be. "The Sage wears haircloth on top and carries the jade next to his heart" (70).

Lao Tzu's inward amorality leads him to what seems at first a cruel and almost sardonic realism. The reader may recall Mr. Creel's criticism of the Taoist as a potential monster.[3] He based it on Chapter 5, which is one of the most crucial in the book, and certainly a puzzle. I hope the reader will be patient, for to get to the bottom of it we shall have to analyze it carefully. Here is a verbatim translation:

> Heaven Earth not good [*jen*]
> Regard Ten Thousand Things as straw dogs
> Sage man not good
> Regards Hundred Families as straw dogs
> Heaven Earth's between [space] it resembles bellows
> Empty but not collapse
> Move and more issues
> Much talk quickly exhausted
> Better keep Middle

"Heaven and Earth" is the Chinese epithet for the whole physical universe. The "Ten Thousand Things" refer to the contents of the universe. The "Hundred Families" refer to mankind. Straw dogs are images for sacrifice. Chuang Tzu says: "Before the straw dogs are set forth they are deposited in a box or basket and wrapt up with elegantly embroidered cloths while the representative of the dead and the officer of prayer prepare themselves by fasting to present them. After they have been set forth, however, passers-by trample on their heads and backs, and the grass cutters take and burn them in cooking. That is all they are good for."[4]

---

[3] See p. 34.

[4] Tr. James Legge, *Texts of Taoism*, Vol. I, p. 352. I have changed his "grass dogs" to "straw dogs."

Mr. Waley renders the chapter thus:

> Heaven and Earth are ruthless;
> To them the Ten Thousand Things are but as straw dogs.
> The Sage too is ruthless;
> To him the people are but as straw dogs.
> Yet Heaven and Earth and all that lies between
> Is like a bellows
> In that it is empty, but gives a supply that never fails.
> Work it and more comes out.
> Whereas the force of words is soon spent.
> Far better is it to keep what is in the heart.

Mr. Waley comments that in the first line the word *jen* (good) is cognate to *jen* (man), although it is written differently. *Jen* (good) originally meant the "men of the tribe," first in contrast to the common people and later in contrast to the people of other tribes. Only men of the tribe were *mei jen* (handsome and good, kaloskagathos). Later, *jen* came to be the Confucian virtue of "humanheartedness," the Highest Good. Mr. Waley lets the reader draw his own conclusions about an important question: how can the Sage have compassion as one of his Three Treasures and yet be ruthless?

Ch'u Ta-kao translates the third line: "The Sage does not own his benevolence." He comments that the Sage neither interferes in the activities of mankind nor does he take credit for them. Men "come into being, grow old, and die away all of their own accord." Mr. Ch'u's implication is presumably that the Sage's benevolence (compassion) should be impersonal: it cannot be his own because if it were it would amount to interest and ultimately interference in the Hundred Families. Thus he is impersonally benevolent, but personally regards the people as straw dogs.

Lin Yutang translates the third verse as "The Sage is unkind" and follows both the foregoing lines of thought. Since the Confucians were the champions of morality and of *jen* as the first moral principle, Lao Tzu, he suggests, is here attacking the Confucian emphasis on "conscious affectation" as opposed to the "unconscious goodness" that comes from the root of our nature. (The Confucians bear somewhat the same relationship to the *Tao Te Ching* as the scribes and Pharisees to the New Testament.) In other words, Lao Tzu is not saying that the Sage is simply not kind: rather, he is not kind-in-the-same-way-as-the-Superior-Man-of-Confucius. Lin Yutang also writes: "Tao resembles the scientist's concept of an impersonal law that makes no exception for individuals." Do we presume, then, the Sage should be as impersonal—as merciless—himself? It must be, for Lin Yutang translates the fourth line, "He *treats* the people like sacrificial straw dogs."

Hu Tse-ling ingeniously makes the verse a question: "Is the Sage unkind regarding all things as straw dogs?" He comments that "Heaven and Earth are very kind: for they produce all things without speaking, possessing, and so on. But their kindness is too great to be described and beyond comparison, so it looks as if they are not kind." This is as ingenious as the French translation of De Harlez: "If Heaven and Earth were without kindness, they would regard all men as straw-dogs."

Cheng Lin picks up the implication of Waley's philological comment and renders it "The Sage is amoral." The Sage, in other words, is not a man of the tribe and the tribal mores have as little importance for him as they have for Heaven and Earth.

These various interpretations complement rather than contradict each other. They explain the special meaning which Lao Tzu attached to *jen*[5] and which made it possible for the Sage to be both unkind and compassionate, indeed, made unkindness a prerequisite of compassion. "Banish humankindness (*jen*) . . . and the people will become compassionate (*tz'u*)" (19W).

They do not explain in my opinion the other problem of Chapter 5, raised most clearly in the version of Lin Yutang. How can the Sage, being compassionate—though unkind—treat the people as straw dogs? It is hard to image a compassion so impersonal that one's fellow men become lifeless images to be crushed with the heel and burned.

First, we must discard Lin Yutang's word "treats." The Sage "regards," he does not "treat" the people as straw dogs. The Chinese original is perfectly clear about this. Second, we must remember that the Sage himself is a member of the Hundred Families. He too is a straw dog. He too may be blotted out by earthquake or flood, along with the just and the unjust, the innocent and those who "deserve" to

---

[5] Not always. According to Chapter 8, the best man chooses to be *jen* in his relations with others.

die. Unless he recognizes this fact, unless he regards mankind as Heaven and Earth regard it, he will be living on false premises. But this realistic analysis of life, which we call "dispassion," does not make the Sage indifferent, as Lin Yutang suggests, to the suffering of others. He may not share their prejudices and desires, and he may therefore seem indifferent, but he is not. On the contrary, he understands more clearly than anyone else how mankind suffers and that in this suffering he is involved. Dispassion brings compassion.

Let us attempt to paraphrase Chapter 5 in the light of the foregoing. "The universe is not moral, not 'our kind,' not kind the way the Rites requires. The universe regards the things in it as straw dogs. The Sage is not moral, not 'our kind,' not kind in the way the Rites requires. He regards men—including himself—as straw dogs. But the universe, amoral as it is, supports us. If we call on its orderliness, it never fails us—any more than the law of gravity will fail us. Try to call on morality the same way, and you will quickly exhaust its support. Forget morality; follow your inner nature."

In the opinion of Lao Tzu, as we shall later see more clearly, our inner nature is an extension of the nature of the universe. To follow one is to be in harmony with the other. Therefore the Sage is a votary of "back-to-nature"; not only in the sense of a return to his own nature as it originally was, but also in the sense of a return by society to its natural state and in another, esoteric sense which we have yet to consider. He understands that a return to "natural" society means the rejection of "ingenious devices"—complex machinery of production and communication, which not only distract the individual from self-cultivation, but represent a form of excessive activity which inevitably defeats itself.

Once I saw a pair of road signs, one of which advertised a gasoline with "Total Power" and showed a car moving at breathtaking speed, while the sign next to it read "Speed Kills." The second sign was a "public service," paid for partly out of profits on the first. Lao Tzu could point to other and graver examples—like the farm surpluses which have resulted from improving our agricultural methods, the population problem which has resulted from improving the medical care of infants, the survival problem which has resulted from improving our knowledge of nuclear physics. In every case, Lao Tzu would counsel us to abandon our ingenious devices, our clever ideas, our improvements, and follow nature.

To follow nature means being ready to accept her support and her cruelty as one. Gentle rains or spring floods, the havoc of a landslide or the beauty of mountain mist—all are parts of the whole to which the Sage himself belongs. This whole, this Mother, is something he both reveres and loves. Whether Lao Tzu's Sage felt the same romantic love of nature as the later Taoists is uncertain.

The idea is not excluded by the indifference to scenery which the Sage displays on a journey. He "will not let himself be separated from his baggage-wagon: however magnificent the view, he sits quiet and dispassionate" (26W). The literal meaning of "baggage-wagon" is "covered-heavy," an allusion to the secret, solid part of his own nature. The man who does not let himself be separated from this original part of his nature is secure. He is what he is, and because he knows that he is what he is, he "cannot either be drawn into friendship or repelled, cannot be benefited, cannot be harmed, cannot either be raised or humbled, and for that very reason is highest [most honoured] of all creatures under heaven" (56W). Some may object that this makes the Sage sound like a monster again, beyond any human appeal. What, for instance, would the Sage do if he found himself in the position of the Good Samaritan? That is a good question. In fact it is the crux of the Christian objection to Lao Tzu. Would the Sage "do nothing" and let nature take its course? Of course he would. But it is part of man's nature to feel compassion and because he feels it, not because he wants to do what is right, he will help the man who fell among thieves. His help will be consistent with the doctrine of inaction which, as we have seen, means not to do nothing, but only to do nothing that is hostile or aggressive.

We have heard *about* the Uncarved Block and in what sense its holder is desireless, dispassionate, natural. But we have not yet learned from Lao Tzu what it *is*. He is not too helpful on this point, until we penetrate to the mystical level of his teaching, as we shall in the next section. He describes the Uncarved Block as blank, childlike, untutored, dark, nameless. It cannot be adequately described. To reach it is to "know oneself" (33), to "return to the root from which we grew," to "push far enough towards the Void, hold fast enough to Quietness" (16W). Pushing towards the Void suggests Chapter 14:

"Endless the series of things without a name on the way back to where there is nothing. They are called shapeless shapes; forms without form; are called vague semblances. Go towards them and you see no front; go after them and you see no rear. Yet by seizing on the Way that was you can ride the things that are now. For to know what once there was in the Beginning, this is called the essence of the Way" (14W). Mr. Waley comments that "what there was in the Beginning" refers macrocosmically to the universe, microcosmically to oneself.

It may have already occurred to the reader that parallels can be drawn between the phraseologies of Lao Tzu and the psychoanalyst. The concept of the Uncarved Block (*p'u*) sounds, for instance, like the unconscious mind. Both are blank and nameless: both are connected with intuition as opposed to discursive reasoning ["the perfect reckoner needs no counting slips" (27) and "the Sage sees all without looking" (47)]: both offer us a way of doing things effortlessly ["the infant is able to scream all day without getting hoarse" (55)]. I do not think we can therefore say that *p'u* is identical with the unconscious. There may be some overlap in the two concepts. But the unconscious is an area of activity, whereas *p'u* is that area's original condition as Lao Tzu supposes it. If we set out to look for parallels between Taoism and psychoanalysis, I think we can find them more easily in method than in concept. I offer some for what they may be worth, partly because no one else, so far as I know, has done so, and partly because they illustrate the ingratiating ease with which Lao Tzu offers himself to all comers for adoption.

During the early phases of a patient's analysis, particularly of the "non-directive" school, the analyst plays a role not unlike that of the Taoist Sage. In listening to his patient, guiding him by question and by silence rather than by command or advice, he seems to be practicing a kind of "actionless activity." Thus he might be said to carry on a "wordless teaching" (2): indeed some analysts, like Dr. Ernest Jones, are reported to say only "good morning" and "good-bye." To them we can apply Lao Tzu's statement "From the Sage it is so hard at any price to get a single word that when his task is accomplished . . . everyone says 'It happened of its own accord'" (17W). Furthermore, the analyst "does not lay claim" to the patient nor "call attention to what he does" (2W). Through transference he "takes upon himself the evils [of the patient]" (78): his "high rank hurts keenly as our bodies hurt" (13W). He absorbs aggression.

In his own analysis the analyst has perfected himself by reaching his original nature. "The perfected man must be the teacher of the unperfected, and the unperfected man must be the stock-in-trade of the perfected" (27). Lao Tzu says that the teacher's duty is to "teach things untaught, turning all men back to the things they have left behind" (64W). Many analysts, Sage-like, have "discarded morality," recognized the relativity of right and wrong, and help their patient to do the same. In the early phases of therapy, at least, they do not goad him with "favour and disgrace." What is their goal? Is it not really their goal to leave the patient contented, quiet, ready to "fill his belly"—"all tangles untied, all glare tempered, all dust smoothed" (4W)? Chapter 37 puts it in another way: "The blankness of the Unnamed brings dispassion: to be dispassionate is to be still" (37W).

How does the psychoanalyst come to understand his patient? Often, it seems, by "banishing wisdom, discarding knowledge" (19W). As Dr. Theodor Reik puts it, the analyst must "forget what he has learned . . . in courses, lectures, seminars, and books . . . and listen to his own response." Thus he can lead the patient back to "the root from which we grew" (16W). For "to know what once there was in the beginning, this is called the essence of the Way" (14W). It might all be summarized in the words of Chapter 71: "The Sage's way of curing disease also consists in making people recognize their diseases as diseases and thus ceasing to be diseased" (71W).

We shall conclude this chapter by trying to visualize the man who "holds the Uncarved Block." How does he appear? Lao Tzu gives us two wonderful and poetic portraits. The first shows him as he appears to himself while still in search of his original nature.

> All men, indeed, are wreathed in smiles,
> As though feasting after the Great Sacrifice,
> As though going up to the Spring Carnival.
> I alone am inert, like a child that has not yet given sign;
> Like an infant that has not yet smiled.
> I droop and drift, as though I belonged nowhere.
> All men have enough and to spare;

I alone seem to have lost everything.
Mine is indeed the mind of a very idiot,
So dull am I.
The world is full of people that shine;
I alone am dark.
They look lively and self-assured;
I alone, depressed.
I seem unsettled as the ocean;
Blown adrift, never brought to a stop.
All men can be put to some use;
I alone am intractable and boorish.
But wherein I most am different from men
Is that I prize no sustenance that comes not from the
      Mother's breast (20W).

The other, equally poetic portrait shows the Sage who has attained *p'u* as he appears to others.

Circumspect [he seems], like one who in winter crosses a
      stream,
Watchful, as one who must meet danger on every side.
Ceremonious, as one who pays a visit;
Yet yielding, as ice when it begins to melt.
Blank, as a piece of uncarved wood;
Yet receptive as a hollow in the hills.
Murky, as a troubled stream—
Which of you can assume such murkiness, to become in
      the end still and clear?
Which of you can make yourself inert, to become in the
      end full of life and stir?
Those who possess this Tao do not try to fill themselves
      to the brim,
And because they do not try to fill themselves to the brim
They are like a garment that endures all wear and need
      never be renewed (15W).

3. Tao

Thus far, in reconnoitering the doctrines of the *Tao Te Ching,* we might compare ourselves to travellers through mountainous country in autumn, when the clouds hang low. We have seen only gentle slopes and valley land—very much like the country we are accustomed to at home. There have been novelties, but nothing transcendental. Where are those mysterious peaks for which Lao Tzu is famous?

They have been right above us all the time, shrouded in obscurity. Let us go up and explore them. As we climb, it may be difficult to understand the terrain. The difficulty will vanish, however, if we remember that the peaks we shall find there poking up through the clouds are continuations of the gentle slopes around us here. That is to say, the doctrines of Lao Tzu have a different look at different levels: his words have a different application at different levels. But they are the same doctrines, the same words.

Now these levels are not abrupt like steps, but are a continuous grade. There is an illusion of abruptness in the cloud—the cloud of mystical experience—that we must penetrate in our climb to the peaks of doctrine. This cloud may tempt us to divide Lao Tzu's world in two—one hidden, accessible only by trance or analyzing the reports of trance (as we are about to do), and the other, quite separate world we see around us down here. To accept such a demarcation makes the *Tao Te Ching* impossible to understand. Usually Lao Tzu speaks at all levels simultaneously, though sometimes he seems to jump back and forth, and indeed he can do so in the middle of a sentence. In his book, ethics, spiritual discipline, and metaphysics blend into one another: the reader can never say with assurance, "This statement is esoteric, that statement is common sense." For example, inaction is a practical, testable doctrine of ethics; it is also part of the regime that leads to trance experience of Tao; it is also an attribute of Tao itself.

The two preceding sections, by keeping the field of vision rigidly confined to the ethical level of the *Tao Te Ching,* presented it falsely. Henceforward, from new vantage points, perhaps we shall be able to see all levels at once. But what is ahead of the reader now is more arduous and more problematical than the teachings of Lao Tzu that he has encountered so far.

Most of us are familiar with the general proposition advanced by Oriental mystics: that everything is God and that by contemplation a man can first perceive and then become identical with God. "Every man," says the Sufi Gulshan-Râz, "whose heart is no longer shaken by any doubt, knows with certainty that there is no being save only One. . . . In his divine majesty the *me* and *we,* the *thou,* are not found, for in the One there can be no distinction. Every being who is annulled and entirely separated from himself, hears resound outside of him this voice and this echo: *I am God:* he has an eternal way of existing and is no longer subject to death." Or, as the Upanishads put it, "That art Thou."

A discussion of mysticism usually begins with the admission that adequate discussion is impossible. Likewise, if we go to the mystic himself and ask for information about what he has experienced, he will tell us that he cannot tell us, and then he will tell us. St. John of the Cross writes: "We receive this mystical knowledge of God clothed in none of the kinds of images, in none of the sensible representations which our mind makes use of in other circumstances. Accordingly in this knowledge, since the senses and the imagination are not employed, we get neither form nor impression, nor can we give any account or furnish any likeness, although the mysterious and sweet-tasting wisdom comes home so clearly to the inmost parts of the soul." Having said that he cannot furnish a likeness, St. John immediately furnishes one: "The soul then feels as if placed in a vast and profound solitude, to which no created thing has access, in an immense and boundless desert, desert the more delicious the more solitary it is."

Lao Tzu is just as inconsistent. He begins his whole book with the sentence, "The Tao that can be told of is not the Absolute Tao." In Chapter 56 he seems to impale himself on a monstrous dilemma when he announces, "Those who know do not speak; those who speak do not know."

But we must not make fun of mystics for inconsistency. If they said no more about their vision than what they could put into precise, apposite terminology, we would learn nothing at all. We must be content with their symbols and similes. We are—to use an analogy that many mystics have used—like a class-room of congenitally blind children hearing a lecture on water colours. The lecturer cannot tell us how colours look; he cannot even prove to us that colours exist. The best he can do is to translate colours into terms of other senses and emotions—soft or hard, quiet or violent, depressed or joyful. Or, if he followed Chinese tradition, he might offer some much odder equivalences: red, he would say, is the colour of seven, green the colour of eight, and yellow the colour of five. All this would be about as helpful to his blind auditors as the mystical hints of the enlightened to the unenlightened.

The unenlightened—and again I suppose this term includes most of us—are skeptical. Confronted by a man who says he frequently sees or is God, we turn upon him with questions. "What is God like?" we ask, "Can you define Him? Can you say where He came from and what He does? Just how did you manage to acquire this extraordinary information? If, as you say, you became God, what are you doing here? And how do you know it isn't all a lot of imagination?"

These questions can be addressed to Lao Tzu as well as to any other mystic who claims special knowledge and experience. Let us examine his answers and see how they compare with the answers given by his peers.

First, what is Tao?

The references to Tao in the *Tao Te Ching* are obscure and in a low tone. They lack the fire, lyricism, and definition which generally characterize mystical writing. There is no sentence like that in the Upanishads which cries out: "Listen, O Ye children of the Immortal, I have found the One Great Absolute Being respendent in his glory beyond a mass of darkness." Instead, Lao Tzu mutters in Chapter 1 about "the Mystery or rather the 'Darker than any Mystery,' the Doorway whence issued all Secret Essences" (1W). In Chapter 6 he amplifies this by telling us that the Doorway is attached to the Mysterious Female who appears to be identical with the Valley Spirit. It is not even clear whether he is talking about Tao at all.

Most mystics and metaphysicians define God in terms of various attributes. Sankara, for instance, the ninth-century Vedantist, writes thus of the union of soul with Being: "I am pure . . . I am eternal . . . the ultimate truth . . . the very image of consciousness and bliss." We are all familiar with definitions of God like the *Universal* or *In-*

finite or *Absolute* or *Pure Being* or *Pure Reality* or *Pure Beauty* or
Pure Love or *Substance* or *Essence* or the *All* or the *One*.

Lao Tzu makes little use of such vocabulary. He does call Tao
"Being" and sometimes "One," in what sense we shall presently see.

Another traditional way of defining God is to say what He is not.
In the pseudo-Dionysius, for instance, we find:

> The cause of all things is neither soul nor intellect; nor has it imagina-
> tion, opinion, or reason, or intelligence; nor is it reason or intelligence; nor is
> it spoken or thought. It is neither number, nor order, nor magnitude, nor
> littleness, nor equality, nor inequality, nor similarity, nor dissimilarity. It
> neither stands, nor moves, nor rests. . . . It is neither essence, nor eternity,
> nor time. Even intellectual contact does not belong to it. It is neither
> science nor truth. It is not even royalty or wisdom; not one; not unity; not
> divinity or goodness; nor even spirit as we know it.

It is to this negative variety that Lao Tzu's only extensive definition
of Tao belongs. In Chapter 25 he writes:

> There was something formlessly fashioned,
> That existed before heaven and earth;
> Without sound, without substance,
> Dependent on nothing, unchanging,
> All pervading, unfailing.
> One may think of it as the mother of all things under
>   heaven.
> Its true name we do not know;
> "Way" is the by-name that we give it (25W).

Does Lao Tzu reach that final stage of negative definition where
God is "nothingness," as Blessed Henry Suso called him, or, in the
words of the great eighth-century theologian, John Scot Erigena, "per
excellentiam nihilum non immerito vocatur"? We can best answer
this by taking up the question, "Where did Tao come from?"

From scattered references in the *Tao Te Ching* it is possible to
deduce a scheme of creation, or cosmogony. But we must not be
stricter in deducing than Lao Tzu in writing, and that, as we know, is
not strict at all. He uses Tao in several senses and for each sense he
uses several synonyms.

In Chapter 4, after praising Tao, he asks,[1] "Was it too the child of something else? I do not know. But as a substanceless image it existed before the Ancestor" (4W). In Chapter 25, after explaining how the universe is conditioned by Tao, he states that "Tao is conditioned by the Self-so." Tao, then, is not the ultimate. There may have been Something Else before Tao and there is even now Something Else beyond Tao on which it depends.

Chapter 40 allows us to go a few steps further. From it we know that "Heaven and Earth and the Ten Thousand Creatures were produced by Being; Being was produced by Non-Being." Since we know from other chapters (42, 51) that it was also Tao which produced the Ten Thousand Creatures, we may equate Tao with Being. As to the production of Being from Non-Being, we met this phrase earlier and in another connection. Chapter 2 gives it an epistemological sense: one can only know a thing in relation to what it is not. ("It is because everyone under Heaven recognizes beauty as beauty that the idea of ugliness exists.") There are several ways these ideas can be utilized in formulating a cosmogony. We can, for instance, imagine a universe packed with primordial substance. Since there is no space—no nothing —to differentiate substance from substance, an observer would not see anything. He would, in effect, see nothing. But now, within this primordial substance, interstices develop. Things take shape. What makes them take shape? The nothing that separates them one from the other. And so out of "nothing," nothing has produced everything. Sophistical as this may sound, I think it is some such picture of creation which Lao Tzu had in mind. Like many archaic pictures of creation, it is vague enough to suggest some of the concepts of contemporary physics. The idea, for instance, of a "nothing" which is packed with substance and out of which the universe was created, would have some resemblance to the "hole theory" of P. A. M. Dirac.[2]

---

[1] Actually, Mr. Waley supplies the interrogative. The literal translation is simply "I do not know whose son it is."

[2] Mr. Dirac, one of the fathers of quantum mechanics, first published the "hole theory" at Cambridge in 1931. It postulated that the vacuum between the particles of the universe might be solidly packed with electrons in a negative energy state. "Energy state" here does not mean electrical charge. The electron has a fixed negative charge, but its energy state may be either plus or minus, according to Dirac, and the number of these possible energy states is infinite. The plus energy states of a given electron vary according to its position in the atomic solar system. No two electrons in a single atom can occupy the same energy state. Each seeks to reach one lower and

In any case the picture which emerges from the *Tao Te Ching* is clear in its outlines: first Tao and then the physical universe—Heaven and Earth and the Ten Thousand Creatures—arose from Something Else.[3] This Something Else Lao Tzu variously describes as the Self-So, the Nameless, or Non-Being. It is symbolized by the Mysterious Female because of the birth motif and by the Valley Spirit because of the motif of emptiness. It "never dies." It is outside time, standing ready, perhaps, to produce new universes ruled by Tao and maintaining the Tao that maintains this one.

But in making this distinction between Tao and the Something Else, we have ignored a mystery like that of the Trinity. Let us look again at Chapter 1, this time in a more literal translation.

"The Tao that can be Tao'd is not the Absolute Tao (*ch'ang tao*)
The name that can be named is not the absolute name."

Tao and the Something Else are, I think, *only aspects of one another.* The Something Else is the *ch'ang tao*—the Eternal, Unvarying, Absolute Tao. It is a Way that we cannot follow. We cannot even give it a

---

is only prevented from doing so because the lower is occupied. Thus each electron, if it could, would cross the boundary of zero energy state and go into the vacuum out of "existence." This may actually happen when an electron collides with a positron, for both disappear, with a release of gamma radiation. Conversely, when a photon of gamma radiation gets far enough into the strong electromagnetic field of an atomic nucleus, the photon disappears and an electron and positron are "created." The explanation of this coming into and going out of existence is a simple one. The positron is really no more than the "hole" left in the substratum when the electron jumps up out of it (that is why this is called the "hole theory"). The height of the jump corresponds exactly to the energy of the photon of gamma radiation which is absorbed when the jump takes place. Being an electron's "hole," the positron's charge must naturally be opposite to the electron's—which it is. There are other pairs of such oppositely charged particles of the same mass, e.g., positive and negative protons and mesons. Each may reflect the existence of a substratum.

Dirac's theory can be interpreted to support the picture of creation outlined above. Originally the universe was a perfect vacuum. Nothing "existed." All particles occupied a negative energy state. Then something happened. Particles were forced from a minus to a plus energy state; they became separated from the substratum and from each other; and so the universe came into being.

Lao Tzu had no better reason to say that Being came from Non-Being than Democritus had for saying that matter consists of qualitatively similar atoms of different shapes. Still, if Dirac proves to be right, Lao Tzu (to the extent that his concept has anything in common with Dirac's) will deserve credit for a first guess.

[3] Cf. Chapter 42. "Tao gave birth to the One; the One gave birth successively to two things, three things, up to Ten Thousand" (42W).

name. And when we give the name "Tao" to its manifest aspect, it is not a true name, for "its true name we do not know" (25W). Therefore this nameable Tao can itself be called nameless, as it is in Chapter 41.

But let us return to Chapter 1. It continues:

"It was from the nameless that Heaven and Earth sprang;
The named is but the mother of the Ten Thousand Creatures."

These two lines tell us little more than we have already learned. The physical universe as a whole—Heaven and Earth—*was* produced from Non-Being, or Tao's nameless aspect. All the things which come and go within the universe—the Ten Thousand Creatures—*are* produced by Being, or the Tao that can be named (here and in Chapters 52 and 59 the name given it is "Mother").

At this point an objection can be raised. Our interpretation is inconsistent, strictly speaking, with Chapter 40, which describes Being as the producer *both* of the physical universe and everything in it. The universe should have been produced by either one aspect of Tao or the other. Which is it? Let us remember our resolve not to construe Lao Tzu too strictly. What he has in mind is probably something like this: Nameless Tao could not produce the universe without becoming nameable. Anything "here" can be given a name. Nameable Tao, in a sense therefore, came into existence simultaneously with the physical universe and yet, in another sense, it antedated and produced the universe since it produced everything in it. To wonder how Nameable Tao could be both simultaneous with the universe and antedate it is like wondering whether the law of gravity antedated matter.

Chapter 1 continues:

> Truly, "Only he that rids himself forever of desire can
> see the Secret Essences";
> He that has never rid himself of desire can see only
> the Outcomes.
> These two things issued from the same mould, but
> nevertheless are different in name.
> This "same mould" we can but call the Mystery,
> Or rather the "Darker than any Mystery,"
> The Doorway whence issued all Secret Essences (1W).

These lines are less formidable when we assume that Tao has two aspects—its public aspect the order of the universe, its secret aspect the Something on which that order depends. All of us are aware of the order of the universe. How are we aware of it? By watching the things going on around us—the "outcomes," the Ten Thousand Creatures. Few of us are aware of the Something on which it depends. Even if we rid ourselves of desire and entered trance, we would still not sense it directly. We would only sense what Lao Tzu calls its "Secret Essences." What are the Secret Essences? They are the manifestations of the inner aspect of Tao, just as the Outcomes are the manifestations of its outer aspect. These two aspects are one and this Two-in-one is the mystery which permits Lao Tzu to say that both Outcomes and Secret Essences "issue from the same mould."

To understand this "mould" better, let us review its dual sets of names: first, the Nameless, the Tao, the Self-so, Non-Being, the Mysterious Female, the Valley Spirit; and next in its other aspect, Tao, Being, the Mother, the One.

By "the One" Lao Tzu means Tao not only as a cosmogonal unity, but as a continuous field in which all physical and moral contraries are reconciled, in which up and down, good and evil disappear. This unity of contraries, including good and evil, was recognized by many of the Indian schools and in the West by mystics like Plotinus, Erigena, and Nicholas of Cusa.

Also under the epithet of "the One," Lao Tzu gives the clearest answer to our question "What does Tao do?"

> As for the things that from of old have understood
> the One—
> The sky through such understanding remains limpid,
> Earth remains steady,
> The spirits keep their holiness,
> The abyss is replenished,
> The ten thousand creatures bear their kind,
> Barons and princes direct their people.
> It is the One that causes it.
> Were it not so limpid, the sky would soon get torn,
> Were it not for its steadiness, the earth would soon
> tip over,

> Were it not for its holiness, the spirits would soon
>   wither away.
> Were it not for its replenishment, the abyss would
>   soon go dry.
> Were it not that it enabled the ten thousand creatures
>   to bear their kind,
> They would soon become extinct (39).

This chapter is Lao Tzu's clearest definition of Tao as the order of the universe. It is the laws of nature, the God that exists by the argument from design; not identical with the universe and yet at work everywhere within it. Tao is impersonal, "unkind," [4] and beyond the reach of prayer. It is real, but no more real than the universe it governs. Here are two important contrasts with other mystical traditions. In the West, mystics generally regard the universe as real and God as personal, while most Eastern traditions regard God as impersonal and the universe as illusory.

Let us pursue for a moment this comparison with other systems of thought. We can find similarities as well as contrasts. We might call Tao similar, for instance, to the Brahman of the Upanishads, whose spark in the individual would therefore be *p'u*. Some scholars have compared Tao to the apex of Plato's hierarchy of ideas, which is perceptible to the eye of the mind and to reach which one goes back past increasingly "formless forms." There is a certain resemblance between Tao and the Logos of Neo-Platonism, whose emanations are then the Ten Thousand Creatures. "Tao gave them birth; the power of Tao reared them, shaped them according to their kinds, perfected them, giving to each its strength [or essence]" (51W). Tao might be said to resemble the potential existence or prime matter of Aristotelianism. In its aspect of Non-Being, it includes everything that ever was (and has now returned to non-being) and everything that ever will be (and has not yet left non-being). Lao Tzu, when he tells us to deal with things while they are yet in Non-Being (64) may be saying more than that prevention is better than cure. He may be urging us to deal with them when we return to Non-Being in trance: that is where we can find them. This suggests a doctrine held by several schools of Buddhism: that past, present, and future are equally real and coexistent. It

---

[4] See the discussion of "unkindness" on pp. 43-44.

makes Non-Being positive, for Non-Being is not what never is, but only what is not at this instant—and that is practically everything. And so forth. Such comparisons are interesting. But, like attempts to show that all great thinkers really thought the same thing, they can muddy rather than clarify our understanding, unless we are careful to think of differences as much as similarities. No two things, in the world or in our minds, are exactly the same. A duck is like a goose, but a duck is not a goose.

We might object to Lao Tzu's metaphysics as too speculative. But mystical, unlike academic, metaphysics is not at all speculative to its adherents. It is eminently empirical. When Lao Tzu tells us about the aspects of Tao, he is faithfully reporting what he has seen with his own eyes—his mind's eyes—in trance. Far from speculating, he offers first-hand experience. We should neither accept nor reject it until we have analyzed and compared it with other trance experience that we accept or reject. Let us recall our example of the lecturer on water colours at the school for the blind. His listeners may not be particularly impressed if he is also blind himself and is merely discussing colour as a quality which ought logically to exist. They will be impressed only if he can discuss colour as something he has *seen*. If they want to decide whether or not he is telling them the truth about it, they will compare his statements with those of other colour-seeing individuals, seeking for inconsistencies and confirmations. That is what we shall try to do now—to compare, that is, the stages and content of trance in Lao Tzu and in other mystics.

Trance, of course, does not necessarily have stages. The form most common in the West is apparently spontaneous, as in the case of St. Paul on the road to Damascus or of converts at revival meetings. (I use "trance" in the broad sense of a state of awareness in which one senses what others do not.) But in the East mystics generally achieve trance by discipline, or, some would say, by a prolonged and carefully regulated program of autosuggestion. Both this discipline and the trance it produces are divided into stages, giving rise to a complex taxonomy. It is not a uniform taxonomy. The Sufis, for instance, distinguish four stages; the Buddhists five; the Tantrists six. It will be convenient to our purpose to say that there are four and to think of them not as stages which must follow one another, but as varieties which can exist independently. Here, then, are the four: (1) visions and voices; (2) non-perceptual awareness of God; (3) merging with God; (4) cessation.

Visions have pictorial explicitness, like a dream. According to Al Ghazzali they "take place in so flagrant a shape that the Sufis see before them, whilst wide awake, the angels and the souls of the prophets. They hear their voices and obtain their favours." The explicitness that we see in this quotation is not confined to religious visions. When Mollie Fancher, the Brooklyn Enigma of the 1870's, went into trance, she would "go out and around and see a great deal. Sometimes I go into a house and view the conditions of the room. Sometimes I see persons and nothing more." In religious visions the explicitness can reflect a well-developed symbolism, as on the occasion when St. Teresa saw Sacred Humanity lying in the bosom of the Father, with the Father in the shape of a huge diamond whose brillance contained the universe.

A sense of brilliance is strikingly common in visions. The great light that shone around St. Paul blinded him for three days. For three days also after a vision the eyes of St. John of the Cross were weak as from the sun. Plotinus wrote: "Everything shines yonder." The first word in Pascal's account of a mystical experience is "Feu." Dr. R. M. Bucke, whose account of conversion is quoted by William James, writes: "All at once without warning of any kind I found myself wrapped in a flame-coloured cloud. For an instant I thought of fire, an immense conflagration somewhere close by in that great city: the next I knew the fire was within myself." And throughout the eighteenth and nineteenth centuries Protestants at their revival or conversion saw a light "like the brightness of the sun." Even after conversion the whole world would sometimes appear bathed in light so that, as a farmer said, "every straw and head of the oats seemed as it were arrayed in a kind of rainbow glory."

When we turn from these images and this glory to Lao Tzu, what does he offer us in counterpart? Not a line. If he has ever had a vision, he does not allude to it. If he has ever found Tao to be luminous, he tells us the opposite: "its rising brings no light, its sinking no darkness" (14W). Possibly he believed, as did St. John of the Cross, that sensible imagery is harmful to mystical development. Possibly illumination occurs only with ecstasy, and, as we shall see, there is no indication that Lao Tzu ever felt ecstasy.

In the second stage of trance, the mystic leaves visions and voices behind him and reaches an immediate awareness of God. "You will ask me what it was that I saw," writes St. Angela of Foligne. "It was Himself, and I can say nothing more. It was a fulness, it was an inward and overflowing light for which neither word nor comparison is worth anything. I saw nothing corporeal." If we turn from St. Angela to a recent Protestant account of ecstacy furnished by William James, to whom I am indebted for many of the illustrations in this section, we read that "God had neither form, colour, odour, nor taste: moreover, the feeling of his presence was accompanied by no determinate localization." It is only a little way from this lack of localization to the sense of oneness, the compelling sense, as St. Angela wrote, that " 'This whole world is full of God.' " Once the oneness of God is perceived, there can be little holding back from union.

Union with God, which I have termed the third stage of trance, is commonly considered the supreme mystical act. For then the individual becomes, as the Sufis put it, "the paragon of perfection, the object of worship, the preserver of the universe." This is evidently an experience more ecstatic than visions or awareness—so ecstatic that it has often been described in the language of sexual love. The opening line of the Song of Solomon, "Let him kiss me with the kisses of his mouth," has been the text for much Christian contemplation. St. Teresa, after telling how in her ecstasies an angel used to plunge his fire-tipped golden dart into her heart, writes: "There takes place then between the soul and God such a sweet love transaction that it is impossible for me to describe what passes." This love transaction resembles the "delicious death" of sexual climax. St. Teresa writes further: "Thus does God when he raises a soul to union with himself suspend the natural action of all her faculties. She neither sees, hears, nor understands so long as she is united with God." The pleasure is even physical. It "penetrates to the very marrow of the bone." Curiously enough, this pleasure, like the masochist's, may be connected with pain. St. John of the Cross, who elsewhere condemns ecstasy as "spiritual gluttony," praises the enrichment of an intuition of God and says that it may be followed by "a strange torment—that of not being allowed to suffer enough." Suso reports that during a rapture in which "his soul was joyful and content . . . his body suffered so much . . .

that it seemed to him that nobody, except in death, could suffer so much in so short a space of time."

Sexual descriptions of union are not confined to Christian writers. The Brihadaranyaka Upanishad has a passage strikingly similar to St. Teresa: "As a man when embraced by a beloved wife knows nothing that is without, nothing that is within, so this person when embraced by the intelligent Self knows nothing that is without, nothing that is within." The word "Beloved" is the epithet of God in Union applied by Plotinus, the Sufis, the Vaishnavas of Bengal, the Guru Granth of the Sikhs.

The language of love is not the only one, of course, to be used in describing this third stage of trance. St. Teresa[5] says of "spiritual marriage" that it is "as if a raindrop fell from Heaven into a stream or fountain and became one with the water so that never again can the raindrop be separated from the water of the stream." The Upanishads contain strikingly similar passages. Or consider the following Sikh poem, quoted by Mukerjee in *The Theory and Art of Mysticism*.

> I do not know why, but when I say "Hail, Master!" the sun and stars seem to run in my breath, my muscles are as if fibres of light, my being flies to strange lands and waters, my lips touch gardens of flowers, my hands I exchange with some other hands, a stranger moves my tongue. The Universe runs into me, and I into the Universe.
>
> I seem a strange misty form. Like vapour I pass into the being of others, and they passing within me become my guests.
>
> It seems fair forms of rolling beauty roll as waves on the sea— Hail, Lord! All are each other's!
>
> Our shape and limbs run into each other.
>
> I find my bones at times strike within me against the bones of someone else.

[5] St. Teresa did not admit that in ecstasy she *became* God. Like St. John and other prudent Christian mystics she kept herself from crossing the narrow line which the Catholic Church has drawn between the Orthodox "union with God" and the heretical "identification with God." Between God and man, that is, a difference must remain, however intimately they are united. Some mystics, like Ruysbroeck and Suso, said that one might be unaware of this difference and, in their daring views, only escaped condemnation because they expressed themselves so ambiguously. Other Catholic mystics, like Eckhart, crossed the narrow line, asserted that in union "We are wholly transformed into God," and were tried for heresy.

Our deeds and thoughts jostle and run into each other.
I see a hundred souls blend in me, and I interchange my blood and
   brain thus with a hundred more in a single breath; and, calm
   in solitude, I find a society.

Now, when we turn from such ecstasies, spiritual marriages, dissolutions, and blendings to the *Tao Te Ching* and seek for parallels, again we find not a one. Lao Tzu makes no use of allegories to describe his experience of Tao. He offers no sexual imagery. He does not even allude to emotions as part of trance. Whereas we have seen how rising ecstasy measures progress up the stages of mysticism, Lao Tzu mentions neither pleasure nor pain, neither hope nor suffering. The closest he comes to it is in Chapter 4 where he tells us that in Tao—and this probably refers to the awareness of Tao as well as Tao itself—"all sharpness is blunted, all tangles untied, all glare tempered, all dust smoothed." This is hardly a report of ecstasy.

Chapter 14 probably comes the closest to being a description by Lao Tzu of the second stage of "non-perceptual awareness" in trance.

Because the eye gazes but can catch no glimpse of it,
It is called elusive.
Because the ear listens but cannot hear it,
It is called the rarefied.
Because the hand feels for it but cannot find it,
It is called the infinitesimal.
These three, because they cannot be further scrutinized,
Blend into one.
Its rising brings no light;
Its sinking, no darkness.
Endless the series of things without name
On the way back to where there is nothing.
They are called shapeless shapes;
Forms without form;
Are called vague semblances.
Go towards them, and you can see no front;
Go after them, and you see no rear (14W).

This is echoed in Chapter 21.

For the Way [Tao] is a thing impalpable, incommensurable.

Incommensurable, impalpable.
Yet latent in it are forms;[6]
Impalpable, incommensurable
Yet within it are entities.
Shadowy it is and dim;
Yet within it there is a force (21W).

Lao Tzu knew that such reports of Tao might disappoint those who sought the emotional and the concrete. In Chapter 35 he says,

Sound of music, smell of good dishes
Will make the passing stranger pause.
How different the words that Tao gives forth!
So thin, so flavourless!
If one looks for Tao, there is nothing solid to see;
If one listens for it, there is nothing loud enough to
    hear (35W).

Worse than the unsatisfactory way in which Lao Tzu refers to his awareness of Tao, it is not certain that he refers at all to *union* with Tao, or even that he believes there is such a thing as a soul to experience union. There appears to be a reference to union in Chapter 28:

He who knows the white, yet cleaves to the black,
Becomes the world's model:
And being such a model,
He has all the time a power that never errs.
He returns to the Limitless.

But this difficult passage can best be interpreted to mean not that the Taoist merges with the Limitless, but rather that he imitates the Limitless by his passivity. Because he understands aggression (the white), yet consciously rejects it ("cleaves to the black"), his passivity works on his fellow men in the same way as the passivity of Tao (the Limitless) works on the Universe. There is a further implication: the Taoist must not be a fool; he must "know his way around"; yet, though he "knows the white" and seems to be worldly enough, all the time he is protected from the perils of worldliness by his dark understanding.

---

[6] Gautama too before his enlightenment saw "an aura and vision of forms."

The key chapter on union with Tao is the sixteenth.

> Push far enough towards the Void,
> Hold fast enough to Quietness,
> And of the ten thousand things none but can be worked
>   on by you.
> I have beheld them, whither they go back.
> See, all things howsoever they flourish
> Return to the root from which they grew.
> This return to the root is called Quietness;
> Quietness is called submission to Fate;
> What has submitted to Fate has become part of the
>   always-so.
> To know the always-so is to be Illumined;
> Not to know it, means to go blindly to disaster.
> He who knows the always-so has room in him for
>   everything;
> He who has room in him for everything is without
>   prejudice.
> To be without prejudice is to be kingly;
> To be kingly is to be of heaven;
> To be of heaven is to be in Tao.
> Tao is forever and he that possesses it,
> Though his body ceases, is not destroyed" (16W).

This chapter touches on so many important points of doctrine that we shall dissect it slowly and carefully. Before taking up its implications on the question of union with God, I think we must digress a moment, and discuss its implications for the question of the soul.

Lao Tzu seems to say here that he *does* believe in the existence and immortality of the soul. At least it is hard to interpret otherwise the lines

> "Tao is forever and he that possesses it,
> Though his body ceases, is not destroyed."

However, such an interpretation must be reconciled with what appears to be a contradiction in Chapter 33.

> "When one dies, one is not lost:
> There is no other longevity" (33W).

These lines read verbatim: "Die but not perish [this is] long-life [*shou*]." Mr. Waley explains[7] them by referring to Chuang Tzu's idea that after death one's left arm may become a cock, one's right arm a bow, one's buttocks wheels. There are no exceptions, in other words, to the law of the conservation of matter and energy. But then what is the "he'" in Chapter 16 who is not destroyed when his body ceases?

These same lines from Chapter 16 are repeated word for word in Chapter 52, but Mr. Waley translates them quite differently. Chapter 16 reads:

> "Tao is forever, and *he that possesses it,*
> *Though his body ceases, is not destroyed"*

while Chapter 52 reads:

> "He who has known the sons
> Will hold all the tighter to the mother
> And *to the end of his days suffer no harm."*

The identical portions are in italics. Verbatim they read: "End (*mo*) body no danger." The problem is: should *mo* be understood as "end" or "to the end"? On such a petty grammatical question depends the existence of the soul in Lao Tzu's teaching. I think we find the answer by examining the clauses of Chapter 52[8] which follow and parallel "end body no danger." In each of them the words "finish body" (*chung shen*) clearly mean "to the end of a man's life." The thought, therefore, is that the Taoist is protected by his imitation of Tao *until he dies.*[9]

When we transfer this interpretation back to Chapter 16, we find

---

[7] The readiest alternative explanation amounts to the rather pointless truism that if a man did not die, he would have long life. Duyvendak suggests that either we understand it in the light of Chuang Tzu or take "to perish" as meaning sudden death, from which the Sage would be protected by his imitation of Tao. Duyvendak also points out that traditional text does not read *wang* "perish," but *wang* "forget." The passage could then be rendered: "To die but not to be forgotten, this is long-life." That seems to make good sense. In effect it is not very different from Mr. Waley's interpretation. An interesting article on this passage by Eduard Erkes and H. H. Dubs appeared in *Asia Major,* III, pp. 157-161.

[8] See p. 69.

[9] This interpretation is supported by the other instances of *pu tai;* cf. Chapters 32 and 44.

that it is consistent with the preceding lines. Lao Tzu is painting a picture of the eightfold path of the mystic. First, the mystic must know the eternal. When he knows it, he will rise to universal understanding; from universal understanding to breadth of personality, and so higher and higher until in the end he assumes the attributes of Tao itself. Then, being completely in tune with the order of the universe, what can harm him? To the end of his life there is no danger. Tao will never fail him. He knows the "sons"—the Ten Thousand Creatures—and, cleaving to their mother, Tao, he manages them. And when, sooner or later, he has to die, is it of any great consequence to him? From the height he has reached his point of view is exceedingly impersonal (though he feels compassion for those who die before they reach that height). His death will furnish physical and spiritual material for future lives. It is as acceptable to him as the fall of a leaf in autumn, whose rotting in spring will nourish the new bud. To the fact that this is the only kind of immortality he is completely reconciled.

Whatever the soul may be, therefore, Lao Tzu does not exempt it from the universal return to non-being. He does not believe in life after death. But this leaves open the question of whether or not there is something in a man which may enter into mystical union with Tao. Two lines in Waley's translation of this same Chapter 16 suggest it: "What has submitted to Fate has become part of the always-so"; "To be of heaven is to be in Tao." Unfortunately, the words "part of" and "in" are due to freedom of translation. Verbatim we have: "Return fate is called eternal"; "Heaven[like] then Tao[like]." I see no justification for reading into this an allusion to mystical union.

Let us return to the first line of Chapter 16. It is a command, literally, to "reach emptiness extreme." What does this mean? A little above (page 63) Chapter 14 was quoted as a description of what Lao Tzu saw in trance:

> "Endless the series of things without a name
> On the way back to where there is nothing."

Literally the second of these lines reads: "reverting returning to what has nothing." Trance, then, is a return to non-being. Now, it can be argued that if you return to non-being, you must unite with it. But, as we have seen, Lao Tzu in his dark chapters on mystical experience does not use the ecstatic language of union. We are once more face to face with the Something Else we discussed in connection with cosmogony. To learn more about "returning" let us re-examine Chapter 40.

> In Tao the only motion is returning;
> The only useful quality, weakness.
> For though Heaven and Earth and the Ten Thousand
>   Creatures were produced by Being,
> Being was produced by Non-being.

The returning motion of Tao has many senses. It refers to the cycle of human events, by which those who are to be abased, are first exalted. It refers to the evanescence of every one of the Ten Thousand Creatures, all of which eventually return to a state of non-being. It refers to the way of the Taoist who erases the marks of society and returns to his original nature. And finally, I think, it refers to another kind of return the Taoist makes—in trance to Non-Being itself.

The experience sounds suspiciously like the fourth and final stage of trance as other mystics have reported it. I called this state "cessation." In a sense all states of trance can be thought of as progressive cessation. When the material world has ceased, a man can have visions; when visions have ceased, he can sense God; when he himself has ceased, he can merge with God. And when God has ceased? That must be the last stage in the progression, though it sounds impious. And yet I think the last stage is something *like* that. In it there is neither desire nor rejection of desire, neither ideas nor absence of ideas, neither ecstasy nor pain. There is, in fact, neither self nor Being. There is simply consciousness that all these have ceased—consciousness, one might say, of Non-Being. It has "the steadiness of the flame of a lamp in a place where there is no wind." Meister Eckhart speaks of this "still desert of the Godhead" as being a place "where never was seen difference, neither Father, Son, nor Holy Ghost, where there is no one at home." "The essence of the soul," Suso tells us, "is united to the essence of Nothingness." Dionysius wrote as follows of the last stage: "Then is he delivered from all seeing and being seen, and passes into true mystical darkness of ignorance where he excludes all intellectual apprehensions and abides in the utterly impalpable and invisible, being wholly his who is above all with no other dependence either on him-

self or any other; and is made one as to his nobler part with the utterly
unknown; and at the same time, in that very knowing nothing, he
knows what transcends the mind of man." This is like the Nirvana of
Buddha and the Nihil of Erigena—though Erigena knew it intellectu-
ally rather than through mystical experience. Consider how Buddha
testified on the progress of cessation: "I have conquered all. I have
known all. I am above all relativities. I have abjured everything. I am
freed from thirst. . . . My mind is tranquil. I have extinguished
everything." Buddha said at another time, "in seeking for salvation I
have reached in experience the Nirvana which is unborn, unrivalled,
secure from attachment, undecaying, unlamenting, and unstained."

With this common negativism in mind and remembering the absence of visions or ecstasy in the *Tao Te Ching,* are we justified in
assigning the mystical experience of Lao Tzu to the fourth and final
stage of trance? Comparison of experiences so subjective is difficult.
But perhaps we can learn a little more by an analysis of the trance-pro-
ducing disciplines. In other words, assuming that like causes bring
like effects, let us find out whether the Taoist discipline resembles
others which lead to the final stage of trance.

Nearly all disciplines begin with meditation, and the object of
meditation is to shut off the outside world. Plotinus writes: "We must
be deaf to the sounds of the sense and keep the soul's faculty of apprehension one-pointed and ready to catch visions from on high." "In
the orison of union," St. Teresa tells us, "the soul is fully awake as regards God, but wholly asleep as regards things of this world and in respect of her self." Al Ghazzali puts it more succinctly: "The first condition for a Sufi is to purge his heart entirely of all that is not God."
A similar thought is expressed in the *Tao Te Ching.*

> "Block the passages, shut the doors,
>   And till the end your strength shall not fail.
>   Open up the passages, increase your doings,
>   And till your last day no help shall come to you."
>   As good sight means seeing what is very small
>   So strength means holding on to what is weak.
>   He who having used the outer-light can return to the
>   inner-light
>   Is thereby preserved from all harm.
>   This is called resorting to the always-so (52W).

"To use the outer light and return to the inner" is parallel to "knowing the white, yet cleaving to the black," discussed above (page 64). "Block the passages" is an important phrase in Taoism. It refers to the Nine Passages[10] of the body, and is repeated in Chapter 56.

> Those who know do not speak;
> Those who speak do not know.
> Block the passages,
> Shut the doors,
> Let all sharpness be blunted,
> All tangles untied,
> All glare tempered.
> All dust smoothed (56W).

Dust, Mr. Waley tells us, is a Taoist symbol for the noise and fuss of everyday life. We have already met four of these lines (pages 48, 63).

Lao Tzu expresses the thought of shutting off the outside world in still another way.

> Learning consists in adding to one's stock day by day;
> The practice of Tao consists in "substracting day by day,
> Substracting and yet again substracting
> Till one has reached inactivity" (48W).

This passage has an ethical sense: subtract every day from your stock of aggressiveness. Esoterically, it is an attack on an intellection. Rather than learning, as all the world tells you, unlearn until you know nothing. When you know nothing, you will know Nothing. We should recall the injunction: "Banish wisdom, discard knowledge" (19). Here we see the highest sense of this phrase that first troubled us when we considered Lao Tzu's attitude towards educators. Lao Tzu believes that God must be approached by ignorance, by the abandonment of reason. In this he is not alone. Following the Neo-Platonist tradition, Nicholas of Cusa wrote: "The place where Thou art found is girt round with the coincidence of contradictories . . . the door whereof is guarded by the most proud spirit of Reason and unless he be vanquished, the way in will not be open."

Meditation, however, is not the essential part of the technique which leads to the final stage of trance, at least not in the East. While

---

[10] Eyes, ears, nostrils, mouth, anus, urethra.

Western mystics like Plotinus and St. Teresa have opposed attempts
to cultivate trance deliberately, feeling that one should not seek it, but
wait for it to come, mystics in the East have employed yoga. Lao Tzu
appears to be no exception. In Chinese, yoga was called *tso-wang* and
later *tso-ch'an*. Although Lao Tzu never used these words, it is probable the practices they referred to are recommended in the *Tao Te
Ching*. Let us consider Chapter 10.

> Can you keep the unquiet physical-soul from straying,
>   hold fast to the Unity, and never quit it?
> Can you, when concentrating your breath, make it soft
>   like that of a little child?
> Can you wipe and cleanse your vision of the Mystery
>   till all is without blur?
> Can you love the people and rule the land, yet remain
>   unknown?
> Can you in opening and shutting the heavenly gates play
>   always the female part? (10W)

Mr. Waley points out that "physical-soul" (*p'o*) had the alternative
meaning of semen; and that "heavenly gates" is an esoteric term for
the mouth and nostrils. The subject of these lines, then, would appear to be a form of sexual hygiene and a breathing technique. Sex in
the *Tao Te Ching* is problematical. We have noted that in his quest
for the Uncarved Block, the Taoist learns to be contented with physical
contentment—as opposed to ambition and greed—but among the varieties of physical contentment sex is not specifically named. On the
other hand it hardly seems likely that a man who discards morality
and does what he naturally wants, will be chaste, unless what he wants
includes a higher stage of trance. Then he may practice continence
much as an athlete, who does not regard cocktails as a sin, goes into
training. There may be a relevant passage in Chapter 55. Comparing
the man of Power (*te*) to an infant, Lao Tzu writes: "[The infant] does
not yet know the union of male and female, yet his little penis is erect.
Indeed he has (or will have) perfection of vitality [or semen]." This,
like Chapter 10 above, could be interpreted to recommend that the
Sage uses continence as an aid in concentrating his energies on trance
and thereby acquiring greater *te*.

Chapter 59 can also be interpreted as a discussion of trance aids.

You cannot rule men nor serve heaven unless you have
　　laid up a store;
This "laying up a store" means quickly absorbing,
And "quickly absorbing" means doubling one's garnered
　　"power" (*te*).
Double your garnered power and it acquires a strength
　　that nothing can overcome.
If there is nothing it cannot overcome, it knows no bounds,
And only what knows no bounds
Is huge enough to keep a whole kingdom in its grasp.
But only he who having the kingdom goes to the Mother
Can keep it long.
This is called the art of making the roots strike deep
　　by fencing the trunk, of making life long by fixed
　　staring (59W).

In the last two lines according to Mr. Waley's translation, Lao Tzu is giving us a prescription for longevity. We have already discussed the return to the root of one's nature and the desirability of a strong trunk —and empty head. "Fixed staring" is the phrase here to be specially noted. Possibly it refers to a technique of self-hypnosis by gazing at a stationary object. Some scholars agree with Waley in taking it thus. Others, like Duyvendak, take it as a synonym for longevity. The literal meaning is "long stare."

The first eight lines of this chapter, which Mr. Waley renders as an esoteric allusion to breath control, can be taken in a purely ethical sense, and that is the case in most translations. "Laying up a store" is literally "moderation," "economy." The eight and ninth lines read, literally, "Having Kingdom's mother (Tao), [one] can thereby last long"; in other words, the man who does not possess Tao, who violates it, will perish. And probably we should take note of the fact that even Chapter 10—the first quotation on yoga—can be given a purely ethical interpretation. Many commentators and translators do so. The vagueness and number of levels which Lao Tzu has written into such passages make them the slipperiest question in the *Tao Te Ching*. If he did intend the book to serve as a manual on yoga, any references to it are so heavily veiled that we cannot interpret them confidently.

We cannot therefore decide very much about the stage of trance that Lao Tzu reached from his methods of reaching it. He reached it by meditation, but this is common to trance in almost all its stages. He probably reached it by yoga, but he does not describe yoga explicitly enough to allow comparisons with other systems of physical aids. He evidently says nothing, for instance, about exercises like turning up the eyeballs at an acute angle, contraction of the abdomen, relaxation in difficult postures, or about fasting or concentration on certain images and ideas—all practices recommended by Patanjali in the Yogasutras. Whether this means that he was unaware of such practices or intentionally omitted them from his book, we cannot tell.

One thing seems likely, however. The many ways of inducing trance besides meditation and yoga, such as the peyote button of the American Indians, the cactus beer of the Mexican Indians, the mass hysteria of the Dervishes, the systematic sexual sublimation of the Tantrists, and the self-mortification practiced by mystics in many times and places—all these were foreign to Lao Tzu. For him trance was something approached by quiet, not by stimulation. Quiet, of course, implies a mild asceticism. But this asceticism cannot be compared to the self-mortification of a fakir, a St. Simon, or a Suso. The *Tao Te Ching* recommends no beds of nails and makes no virtue of lice— the "celestial pearls" of St. Francis. Rather, it recommends moderation. Let us recall Chapter 12, already quoted.

> The five colours blind the eye,
> The five sounds deafen the ear,
> The five tastes spoil the palate (12).

We can understand this now at an esoteric level; not merely as ethical comment, but as advice on how to reduce impediments to trance. When colours, sounds, and tastes are reduced, the Taoist will be ready to see the Secret Essences; in seeing the Secret Essences, he returns to Non-Being; in returning to Non-Being, he reaches the final and highest stage of mystical experience.

Perhaps we are ready to consider the last of the questions that we addressed to Lao Tzu: How does he know that his trance experience is not a lot of imagination?

Other mystics usually answer this question: "Because we *know.*" They feel "the undemonstrable, but irrefragable certainty of God." St.

Teresa tells us: "I shall never believe that any soul who does not possess this certainty has ever really been united with God."

To many of us, though we would agree with St. Teresa, certainty cannot be effectively communicated. We find too many instances of the dubious subjective experience. We think of the schizophrenic, who is just as certain as the mystic of the truth of his hallucinations. We think of our experiences in sleep. We think of hysteria, hypnosis, and anaesthesia.

With such things in mind those of us who are dubious about mystical certainty can probably be pardoned. But we have to reckon with another argument advanced by mystics. This argument bases itself on mysticism's physical phenomena: the stigmatizations, tokens of espousal, marks of wisdom, levitations, immunities to fire and frost, incorruption after death, total abstinence from food and drink, clairvoyance, telekinesis, longevity, and all the other accomplishments that trance is said to make possible in the public, physical world. "If visions are not veridical," mystics ask, "then how do these things happen?"

If we are skeptics, we answer "They don't happen." In giving this answer we reject a vast accumulation of evidence. This is not the place to consider whether it is good or bad evidence. But at least we should see where Lao Tzu stands in the matter. Does he support his claims to veridical mystical experience with references to miracles or other phenomena which impress us, though they may tax our belief?

In general he does not. Much of the miraculous has been read into the *Tao Te Ching* that is not justified by a close examination of the text. Let us see for ourselves.

Chapter 55 seems to make the most specific claim to paranormal powers.

> The impunity of things fraught with the "power"
> May be likened to that of an infant.
> Poisonous insects do not sting it,
> Nor fierce beasts seize it,
> Nor clawing birds maul it (55W).

Does Lao Tzu mean that Taoism is effective as an insect repellent? No, I think his meaning is quite different. It is not the Taoist who is immune to insect stings, but the child to whom the Taoist is likened. Lao Tzu is referring here to a popular myth, found in many folklores, that children because of their innocence survive in the wilderness, and are sometimes even adopted by the fierce beasts and clawing birds. "Even like these children," he tells us, "the power of innocence will protect you in the human jungle."

Another reference to immunity from wild animals can be found in Chapter 50.

> He who aims at life achieves death. If the "companions of life" are thirteen, so likewise are the "companions of death" thirteen. How is it that the "death-spots" in man's life and activity are also thirteen? It is because men feed life too grossly. It is said that he who has a true hold on life, when he walks on land does not meet tigers or wild buffaloes; in battle he is not touched by weapons of war. Indeed, a buffalo that attacked him would find nothing for its horns to butt, a tiger would find nothing for its claws to tear, a weapon would find no place for its point to enter in. And why? Because such men have no "death-spot" in them (50W).

Note that here the whole section on immunity to wild animals is prefaced by the words *kai wen,* "now [I have] heard." Once again Lao Tzu is drawing on folklore for an illustration. The point is the same as in Chapter 55. When the Taoist is attacked, he presents no resistance; there is nothing to "butt," there is no place for a weapon to enter. "This is called the power that comes from not contending."

This same Chapter 50 is sometimes interpreted as claiming physical immortality for Taoists, since it says they "have no death spots," or, literally, "because them no death place." This can be rendered as "beyond death," "out of the way of death," or "immortal." But, as Mr. Waley points out, "death spot" is a military term, something like our "Achilles' heel." The subject of this chapter is not physical immortality, but rather a kind of survival value.

Our thirteen senses and bodily activities—nine openings and four limbs—can be used by a man either to preserve or destroy himself. If he is sensual and aggressive, he aims at life, but achieves death. The hand he raises against his victims is really raised against himself. The mouth he stuffs at others' expense will some day be the death of him. Each of his organs is an Achilles' heel. In perfect contrast is the Quietist. He verily does not have an Achilles' heel in his body, but thrives to a ripe old age on moderation, compassion, and humility (and, as some people might add, because he avoids nervous tension).

A ripe old age has always been considered a great blessing by the Chinese, and is one of the physical phenomena most commonly associated with the mysticism of the *Tao Te Ching*. Marvelous longevity is a feature of the legends about Lao Tzu and later became the central goal of the Taoist movement. Lao Tzu himself, however, at no point promises his followers more than their natural span. Though he calls Tao the way of "long life" (59), he never specifies *how* long.

The Sage's "long life," his survival value, his immunity to the fierce beasts of the human jungle are the result of the way he goes about things, of his innocence and his Three Treasures. They are also the result of the *te* that he acquires through trance. "He who has achieved it [trance] . . . cannot be benefited, cannot be harmed" (56W).

There is one "miracle" to which Lao Tzu refers and for which parallels can be found in other mystical writings. This is a kind of clairvoyance, a direct apprehension of how the universe works.

The theosophist Jacob Boehme tells us that after a trance, "viewing the herbs and grass of the field, in his inward light he saw their essences, use, and properties." George Fox had a similar experience. Plotinus invested animals, plants, and even inanimate stone with souls participating in the One. Anuruddha, Buddha's disciple, wrote that in the fifth dhyana or stage of trance he knew "the destinies of others' lives, whence beings come and whither they go."

With such examples in mind, let us consider the sentence already quoted from Chapter 52 of the *Tao Te Ching*. "He who knows the Mother, thereby knows the sons." The Mother, of course, is Tao; the sons are the Ten Thousand Creatures. Lao Tzu is saying that if you understand the order of the universe, you will understand everything in it. This does not sound particularly esoteric. Chapter 47 may be more so:

> Without leaving his door
> He knows everything under heaven.
> Without looking out of his window
> He knows all the ways of heaven.
> For the further one travels
> The less one knows.
> Therefore the Sage arrives without going,

Sees all without looking,
Does nothing, yet achieves everything (47W).

Of course it is possible to interpret this rationalistically. It may again
refer to the results of understanding the order of the universe or it
may be one of those syncopated passages in which an important quali-
fication is left out to make it more striking. For instance, Lao Tzu
may mean that the Sage, without leaving his door, knows everything
that is worth knowing. But the flavor is esoteric, like the question in
Chapter 10: "Can you penetrate without knowledge to the four cor-
ners of the land?"

Some parapsychologists believe that clairvoyance and pre-cognition
are aspects of a single extrasensory power. It is therefore interesting
that Lao Tzu specifically rejects pre-cognition—if, that is, we go
along with Mr. Waley on Chapter 38: "Foreknowledge may be the
'flower of doctrine (Tao),' but it is the beginning of folly." To call pre-
cognition "the beginning of folly" has a fine, skeptical ring. Are we
justified, therefore, in guessing that Lao Tzu would stand for no extrasensory nonsense?

Unfortunately this is another of those very moot passages. It may
alternatively mean that "former" knowledge (tradition) is the beginning of folly, or the word "foreknowledge" may have the sense of
foresight and planning"—as opposed to living by intuition. The doctrine referred to may not be the Tao of Confucius, as Mr. Waley
thinks, but the Tao of Lao Tzu. Both schools used the word to denote
their Way. In that case, since "flower" has a pejorative sense—more
fluff as opposed to solid fruit—the sentence becomes an attack on tradi-
tionalism: "The 'former knowledge' is the superficial understanding
of the Tao and the beginning of foolishness" (Hu Tse-ling).

Let us move on to a general conclusion. Lao Tzu nowhere specifies
that he acquires information in trance about physical objects beyond
the reach of his five senses. What he acquires seems, rather, to be an
intuitive and ultimately mystical understanding of Tao, of people, and
of life. Without leaving his door he knows everything, in the sense
that, as Mencius put it, "he who completely knows his own nature
knows Heaven."

In this and in all other respects I think it is impossible to extract
any claims from the *Tao Te Ching* that are explicitly miraculous or

paranormal. There is nothing as explicit, for example, as the claims of Patanjali, who said that the Yogi could see past and future, enter another's body, float on water, walk on thorns, become invisible, and so forth. The whole literature of mysticism is full of the most extraordinary physical phenomena, vividly and enthusiastically related. Such material is absent from the *Tao Te Ching*.

And yet, after making an interpretation which rationalizes away all hints at the paranormal, one is left with the feeling that something has been glossed over. Just as the experience of trance is a mystery that outsiders cannot penetrate, so the power that comes from trance is in some way mysterious. Lao Tzu calls it mysterious. It is not enough to explain *te* ("power" or "virtue" like the Latin *virtus*) as the ability of the Sage to turn the human forces around him to his own advantage because he understands them. He is more than a specialist in "human engineering." The role of trance is more than hygienic.

"[The Taoist] has all the time a Power that never fails" (28).

"What knows no bounds
Is huge enough to keep a whole kingdom in its grasp" (59W).

"Push far enough towards the Void
Hold fast enough to Quietness.
And of the ten thousand things none but can be worked on by
you" (16W).

"If one uses [Tao], it is inexhaustible" (35W).

Lao Tzu, I think, is talking about a kind of irresistibility that is sometimes found in great prophets, a force of personality that we cannot rationally account for. He believes that through trance such a force can be cultivated.[11]

This concept has the lack of definition that characterizes the *Tao Te Ching*. We cannot say where it ends and where it begins. Consider, for instance, Chapter 27:

[11] Confucius too seems to have believed in this force, not as something to be acquired through trance, but through knowledge of the Rites. Once he said: "Anyone who knew the meaning of the Ancestral Sacrifice could cope with the empire as easily as I put this here" and he touched his finger to his palm (*Analects* 3:11). Surely this cannot be explained merely in terms of the power of example.

Perfect activity leaves no track behind it;
Perfect speech is like a jade-worker whose tool leaves no mark.
The perfect reckoner needs no counting-slips;
The perfect door has neither bolt nor bar,
Yet cannot be opened.
The perfect knot needs neither rope nor twine,
Yet cannot be untied (27W).

All this can be interpreted as referring to the power of *p'u*—the capacity of the unconscious mind to do work. The man who struggles to carve a piece of jade will mar it, but if he lets his hands guide themselves, the work is easy and perfect. Search our brain for the forgotten word and it never comes; do not search and it comes at once. Let the childless couple adopt a child and they will soon conceive their own. Certain ends are best accomplished without the use of conscious means. The theme here of "ends without means" takes us back to the power of inaction. The Taoist who acts by inaction provides in the ordinary person's view a prime example of obtaining one's ends without the use of means. His "perfect activity leaves no track behind."

Yet such a rational explanation does not seem to be enough. It is too much confined to the behavioural, ethical level of Tao. At the mystical level it is necessary to attribute this "perfect activity" at least in part to a power which, though natural, is unrecognized by Western science.

We embarked on this discussion of miracles and magic to find out how Lao Tzu supported his claims to valid trance experience, how he knew that it was anything more than imagination. This we have not found out, and of course we never can. From the scholar's point of view, it is a waste of time to speculate whether or not Lao Tzu *really* saw the Secret Essences: the important thing is to relate the *Tao Te Ching* to the development of Chinese thought and literature. But from a philosopher's point of view, there is still something to be said about it, which we shall reserve for the last chapter.

One final topic under the heading of mysticism requires attention: the role of the mystic in his community. Does Lao Tzu envision him as a hermit who keeps to his mountain hut and will not stir a step down the path that leads to the dust and noise of the distant village?

That is the traditional picture of the Taoist Sage and the one that Mr.
Waley seems to accept.[12]

From Chapter 27, the beginning of which we have already examined, we learn that the Sage spends his whole life helping his fellow
men.

> Perfect activity leaves no track behind it;
> Perfect speech is like a jade-worker whose tool leaves no mark. . . .
> Therefore the Sage
> Is all the time in the most perfect way helping men,
> He certainly does not turn his back on men;
> Is all the time in the most perfect way helping creatures,
> He certainly does not turn his back on creatures.
> This is called resorting to the Light.
> Truly, "the perfect man is the teacher of the imperfect;
> But the imperfect is the stock-in-trade of the perfect man."
> He who does not respect his teacher,
> He who does not take care of his stock-in-trade,
> Much learning though he may possess, is far astray.
> This is the essential secret (27W).

"Resorting to the Light" is parallel to "essential secret." This enlightenment, this secret, is the wisdom that makes possible the "perfect
activity" of the first seven lines.

On the face of it, the chapter would seem to dispose of the Sage as
hermit. How can he possibly take care of his "stock-in-trade"—his
pupils—if he is separated from them by several miles of woodland?
But this is reckoning without his "mysterious power" or, as Mr.
Waley describes it, his "magical passivity." If we assume that its
magic is powerful enough, he need never leave his door.

However I do not see the need for making this assumption. As
we have seen, the nature and extent of the "mysterious power" is never
defined. A far more economical hypothesis would be that *Te,* while it
can be mysterious, is not specifically magical and that the wordless
teaching carried on by the Sage involves a physical relationship, however indirect, between the Sage and his pupils. I think this hypothesis
is supported by the phraseology of the book.

Seclusion, of course, is necessary to any Taoist, whether he is a

[12] See *The Way and Its Power,* p. 92 and p. 177, note 2.

sage, a ruler, or a layman (the categories are not exclusive). But it is necessary in varying degrees. The layman must have it for self-analysis and understanding Tao if he is ever to return to his original nature and practice inaction. The ruler, whose inaction can facilitate the layman's return, must be that much surer that he has returned himself. His periods of seclusion will therefore be longer. For the Sage—the *sheng jen* or "holy man"—seclusion is most necessary of all. He practices not merely the ethics, but the mysteries of Taoism, and these can only be achieved when he has entirely shut off the outside world. This means long and arduous seclusion. But once the work of seclusion is done, every Taoist, whether layman, ruler, or Sage, returns to live in the world.

How can we know that he lives in the world? Because, as the perfected man, he does not hoard his wisdom. Rather, he "uses up his own last scrap in giving to others" (81). Ignorance is a disease. "The Sage's way of curing disease also consists in making people recognize their diseases as diseases and thus ceasing to be diseased" (71W). Do this teaching and this therapy sound like "absent treatment"?

Then consider Chapter 49.

> The Sage lives in the world carefully.
> Deals with the world carefully.
> He fills his heart with care for everyone.

Does this sound like anchoritism?

Chapter 69 tells us that the Sage plays the debtor's role; in other words, he finds it more blessed to give than to receive. Contracts in China were written on two matching slips of bamboo, the left-hand one being held by the debtor and the right-hand one by the creditor. "The Sage behaves like the holder of the left-hand tally who stays where he is and does not go round making claims on people. For he who has [te] is the Grand Almoner; he who has not [te] is the Grand Perquisitor" (79W). It is hard to see how the Sage can be the Grand Almoner if he never leaves his cave. And, if he sticks to his cave, why is it necessary that he "wear haircloth on top, but carries the jade next to his heart" (70)? [13] How, if people are unaware of

---

[13] Mr. Waley himself says this is "not in the sense that he flies in panic from the horrors of the world." In *Three Ways of Thought in Ancient China*, pp. 83 and 108, he agrees that for Chuang Tzu, at least, the Sage is not a hermit.

his existence, does it happen that they are "unable to understand him" (70W)?

In maintaining that Lao Tzu's Sage "lived in the world" I mean only that at least *some* human beings were exposed to his personality, and that if not directly, then through them he influenced humanity at large. He may have been a recluse with a little circle of disciples; he may have been a boatman or a charcoal seller, plying an obscure trade among the people; he may have been chief minister or even the ruler himself—to whom, after all, the *Tao Te Ching* is directed. But whatever his place in life, he was a "perfected man" who taught the imperfected with a wordless, but unmagical, teaching: by example, by love, humility, and compassion, and by a mysterious, but natural power of his personality.

4. Seeking the Ancestry

> My words have an ancestry,
> My deeds have a lord.

By this Lao Tzu means that a system underlies his philosophy. "It is precisely because men do not understand this that they are unable to understand me." But once the system has been grasped, "my words are very easy to understand and very easy to put into practice" (70W).

We have examined the separate parts of the system. Let us try now to put them together. We have noted that there are several distinct doctrines; that each doctrine can be interpreted at several distinct levels; but it must already be evident that such distinction is artificial. The doctrines interlock with one another and the levels blend into one another. They make a coherent whole that resists analysis and yields to intuition.

Our study of the *Tao Te Ching* began with *wu wei*. By this we understood inaction as a technique for handling people. It is futile to push people around. The harder you push the harder they resist. "Therefore," Lao Tzu might be paraphrased, "therefore *stop* pushing. Become the kind of person whose wish is infectious. Then what you want, others will want, and while you seem to do nothing (*wu wei*), everything will be done. The power of the infectious wish comes from certain virtues: compassion, moderation, and humility. These virtues and their power are *te*.

"*Te* cannot be achieved, however, until you have erased the aggressive patterns etched by society into your nature. You must return to your natural self, to *p'u*. You must discard morality and ambition, for if you keep these you will never be capable of compassion, moderation, and humility. When you discard some of your wishes, you will have them all."

All the above deals with outward inaction, outward virtue, and the discarding of outward impediments. But it invites a series of in-

ward extensions. "For," continuing the paraphrase, "to achieve the outward *p'u* you will have to cultivate a *wu wei* of the mind. And when
the mind is quiet, *p'u* will deepen. It will become a faculty for intuitively sensing the order of the universe—the Tao that can be named.
This Tao is itself characterized by *wu wei*. It does not act, yet by it
all things are acted upon. Sensing it gives you a new kind of *te*. This
te is no longer the effectiveness of outward inaction, but of understanding how and why everything works. With it you can detect
things in the earliest stage of their development, be inspired to art and
poetry, and see into the bottom of people's hearts. For all these reasons
te will make your outward inaction more effective.

"Still you are not far inwards. But practicing *tso-wang* (yoga)
your mind grows quieter, its *wu wei* more complete. The passages are
blocked. The outside world vanishes. You are in trance. Past formless
forms you go back to what you were in the beginning. You approach
the Void. Nothing here has a name, neither Tao, nor its attributes, nor
yourself. But among the attributes of this Absolute Tao is an extension
of the term *wu wei*: the self that is left of you is an extension of the
term *p'u* and its *wu wei* is as complete as Tao's. The *te* of this Tao is
infinite. For what is it that does not come from Non-Being? Your
own *te* is infinite and, when you return to awareness of the physical
world, this infinite *te,* which is more than the effectiveness of outward
inaction and more than the power of intuitive understanding, will
protect you from all harm to the end of your days. There is little
that you cannot do then. You can turn black into white, evil into
good, and harm into help, for in the Absolute Tao all contraries are
one. Indeed, you are now beyond harm, a secret soldier in the army of
Non-Being to whom only Nothing is ultimately important."

Is it necessary that a man reach these innermost mysteries to be
called a Taoist? Paradoxically, the nearer he approaches them, the
easier Taoism becomes. It is hard to follow an ethic because it is logically correct. It is easy if a man can borrow the strength of something
he finds greater than himself.

Lao Tzu tells us, for instance, that our response to hatred should
be *te*. By this he means that when we are attacked, in most cases we
should be passive and in all cases we should regard the attacker with
love, moderation, and humility. This makes an impossible demand
on social reflexes that have been conditioned for survival and success.

And so Lao Tzu tells us that our social reflexes must be erased. But to erase them because it is logically correct is no easier than to respond passively to attack because it is logically correct. There is only one answer: to dissolve reflexes and response alike in a stronger experience, or rather in our memory of it. To do nothing when our cheek stings from the blow, we must remember the time when we knew nothing— a Nothing so overwhelming that the stinging blow is faint, and anger seems irrelevant.

Still, although Taoism becomes easier to practice as we approach its mysteries, it does not insist that we approach them. That is why the *Tao Te Ching* was written in levels, to yield a little or a great deal, depending on the needs of the reader. To the reader unprepared for inner experience, it offers practical advice, which, to the extent that he is able to take it, will help him. For the reader with mystical inclinations it points a way which he can follow as far as he may wish. But to all men it offers a degree of comfort—a cold comfort, it is true, not like the comfort of prayer to a merciful God who may, if he chooses, suspend the order of the universe for the sake of a single penitent. Tao can never be suspended. Dark, infinite, and unchanging it is something a man can depend on to the end of his days. Rationally, intuitively, he can know it, accept it, and bring himself into harmony with it, and mystically he can penetrate to something darker behind it. At each step his comfort will grow, until at the last he feels that "mysterious power" which all of us need to feel, confronted by the hostile immensity of the universe. There is little that we cannot face then. It is a wonderful, almost a miraculous thing that for Lao Tzu this hostile immensity becomes the Mother, symbol of all that is warm and protective.

Thus, in writing levels into the *Tao Te Ching* Lao Tzu did not seek to discourage people from reaching its highest level, but to entice them towards the highest level of which they were capable. Society is not to be envisioned as a hierarchy of castes—layman, ruler, and Sage. The layman can be a Sage and the Sage a ruler. But since the Sage is the "perfected man" he exemplifies *te* in all its senses. Therefore we have license to make his attributes the ideals of the ruler and layman. We may not say of a passage, "Here Lao Tzu is talking about the Sage and so this is inapplicable to the man in the street." Lao Tzu hoped that everyone would become Sage-like. Then society might come back to what it was in the beginning. That is why the ruler must keep his people ignorant and desireless. For if they are ignorant of money and power and feel no desire for them, there will be fewer impediments to their following the Way. They will be able to practice inaction with increasing inwardness. In the end they may return to the Absolute Tao. In other words, there is hope for us or, even for those of us who feel incapable of the mystical life and, perhaps, beyond salvation.

Tao provides the underlying unity in the *Tao Te Ching*. All things come from it and to it all things return. It has many aspects. It is the way of life the Taoist follows, at whatever level. It is the order of the universe. It is the Absolute Non-Being behind that order. Tao is amoral (*pu jen*), but because in its impersonal and relentless functioning, it preserves the Quietist and punishes the aggressor, some may call it a moral order.

English translations of Tao are many: Nature (Watters), Reason (Carus), Logos (Legge), Truth (Cheng Lin), the Undifferentiated Aesthetic Continuum (Northrop) and, most often, the Way.

Tao is the underlying unity: *te* is its power and the power of the man who follows it; *wu wei* is the attribute of both; and *p'u* is the reflection of the former in the latter.

What does it mean to say that *p'u* is the reflection of Tao in man? We have a microcosm, man, and a macrocosm, the universe. Human reason, the nameable Tao of the microcosm, reflects natural law, the nameable Tao of the macrocosm. For, in both, effect follows cause, one and one make two, and mutually exclusive conditions cannot coexist. But human reason is not the ultimate *p'u*. The ultimate *p'u* cannot be named. It is our original nature in the sense of the blank non-being from which we began. The universe also began from non-being. This non-being is beyond reason and natural law. In it one and one can make seven and mutually exclusive conditions flourish together. It has the illogic of the deepest regions of the subconscious, of other realities than our own in space and time.

The doctrine of Tao supplies all the conventional branches of Western philosophy: a metaphysics based on the cosmogony and ontology of Tao itself; a relativistic epistemology with aesthetic corollaries (beauty makes ugliness); and a joint ethics and politics in which *wu wei, p'u,* and *te* are both means and ends. Only a logic is missing. No one would accuse Lao Tzu of making a contribution to logic.

It might be said that to the extent Tao is considered divine, the metaphysics becomes a theology and Taoism a religion. In that case it is a very curious religion. It is not based on faith, but on direct experience of God. It has no place for ritual or priests or church. It promises no response to prayer while we are in this world, and as to the next world, that does not exist—unless it be the state of non-being, which does not sound particularly lively. It vigorously attacks morality and government—two institutions that religion generally supports. And most curious of all, the mystical experience it offers is not ecstatic, but dark, neutral, and uncertain.

For these reasons Taoism as a religion was no success at all. Or rather the highly successful religion which came to be called Taoism has almost nothing to do with the *Tao Te Ching.* This evolution is the subject of the next part of the book.

Part Three: THE TAOIST MOVEMENT

1. The Beginnings of Taoism[1]

Lists of the world's principal religions usually include "Taoism." We might therefore suppose that "Taoism" was a religion comparable to Christianity, Buddhism, or Islam. We might suppose that like them it could be traced back to a founding prophet—in its case, Lao Tzu—whose followers set up a church—the Taoist church; that various branches of Taoism developed as the church divided into sects; and that the church and its doctrines, originally pure, became corrupted with the passing of centuries until they ended up as the Taoist priests and sorcery of today.

This is almost wholly mistaken. Taoism cannot be traced back to Lao Tzu or any other single man. Its principal branches were not offshoots of the Taoist church. Those who set up the church were not followers of Lao Tzu (they turned their backs on almost every precept in his book). The doctrines of Taoism are no more "corrupt" today than they were when it began. And to call it a religion at all is misleading because, though it included a religion, its other elements were equally important.

These other elements were oddly assorted. There was, for example, the science of alchemy; maritime expeditions in search of the Isles of the Blest; an indigenous Chinese form of yoga; a cult of wine and poetry; collective sexual orgies; church armies defending a theocratic state; revolutionary secret societies; and the philosophy of Lao Tzu. Since all these things can properly be termed "Taoist," it is, as you can see, a very broad term indeed, which has proved confusing for students of the Far East and of the history of religion.

No less confusing has been the primary source on Taoism—the Taoist Canon or Tao Tsang. This is a bible in 1,120 *volumes*—not pages—compiled over a period of fifteen centuries. Many of the books

---

[1] Those who would like a fuller set of footnotes for the material covered in these first five sections may consult my paper, "Syncretism in the Early Taoist Movement" printed in the *Papers on China*, Vol. 10, at Harvard University, 1956.

that compose it use an esoteric vocabulary which only initiates were meant to understand, and in some cases the last initiate may have died a thousand years ago. It includes books of divine revelations received by the adept in trance, which are partly or wholly incoherent. Almost no book bears a date or the name of its author. We do not even know the order in which the Canon was written.

It would take decades and whole teams of scholars to make order out of this vast heap of textual material, and more decades to collate it with the related material, even larger in bulk, that may be found in the dynastic histories and collections. The task is so lengthy that it is never likely to be undertaken. But until it is, all discussion of the history of Taoism must be tentative.

To find his way through the complexities ahead the reader may want to equip himself with a map. Let him think of Taoism, then, as a river which united four streams. None of the four was bigger than the others, so none can be singled out as the real headwaters. The river simply began where they met. Lower down in its course it was joined by other streams. Only a little lower, as it approached a long delta, it began to throw off branches. Many of these branches can be identified as the same streams that had flowed in higher up. It was indeed a strange sort of river, with currents flowing side by side, half mingling, half separate. Finally as it broadened towards the mouth at which we stand today, there developed a crisscrossing of watercourses, branching off not merely from our Taoist river, but from the rivers of Confucianism and Buddhism which share the same delta. A complicated picture! But it is no more complicated than the facts.

The four streams which were later to converge in the river of Taoism appear to rise into history about the middle of the fourth century before Christ. It was probably between 350 and 250 B.C. that the names of Lao Tzu, Chuang Tzu, and Lieh Tzu became associated with what we shall call "philosophical Taoism"; their books testified in turn to the existence of a "hygiene school," which cultivated longevity through breathing exercises and gymnastics; early in the same period the theory of the Five Elements was propounded by Tsou Yen, whose followers are thought to have started research on the elixir of life; and lastly, along the northeastern coasts of China, ships began to sail out in search of the Isles of the Blest, hoping to return with the mushroom that "prevented death." Notice that the pursuit of immortality is an element common to three of the four streams I have just mentioned. For the Chinese of that time immortality could only be physical. This was because they considered the personality a composite of several complementary souls that dispersed at death.[2]

Though in history as we have it the appearance of the four streams of Taoism is sudden, clearly each must have had a long period of development. In this development—in the watersheds, so to speak, of the streams—some contribution was probably made by the ancient Chinese shamans who danced and prophesied in trance; by the mediums who represented the dead at funerals; by the anarchistic hermits and agriculturalists mentioned in the Confucian *Analects;* by men like Yang Chu and Sung Tzu; and by experts in the *I Ching,* the oldest scripture we have on divination. But just what their contributions were, we can only conjecture.[3]

We have already discussed the first of the philosophical Taoists, Lao Tzu. What about his successors, Chuang Tzu and Lieh Tzu? They are figures almost as shadowy and controversial as he was. The *Chuang Tzu* was probably compiled during the early decades of the third century B.C. and the *Lieh Tzu* either shortly thereafter (in the opinion of earlier scholars) or in the third century A.D. (according to modern scholars). The doctrines that both these books expound are essentially the same as those we have met in the *Tao Te Ching:* inaction, government by *te,* the relativity of opposites, the search for Tao through meditation, and so forth. There are differences, however, especially in emphasis. Lao Tzu emphasized humility while Chuang Tzu emphasized the danger of high position. From Chuang Tzu we learn more specifically than from Lao Tzu that the artist creates not by reason, but by intuition, not by the study of books and rules, but by losing himself in what he creates—a doctrine that was eventually to determine the course of Chinese art. Chuang Tzu attacks by name the sainted kings of antiquity and ridicules Confucius, who held them up as a model. Lieh Tzu, on the other hand, emphasizes determinism. He taught that cause and effect rather than fate are responsible for the vagaries of life. One chapter of his book is

---

[2] This is further explained on p. 112.

[3] For a good discussion of the origins of philosophical Taoism, see the Introduction to Arthur Waley's *The Way and Its Power.*

devoted to the doctrines of a certain Yang Chu, who shocked the Confucians by saying that a Sage would not sacrifice one hair from his body to save the whole world (on the principle that if everyone did this the world would be saved). Yang Chu's heroes were men who devoted themselves to the most stupefying debauchery. The stupefaction of debauchery was an analogue and perhaps a substitute for the stupefaction of trance. Chuang Tzu and Lieh Tzu, unlike Lao Tzu, were the first Chinese thinkers to suggest that the physical world might be illusory. Each of the three, incidentally, has his own special flavour. While Lao Tzu is reserved, Chuang Tzu is exuberant and imaginative, and Lieh Tzu is ironically witty.[4]

I have not yet mentioned their most interesting difference. There are certain passages where Chuang Tzu and Lieh Tzu allude to magic islands and describe the apparently magic powers of the individual who has perfected himself in Tao. These passages, which have no parallel in Lao Tzu, have been misunderstood, and their misunderstanding has been partly responsible for the development of the Taoist movement. We must give them close attention.

Chuang Tzu tells us, for instance, that on the river island of Ku I there is a Spiritualized Man (*shen jen*) whose skin is white, who does not eat the five grains,[5] but inhales air and drinks dew. He can mount the clouds and drive flying dragons; he can save men from disease and assure a plentiful harvest. He is immune to flood and fire.

In many similar passages Chuang Tzu attributes these and other magic powers to his idealized individual, emphasizing particularly the purity of the latter's essence or breath (*ch'i*). He calls him *chen jen* (Realized Man), *chih jen* (Perfected Man), and *sheng jen* (Sage). There are parallel passages in Lieh Tzu. From Lieh Tzu we also hear for the first time about the Isles of the Blest. They lie in an archipelago

---

[4] Complete English translations of Chuang Tzu have been made by James Legge and Herbert A. Giles. Fung Yu-lan has translated the first seven chapters. Extensive selections will be found in Lin Yutang's *The Wisdom of Lao Tzu* and in Arthur Waley's *Three Ways of Thought in Ancient China*. There is a nearly complete translation of *Lieh Tzu* in two volumes of the Wisdom of the East series: *Taoist Teachings* and *Yang Chu's Garden of Pleasure* by Lionel Giles and Anton Forke respectively. I recommend Chuang Tzu to the attention of readers who do not know him. From a literary point of view his book is superior to the *Tao Te Ching,* and perhaps to any other book in Chinese. Mr. Waley's translations are excellent.

[5] Rice, millet, wheat, barley, and beans. Lists vary. This passage is from *Chuang Tzu* I, 5.

far out to sea. The most famous is called P'eng-lai. On these islands the buildings are gold; all living creatures are white; "immortal sages" live there, who eat sweet flowers and never die. The word used for "immortal" is *hsien*.

We are faced here with a choice that will determine our picture of how the Taoist movement developed. Do Chuang Tzu and Lieh Tzu intend their descriptions of magic powers and islands to be taken literally or allegorically? The argument for taking them literally is strong. A few centuries after Chuang Tzu the Immortals, or *hsien,* took over the center of the stage in Taoism. They became the celestial officials who governed the world from Heaven and, who, though born as men, had won magic powers and immortality through the practice of hygiene. By purifying their breath or essence they acquired immunity to fire and water, could ride the wind, and became immortal; if only the adept could win their favour, they would teach him how to follow in their footsteps.

These later *hsien* were no longer an incidental feature of the misty Isles of the Blessed. They were the saints and archangels of the Taoist pantheon. But it certainly sounds as though they had originated in the philosophical Taoists' descriptions of the Realized Man and the island of P'eng-lai. To a large degree this is true, but it was not, I think, the intent of the philosophical Taoists that it should happen. There are good reasons for supposing that the magical passages in Chuang Tzu and Lieh Tzu are really allegorical, and that it was a literalistic misinterpretation of these passages which was responsible for the later union between the "pure" stream of philosophical Taoism and the "impure" streams of the search for immortality. What are these reasons?

First of all, the *hsien* of later centuries acquired immortality, as I have said, through the practice of hygiene. If Chuang Tzu embraced the cult of *hsien,* we should be able to find people in his book who indulged in that cult's typical pursuits: searching the woods for herbs, living on famous mountains, preparing medicines, retaining and circulating their breath, and practicing gymnastics. And we can find such people. The trouble is that Chuang Tzu unequivocally condemns them. He ridicules those who dwell in solitary places, those who "pant, puff, hail, and sip," who practice "bear-hangings and bird-stretchings" in order to "nourish the body" (*yang hsing*) and live as long as P'eng

Tsu, the Chinese Methuselah.[6] He contrasts them unfavourably with the true Sage, who attains old age without hygiene or anchoritism. In this respect, at least, the Sage is not a *hsien*.

The second respect in which he differs from the *hsien* is in his "lyrical acceptance of death," as Mr. Waley has so well described it. Chuang Tzu's idealized individual not only "offered no resistance to death," but he embraced it with joy. This doctrine, which is implicit in Lao Tzu, becomes explicit in Chuang Tzu and has the highest significance. It is a wholly original answer to the dread that has converted most of mankind to organized religion. Chuang Tzu says that life and death are one, for they are phases of the grand process of Nature in which death can no more be avoided than life and to which submission is the only wisdom. In death the spirit decomposes along with the body, but even physical decomposition is, in Chuang Tzu's view, something wonderful and moving, for new life arises from the materials of the old. Thus it is that the transformations both of living and of dying "afford occasion for joys incalculable. . . . Early death or old age, beginning or end, all are good." [7]

When Chuang Tzu himself was about to die, his disciples expressed a wish to give him a splendid funeral. He said: "With Heaven and Earth for my coffin and shell; with the sun, moon, and stars as my burial regalia; and with all creation to escort me to the grave—are not my funeral paraphernalia ready to hand?"

"We fear," argued the disciples, "lest the carrion kite should eat the body of our Master"; to which Chuang Tzu replied: "Above ground I shall be food for kites; below I shall be food for mole-crickets and ants. Why rob one to feed the other?" [8]

There is danger of a misunderstanding here. I do not mean that Chuang Tzu was lyrical in accepting *premature* death. Death was something that should only come in its time. Immortality in Chinese is *ch'ang sheng pu ssu,* "long life no death." Chuang Tzu does accept the ideal of "long life"; he does not accept the ideal of "no death." The Sage lives long because he models himself on nature, and because he models himself on nature, he has to die.

The third reason we may know the Sage is not a *hsien* is because

[6] *Chuang Tzu,* XV, 1.
[7] *Chuang Tzu* VI, 6 (tr. Legge).
[8] *Chuang Tzu* XXXII, 14 (tr. H. A. Giles).

at the end of some passages on magic powers Chuang Tzu and Lieh Tzu take us behind the scenes and either give us a rational explanation of what was apparently magical or say point blank that it was only an allegory. In *Chuang Tzu* XVII, 7, for instance, we find an example of the former. "He who knows the Tao . . . is sure to understand how to regulate his conduct in all varying circumstances. Having that understanding, he will not allow things to injure himself. Fire cannot burn him who is perfect in virtue, nor water drown him; neither cold nor heat can affect him injuriously; neither bird nor beast can hurt him. This does not mean he is indifferent to these things; it means that he discriminates between where he may safely rest and where he will be in peril; that he is tranquil equally in calamity and happiness; that he is careful what he avoids and approaches; so that nothing can injure him" (Legge translation).

Lieh Tzu gives a similarly rational explanation of immunity to wild animals, and as to the magic islands in his book, they evidently belong to the same allegorical category as the other magical regions he mentions. Such regions are beyond the reach of mortal foot. "Only the soul can travel so far." [9] Journeys of the soul are one of the themes of the philosophical Taoists.

Finally, I think that a literal interpretation of these magic powers and islands is simply against good literary instinct. Chuang Tzu was a poet, though he wrote in prose. He is reaching out for the infinite and wishes us, too, to reach for the infinite. To help us, he gives our imagination the shock treatment. He wants to knock the sense out of us, to make us realize that up is down, asleep is awake, and that we are gross and dull compared with those who have lost themselves in Tao. To take him literally is completely to miss the spirit in which he wrote. He no more intends us to believe that his Spiritualized Man actually rode the clouds or avoided cereals than that the *p'eng* bird was actually many thousand miles in breadth or that Tzu Yü's cheeks were actually level with his navel. Not that I think such fabulous beasts and saints were manufactured out of whole cloth. Probably they were based on folklore that was current at the time. The search for the Isles of the Blest had already begun along the northeastern coast when the *Chuang Tzu* and *Lieh Tzu* were written. To utilize them in allegory was altogether natural.

[9] *Lieh Tzu* II, A.

It is my own opinion,[10] therefore, that though the word *hsien,* or Immortal, is used by Chuang Tzu and Lieh Tzu, and though they attributed to their idealized individual the magic powers that were attributed to the *hsien* in later times, nonetheless the *hsien* ideal was something they did not believe in—either that it was possible or that it was good. The magic powers are allegories and hyperboles for the *natural* powers that come from identification with Tao. Spiritualized Man, P'eng-lai, and the rest are features of a *genre* which is meant to entertain, disturb, and exalt us, not to be taken as literal hagiography. Then and later, the philosophical Taoists were distinguished from all other schools of Taoism by their rejection of the pursuit of immortality. As we shall see, their books came to be adopted as scriptural authority by those who did practice magic and seek to become immortal. But it was their misunderstanding of philosophical Taoism that was the reason they adopted it.

I have given so much space to this question of magic versus allegory not only because the Western reader is in danger of going astray if he should turn to certain pages of Chuang Tzu or Lieh Tzu, but also to support the thesis that the four streams of Taoism—philosophy, P'eng-lai, alchemy, and hygiene—were *separate* when they flowed into history in the middle of the fourth century B.C. Expeditions were by then sailing out in search of the mushroom of immortality, but I do not think Chuang Tzu or Lieh Tzu would have advocated either joining the expeditions or eating the mushroom. In both of their books there is opposition to hygiene and in neither of them is there reference to alchemy. As for Lao Tzu, he does not allude to magic islands or to alchemy. Whether he alludes to breathing exercises is uncertain, but if he does, they are exercises undertaken as a part of meditation leading to union with Tao, not as hygiene leading to immortality. Lao Tzu does refer to immunity from wild beasts—a standard privilege of the later *hsien*—but the first reference is presented as hearsay and the

[10] In contrast to the opinion of Henri Maspero, the great French Sinologist, who took Chuang Tzu literally. See his *Le taoisme,* pp. 201-218. I have been encouraged to find that H. G. Creel agrees with me on this and other conclusions. Indeed there are such close parallels between his paper *What is Taoism?* and my nearly simultaneous paper *Syncretism in the Early Taoist Movement* that I take this opportunity to say that neither of us was aware of the work of the other.

second as a simile.[11] Immunity in the *Tao Te Ching* is of the same nature as immunity in Chuang Tzu and Lieh Tzu.

So much for the philosophical Taoists. So much for the hygiene school, there being little we can add to our knowledge of the school at this early period beyond what we have noted in Chuang Tzu.[12] There is still something to be said about the other two currents of early Taoism: alchemy and P'eng-lai.

The works of Tsou Yen, to whom the origin of alchemy is usually traced, have been lost. But from quotations and discussions of his works we know something of his theories. He believed that the physical processes of the universe were due to the interaction of the five elements of earth, wood, metal, fire, and water. In that order they destroyed one another, and dynasties, each governed by an element, succeeded one another. Tsou Yen was also one of the first geographers. He regarded China as only a small part of the world. In none of this is there anything specifically alchemistic.

Tsou Yen flourished about 325 B.C. A little before 200 B.C. magicians appeared along the northeastern coasts who "transmitted his arts without being able to understand them." Specifically, they "practised the Tao of recipes and immortality (*fang hsien tao*). Their bodies were released, dissolved, and transformed. They relied on serving ghosts (*kuei*) and spirits(*shen*)."[13] We are going to hear a lot about these magicians. They were known as *fang shih,* or "recipe gentlemen."

The magic they practiced is no evidence that Tsou Yen was an alchemist or, for that matter, that they were alchemists. Alchemy, in China, was the search for a chemical elixir of immortality. Their elixirs may have been herbal. Furthermore, we do not know whether they compounded them in spite of or because of their "misunderstanding" of Tsou Yen's arts.

By 100 A.D., however, Tsou Yen had come to be *regarded* as an alchemist. This is clear from a reference in the history of the Early Han dynasty, which was compiled about that time. I think we can conclude that, although Tsou Yen gradually acquired alchemistical stature, he himself knew nothing of the art. It was probably developed

---

[11] See pp. 74-75.
[12] See p. 92.
[13] *Shih Chi,* 28/10b.

by those of his followers who became interested in physical experimentation with the Five Elements. The first elixir they developed was cinnabar, or mercuric sulphide. Arthur Waley has pointed to the use of cinnabar as a pigment on early grave ornaments and suggested that it was thought to have "life-giving" properties. This might have been the germ of the theory that, when properly purified and eaten, it confers immortality. It is actually a poison.

We come finally to the magic island of P'eng-lai, not as a feature of allegory, but as the object of serious maritime expeditions. Ships were sent out as early as the reign of Duke Wei of Ch'i (357-320 b.c.). By the time of Ssu-ma Ch'ien, whose history alludes to these expeditions, the magic islands were no longer thought of as inaccessibly remote, but nearby in the Gulf of Chihli. They might just as well have been remote, however, for everyone who approached them was either blown away by headwinds or found the islands upside down in the water. Nonetheless, because P'eng-lai had "the drug that prevented death . . . there was not one of the feudal lords who would not like to have gotten there."

The origins of the P'eng-lai cult are as obscure as the origins of alchemy. But it may have begun like the legends of other maritime peoples. Traders and fishermen are blown out to sea, land on *terra incognita,* and, when they get home, spin a good yarn about it. Eventually it develops into the Isles of the Hesperides or Prospero's Bermuda. We have no right to scoff at a civilized people like the ancient Chinese for taking such things seriously. There is a parallel here and now in the cult of flying saucers. Other planets take the place of magic islands. Their inhabitants take the place of the Immortals. Already these "Masters" are making their presence known to the adepts of today. I suppose we shall soon have books of revelation, dictated to the adepts by our interstellar visitors in remote and secret places. That, at least, was the way it developed in China.

2. *The Period of Syncretism*

The century from 220 to 120 b.c. was the period in which the four separate streams we have been discussing met to form a broad river. They met for a good reason. As I have pointed out, all of them had in common the pursuit of immortality—all, that is, except the philosophical

Taoists, and the same pursuit could, through misinterpretation, be attributed to them.

The principal agents of syncretism were the magicians, or *fang shih,* from the northeastern littoral. After the first Emperor, Shih Huang Ti, united China in 221 B.C., these specialists in immortality flocked to his court. I have already mentioned them in connection with Tsou Yen, whose theory of the Five Elements they had adopted. They persuaded the First Emperor to adopt it too. His dynasty, the Ch'in, was considered to represent the element *water* and the colour *black.* This was because it had destroyed the Chou Dynasty, which represented *fire* and *red,* and water is the destroyer of fire.

Furthermore, the magicians had become experts in the search for P'eng-lai, which had been carried on for more than a century in their part of China. Thus they persuaded the First Emperor to equip maritime expeditions, the most famous of which were led by the magician Hsü Fu. Some were on a vast scale. One carried 3,000 youths and maidens as well as the seeds of the five grains and artisans of every kind. Although Ssu-ma Ch'ien makes contradictory references to Hsü Fu, it seems clear that he always returned empty-handed.

Another magician named Master Lu urged the Emperor to conceal his whereabouts and thereby to avoid evil spirits and attract the Realized Man (*chen jen*). "Realized Man" was one of the epithets that we may remember Chuang Tzu applied to his ideal individual.[1] The influence of Chuang Tzu here is further suggested by the terms in which Master Lu described him. "The *chen jen,*" he said, "enters water without getting wet and fire without getting burned. He rides the clouds and mists. He is as eternal as Heaven and Earth. . . . Your majesty governs the Empire without rest. We want your majesty to permit no one to know what palace you are in. Thereafter the drug of immortality may be found." [2] The line of reasoning in this curious statement may escape us, but it pleased the First Emperor. He began to call himself "Chen jen" and to conceal his whereabouts. He ordered that his 270 palaces, which covered some twenty square miles, be connected by covered ways, so that no one could see his coming and going. Those who mentioned where he was were executed. He went incognito even on his frequent journeys to the

---

[1] See p. 91.
[2] *Shih Chi,* 6/23b.

northeast coasts, where he used to range the beaches hoping for a glimpse of P'eng-lai.

Ch'in Shih Huang set himself a daily quota of a hundred pounds of documents. Until he had personally reviewed and acted upon them, he would not retire to bed. That is presumably why Master Lu had protested that the Emperor governed "without rest." He and the other magicians must have feared lest the imperial work day impair the life that they were committed to prolong. Finally Master Lu fled from court. Ch'in Shih Huang was so annoyed that he executed 460 magicians and scholars. Two years later he was on the coast again, where he fell ill and died. His last act had been to shoot a large fish that was said to bar the way to the magic islands.

Such was the influence of the magicians on the First Emperor. A century later they repeated and redoubled their successes, this time with the most famous Emperor of the Han Dynasty, Wu Ti (140-87 B.C.).[3] One after another, the *fang shih* came to court and won his favour. The first of them was Li Shao-chün.

Li Shao-chün represents a new phrase. He trafficked not in the Five Elements, like the magicians of a century before, but in alchemy proper. His emphasis was not on P'eng-lai's "marvelous drug," but on the *hsien* who lived there. He believed it possible for a man to become a *hsien* and that, when he did so, he would not only be immortal, but acquire magic powers like invisibility. Thus the *hsien,* who began as an incidental feature of P'eng-lai, acquired the magic powers with which the Realized Man had been invested by Chuang Tzu and the immortality with which he had been invested by Master Lu. One might say that the cult of *hsien* had now begun. This is only a small part of what Li Shao-chün contributed.

Let us consider his experiment in alchemy. In 133 B.C. he persuaded the Emperor Han Wu Ti to seek for immortality by transmuting cinnabar into gold. This is the earliest clear instance of alchemy recorded in East or West. It is important, however, to note certain differences from alchemy as it later developed in China: the transmuted cinnabar is not to be eaten, but to be eaten out of (after being made into vessels); and it does not confer immortality, but only longevity. Given longevity, one can see the *hsien* on P'eng-lai. "When

---

[3] Here and below the dates given for a ruler are those of his reign, not of his life.

you have seen them and made the *feng* and *shan* sacrifices, then you will not die." [4]

The first step in transmuting cinnabar, as proposed to Wu Ti by Li Shao-chün, was sacrifice to the Stove. The God of the Stove (Tsao Chün) was to become one of the great divinities of Taoism. Under the title of Director of Destinies (Ssu-ming) he kept a register of men's good and bad deeds and determined the length of their lives through his recommendations to Heaven. By the third century A.D. he had acquired a niche in the house, and even today, as the Kitchen God, he is worshipped in almost all Chinese families, who sacrifice and feast at New Year's on the occasion of his annual trip to report to the Jade Emperor.

Tsao Chün's entry onto the scene is significant not only because it shows that the early alchemists considered divine favour necessary for success, but also because he is the first clearly identified divinity to be associated with any current of Taoism. For at least a century before, anonymous spirits (*shen* and *kuei*) had figured in the cult of P'eng-lai and magic recipes. But they had no well-defined function, place in Heaven, or mode of worship.

The God of the Stove, as I say, had another title: Director of Destinies, or Ssu-ming. This title originally may have represented a separate divinity and one which had had a long history. At least as early as the eighth century B.C. the Book of Documents[5] tells us: "Heaven, looking upon men below, keeps a record of their righteousness and accordingly bestows on them many years or few." There is a bronze from the sixth century B.C. that records offering two jade goblets and eight tripods to Ta Ssu-ming, the Great Director of Destinies. This bronze comes from Ch'i, the land of the shamans and magicians. In the fourth or third century B.C. Ssu-ming was a god with whom the shamans of Ch'u sought mystical dalliance. For them he was already the regulator of the length of human life. He was still being worshipped by the Ch'u shamans a few years before Li Shao-chün appeared at court. If, as the *Li Chi* indicates, Ssu-ming had *already* been identified with the God of the Stove when Li Shao-chün sacrificed to the latter in 133 B.C., then the God of the Stove is not a new divinity, but only new to Taoism. Ssu-ming is a good example of the difficulties

[4] *Shih chi,* 28/21b.
[5] *Shu ching, Kao Tsung jung jih,* 3.

we meet in tracing the origin of elements of the Taoist movement, especially of the problematical role played by the shamans.[6]

We must return now to Li Shao-chün, and discuss the background for another aspect of his activities.

Li was apparently the first of the magicians to take up hygiene. The hygiene school had not been quiescent during the two centuries since it was first mentioned by Chuang Tzu. There are passages in other and later books on meditation and breathing exercises. The *Lü Shih Ch'un Ch'iu* (written before 235 B.C.) tells us, for instance, that the adept must keep his body and breath in motion to prevent decay. "If the vital breath is renewed every day and the bad breath entirely leaves the body, then man may reach the age of Heaven itself." [7] In the biography of Chang Liang, we read that after he had helped win the empire for the Han Dynasty, he retired to practice gymnastics and abstain from cereal food. This is the first instance we have seen of grain avoidance since Chuang Tzu mentioned it in his allegory of the Spiritualized Man.[8] It may be as legendary as many other details of Chang Liang's biography.

Li Shao-chün, however, was a contemporary of Ssu-ma Ch'ien and there is no reason to question as legendary the historian's statement that he practiced the "grain method" (*ku tao*). What might be questioned is whether he also practiced breath control and gymnastics. Perhaps the magicians had yet to take up these chief practices of the hygiene school.

Li Shao-chün not only promised the Emperor immortality after seeing P'eng-lai, but he said that he himself had been to P'eng-lai. Li Shao-chün was presumably, therefore, already immortal, and in fact that is how he advertised himself, for he "knew the art of avoiding old age" and in several famous episodes showed his familiarity with the events of hundreds of years before. It might be supposed that his death would have shaken the faith of Han Wu Ti. On the contrary, the

---

[6] The shamans as such never seem to have been absorbed into the Taoist movement, although some of their activities, like divination, exorcism, medicine, and preparation of elixirs, were parallel to those of their Taoist counterparts, the *fang shih* and *tao shih*. Governmental discrimination against the shamans began in 31 B.C. when their seances were barred at court, and ended in their complete proscription from the Sung Dynasty onwards.

[7] *Lü Shih Ch'un Ch'iu*, IV, 3.

[8] See p. 91.

Emperor decided that "he had been transformed and departed and had not died." The French scholar Henri Maspero considers this the first instance of "Liberation from the Corpse" (*shih chieh*) which in later centuries came to be considered the regular demise of the *hsien*. To avoid creating a sensation when they achieved immortality, they would go through the motions of death and burial. If at some later time their graves were opened, only a cane or a sword and some loose clothes would be found.

If we add up Li Shao-chün's accomplishments, the total is impressive. So far as we know, he was the first alchemist; the first man to worship a clearly identified Taoist divinity; the first *fang shih* to take up hygiene (though probably only grain avoidance); the first man to "die" like a *hsien;* he was an expert in the cult of P'eng-lai; and some of his ideas, like magic powers and grain avoidance, may be traceable to the texts of philosophical Taoism. Here is syncretism far advanced. On the other hand, there is no evidence as yet that the *adherents* of philosophical Taoism were having traffic with Li Shao-chün or any other magician.

This last statement, which would be an important one if it could be proven, is to some extent confirmed by the position of Ssu-ma Ch'ien. A later historian asserted that Ssu-ma honoured the words of Huang-Lao[9] more than the Five Classics. In his history, the Taoists are treated by far the most favourably of all the philosophical schools. And yet there is no question about Ssu-ma Ch'ien's attitude towards the magicians. He considered them charlatans and despised them. This suggests a clear distinction between other currents of Taoism, now merging at the hands of the magicians, and the philosophical Taoists, who "practised the words of Huang-Lao."

After the death of Li Shao-chün developments came thick and fast.

Before 122 B.C. another magician, Miu Chi, memorialized the Emperor concerning the worship of T'ai I, or the Grand Unity, saying that he was the noblest of the gods. Here we have the second new

---

[9] I.e., Huang Ti and Lao Tzu. Huang Ti was the mythical Yellow Emperor. One of the early Taoist books (now lost) bore his name. Since about 200 B.C. "Huang-Lao" had figured in the vocabulary of the philosophical Taoists. An early Han general studied how "to cultivate Tao in honouring purity and calm" from a man who excelled in practicing the sayings of Huang-Lao. The Dowager Empress Tou (d. 135 B.C.) also practiced the sayings of Huang-Lao. This pair of authors was later to become Huang-Lao Chün, the god of the Yellow Turbans.

divinity in Taoism, and one who was to have as important a place for a time as the God of the Stove.

T'ai I presents us with many problems. While some of his roots are to be found in philosophical Taoism, others are certainly in shamanism. Like the Director of Destinies, he is mentioned in the Nine Songs.[10] In fact, the first of the nine takes his name as its title and celebrates the offering of meats and wine to please the "Monarch on High," as it calls him. By the time of the Han he had come to reside in the Pole Star.

T'ai I's roots in philosophical Taoism may go as far back as Lao Tzu. Chapter 42 of the *Tao Te Ching* states that "Tao produced the One; One produced Two; Two produced Three; Three produced the Ten Thousand Things." Chuang Tzu speaks of the Great Unity (Ta I) and the Grand Unity (T'ai I). A half-century later, after ideas of *yin* and *yang* had spread through China, we learn from the *Lü Shih Ch'un Ch'iu* that "T'ai I produced the Two Forms; the Two Forms produced *yin* and *yang*." [11]

Philosophically, then, T'ai I represented the attempt to find a unity underlying the diversity of the universe. At first it was thought of as the unity that antedated creation: later it was also the unity in which the opposites, Yin and Yang, were reconciled.

I suspect that the T'ai I of the shamans and the T'ai I of the philosophers came into being independently and that they were united at the hands of the magician, Miu Chi. Whatever the truth is, Wu Ti eventually became enthusiastic about T'ai I and sacrificed to him on several occasions.

Soon after Miu Chi's successes, someone proposed the worship of the Three Ones, San I, a triad that *included* T'ai I, as well as T'ien I, the Heavenly One, and Ti I, the Earthly One. From now on, Taoist theology was never without three supreme divinities, though their identity was often to change. The Three Ones may be connected with the Three that arose from the Two that arose from the One according to Chapter 42 of the *Tao Te Ching*.

This triad raises questions. If T'ai I was all-embracing unity, why

---

[10] The mystical hymns attributed to the shamans of the fourth and third century B.C. in the southern kingdom of Ch'u. Arthur Waley's translation, *The Nine Songs,* is the best English source on Chinese shamanism.

[11] *Lü Shih Ch'un Ch'iu,* V, 2.

was he not three in one rather than one of three? According to Miu
Chi, the Five Emperors served him as assistants. They were the gods of
the five elements and of the corresponding five seasons, directions,
colours, and so forth. What relation do they have to Ssu-ming and Ta
Chin who are also called his assistants? This is only a foreshadowing
of the vast and hopeless confusion that arose as Taoist divinities multi-
plied in the Six Dynasties. Now, as then, we must not expect to be
able to draw up a consistent scheme. We might note this much, however. Ssu-ming, or the Director of Destinies, was identified with the
God of the Stove. Therefore the God of the Stove, worshipped by the
first magician, Li Shao-chün, was the assistant of T'ai I, the Grand
Unity, worshipped by the second magician, Miu Chi, and both these
divinities were worshipped by Shao Weng, who was magician number three in the series who won the favour of Han Wu Ti.

We have seen how the magicians wove together the various threads
of Taoism. They did not, however, have any monopoly on the Taoist
movement. Outside their circle the philosophical Taoists had continued to study the teachings of Lao Tzu and Chuang Tzu, and some
of them took up the study of alchemy. The most important of the
philosophical Taoists were members of the Imperial family.

The Emperor Han Wen Ti (179-157 B.C.) is often called a Taoist,
and his wife was certainly one. He established professorships, all but
one in non-Confucian philosophies. He patronized the worship of the
Five Emperors by a pair of charlatans who were finally exposed in
164 B.C. But, most interesting to us, he applied the political doctrines of
Lao Tzu to the government of the Empire. Wen Ti was one of the
best emperors the Chinese ever had. He abolished mutilating punishments. He abrogated the law that a whole family must be exterminated
for the crime of one of its members. He reduced and at one time
wholly abolished the land tax. Rather than waging war against the
barbarians who threatened the northern marches, he pursued a policy
of friendship, gifts, and trade. He practiced economy and interfered
in the affairs of his people as little as possible. As a result China became more prosperous than it had been for many centuries.

Wen Ti's son, Ching Ti (156-140 B.C.), was the first emperor to
recognize the *Tao Te Ching* as a classic. His nephew, Liu An
(Huainan Tzu), was the author or at least the patron of one of the
later texts of philosophical Taoism, the *Hung Lieh*. Liu An is also

credited with several books on alchemy, which have been lost. Dying in 122 B.C., he appears to have been an important figure in the history of Taoist syncretism, for he was both an alchemist and a follower of Lao Tzu and Chuang Tzu, and thus represented the first breach in the "purity" of philosophical Taoism.

The last member of the Imperial family whose Taoist activities we shall mention is Liu Hsiang. In 60 B.C. he persuaded the Emperor Han Hsüan Ti that with certain books of Liu An which he had acquired, he could make the elixir of immortality. Naturally the Emperor was intrigued. If his cousin could make the elixir, his reign would last forever and he would succeed where Ch'in Shih Huang and Han Wu Ti had failed. He ordered that Liu Hsiang be given all financial assistance. The years passed: the elixir was not forthcoming. In 56 B.C. the Imperial patience ran out and Liu Hsiang was sentenced to death. Fortunately, his brother was able to ransom him, so that he lived on to become a prolific writer and bibliographer. The incident is important, however, because it was to be many years before alchemy recovered the prestige it had lost in this notorious fiasco.

3. The First Four Centuries A.D.: The Interior Gods Hygiene School

We have now reached the Christian era. We have seen how P'eng-lai, *hsien,* alchemy, gods, and hygiene have gradually become the branches of a single science of immortality: only philosophical Taoism has not been brought fully into the stream, but it is beginning to be.[1] Standing at this point in history it is hard to see what further development was possible beyond the completion of the syncretic process. But the next three centuries were to see new and surprising departures in Taoism: first, the rise of what I shall call the Interior Gods hygiene school; and second, the sudden spread of collective worship under a fighting church. At the same time there was a renascence

[1] H. G. Creel in *What is Taoism?* (p. 150) calls attention to some very significant passages in the *Lun Heng* written by Wang Ch'ung (27-*ca.* 100 A.D.). Wang Ch'ung refers to a belief that immortality can be won by means of the doctrine of Lao Tzu. He calls Han Wu Ti's magicians *tao shih* (the term later used for Taoist priests). He attributes the practice of hygiene to the *Tao chia* (a term usually applied to the *philosophical* Taoists). Prof. Creel is surely right in considering this evidence of a great advance in syncretism during the preceding century. There is other evidence; e.g., about 30 B.C. a shaman-physician named An-ch'iu Wang-jih was known as an outstanding authority on the *Tao Te Ching.*

of philosophical Taoism under the label of "Pure Conversation." This renascence presaged a change in the developmental process: syncretism was reversed. Currents now began to branch off as well as to join in. First alchemy and then hygiene largely separated from the main stream. Some currents, like the search for P'eng-lai, simply vanished. From this time on, many of the important figures were eclectics who mixed their own brand of Taoism. Ko Hung is a good example.

All this makes it even more difficult than before to trace the development of the Taoist movement and to fix its chronology. The difficulty is aggravated by the fact to which I alluded at the beginning of the chapter: very few of the books in the Taoist canon bear the name of an author or a date. Their provenance can only be determined by internal evidence or by their mention in a text whose date we know.

That applies particularly to the Interior Gods hygiene school, an offshoot of the main hygiene school, by which it was both preceded and survived. This was the school which the late Henri Maspero studied for better than thirty years and on which he must be acknowledged the outstanding Western authority.

What he considered the basic text, the *Jade Classic of the Yellow Chamber*,[2] was probably written in the first two centuries A.D. It is confused and cryptic. Its content was systematized in the *True Classic of the Great Mystery*[3] which in turn was the authority for a series of five texts in the Taoist canon written in the fourth to sixth centuries A.D. In the sixth century the school died out because of the competition of the Ling-Pao doctrines.[4] During its flowering, however, it introduced ideas that were certainly novel.

One idea was that every man has three vital centers in his body, one in the head, one in the chest, and one in the abdomen. They are called Fields of Cinnabar (*tan t'ien*), which suggests that alchemists must have played a role in the founding of the school. Furthermore, every man's body is inhabited by 36,000 gods—the same gods who, as celestial bureaucrats in their various heavens, govern the physical universe. Thus the body is a microcosm of the universe. My left eye is the sun, and in it lives the sun god. My right eye is the moon, and so forth. The most important divinities are the Three Ones (San I),

[2] *Huang T'ing Yü Ching*
[3] *Ta Tung Chen Ching*
[4] To be explained on pp. 136-137.

each presiding over a Field of Cinnabar. They, in turn, are presided over by T'ai I,[5] who lives in one of the nine compartments that comprise the Field of Cinnabar in the head. In a neighbouring compartment lives the Director of Destiny (alias the God of the Stove). There, as in his palace in Heaven, he keeps the Book of Death (listing those who must die) and the Book of Life (listing the Immortals). The object of hygiene is to be transferred from the first to the second. Thus we find here, shifted to the body, the theological system of Han Wu Ti's magicians.

But we also find someone whom, in Han Wu Ti's time, the magicians had not begun to worship. That is Huang-Lao,[6] now reduced to a single individual and elevated to the status of a god, Huang-Lao Chün. He governs the world, but does not interfere in it. Lao Tzu was one of his avatars. He is a member of the Supreme Triad, which appears to be distinct from the Three Ones, although, like them, it resides in the body. The Supreme Triad is probably a later accretion than the Three Ones and represents an attempt to capitalize on Huang-Lao Chün's growing popularity in the second century A.D.

It is essential to understand that in all the non-philosophical schools of Taoism, the pantheon was continuously growing and shifting. Existing gods were accepted from every source. Even Confucius eventually became one (with the title of "Duke Superior Truth of the Grand Ultimate"). At the same time new gods were created on a scale that can only be called mass-production. This was because every adept had a god as his patron, from whom he got instruction in hygiene. The objective was to get instruction from as highly placed a god as possible; but not everyone could begin as the client of T'ai I or Huang-Lao Chün. When the clients of lesser gods came to write their books, they naturally assigned their patrons a place in heaven—and the higher the better. This made for vast confusion.

In general, the pantheon was modelled on the Chinese imperial government. There were departments in charge of the various processes of nature—thunder, rain, the sun, and so on. The adept who attained immortality as a *hsien* was admitted to one of these departments, his rank depending on his merit and his skill in hygiene. As Maspero

[5] The Grand Unity, or Grand One.
[6] See note on p. 102.

puts it so well: "Even in the divine world the Chinese could think of no greater felicity than to be a bureaucrat." [7]

According to the Interior Gods school of hygiene, as I have said, the whole celestial pantheon is inside the human body. Its 36,000 divinities are necessary for life. When they depart, the adept dies. Hence his task is to keep them at their post. This he accomplishes by the "interior vision," reviewing in trance the five gods of the spleen, the seven gods of the kidneys, and so on, but most particularly visualizing T'ai I. Unfortunately these gods detest the smell of wine and meat. Hence the adept avoids eating them. Furthermore, besides the 36,000 gods, man is host to the Three Worms, one in each Field of Cinnabar. They are the cause of disease, old age, and death. What do they live on? The five grains. These too must be avoided, which hardly permits the adept a well-balanced diet. Some got down to eating nothing but jujubes.

The most advanced adept eats no solid food at all. This is because solid food fills the body with excrement, and excrement inhibits the circulation of breath. To open up the channels of circulation the adept practices gymnastics, *tao yin,* stretching like a monkey and twisting his neck like an owl. Having cleared his interior channels, he can undertake Embryonic Respiration.

Embryonic Respiration means a breathing like a child in the womb. Shortly before dawn the adept retires to a square chamber, closes the doors, and stretches out on a soft bed with a pillow two and one-half inches thick. He folds his hands and closes his eyes. Then he commences to hold his breath. Holding it for 12 heart beats is a "little tour." Holding it for 120 heart beats is a "big tour." If he can get up to 1,000, he is approaching Immortality. Not merely does the adept hold his breath; he guides it through his body. This is called *hsing ch'i.* The air that ordinary people inhale goes down through the heart and spleen to the liver and kidneys (its passage through the spleen, incidentally, is what pumps the blood out into the veins). But the adept knows how to conduct his breath beyond the liver and kidneys to the Lower Field of Cinnabar, thence to the soles of the feet, up the spine to the brain, down to the chest, and up again to the throat. He guides it by the same "interior vision" that enables him to see the

---

[7] *Le taoism,* p. 31.

gods inside his body.[8] He is careful to send it coursing through any afflicted areas, since poor circulation is the cause of disease.

All this time he has been accumulating saliva, or Jade Liqueur, by keeping his tongue arched against the roof of the mouth. After he has conducted a mouthful of breath to the back of the throat, he swallows it down with a liquid "cork." Breath and saliva are the purest nourishment. If the adept can learn to make them his exclusive diet, his body will become light and so transparent that it casts no shadow. He will be able to ride the wind. Of course there is a certain knack to these "feasts of emptiness." If the adept has not acquired it, even eating them forty or fifty times a day will leave him with a hungry feeling.

One of the vital steps in hygiene is to unite breath with semen accumulated[9] in the Lower Field of Cinnabar, and thus to form the Mysterious Embryo. It is the Mysterious Embryo that is nourished on breath and that gradually develops into a new, pure body inside the old one. When the adept "dies," this pure body is released from his corpse,[10] and he becomes an Immortal.

It must not be thought that the adept found hygiene an easy vocation. Even if he limited his dieting to the elimination of grains, wine, and meat, we are told that he suffered from dizziness, sleepiness, diarrhea, and constipation. For the first month or so, he had to fortify himself with drugs—digitalis, for example. Embryonic Respiration could also be uncomfortable. After the adept had held his breath for a period of 300 heartbeats, his "ears no longer heard, his eyes no longer saw, his mind no longer thought. . . . In a while he had a stomach ache." To practice Embryonic Respiration several hours a day, to live on a diet of roots and berries, and to devote the necessary time to study and meditation hardly permitted the adept to hold an ordinary job. Hygiene was his life work and so intricate and rigorous that he had to commence it while still young if he was to have any hope of success.[11]

---

[8] This "interior vision" was probably facilitated by CO_2 intoxication that must have resulted from holding his breath so long. CO_2 intoxication, which resembles the effect of some hallucinagenic drugs, would account for the vividness of what the adept saw inside his body, such as the God of the Spinal Column three and a half inches tall, dressed in white.

[9] By such methods as those described on pp. 120-121.

[10] *Shih chieh.* See p. 102.

[11] Once again we have no right to scoff at the Ancient Chinese for taking such

The Interior Gods school was responsible for an important innovation in hygiene: good works. The gods in the adept's body would not cooperate unless he was virtuous and public-spirited. Hence Taoists began to repair roads and bridges, endow orphanages, care for the poor, and minister to the sick. There was a sliding scale of rewards and punishments. For example, 120 sins resulted in illness; 530 in stillborn children; 10,000 in being publicly executed with all one's family. On the other hand the adept who performed 300 good deeds became an

things seriously. There is a parallel to Taoist hygiene in America today and it is even closer than the parallel, suggested above, between the Immortals and men from Flying Saucers. I have in mind the cult of Breatharianism, propagated by the Natural Science Society of Maitland, Florida. According to Breatharian doctrine, eating is the cause of death. Meat and wine are poisonous; vegetables are even more poisonous (the Breatharian, like the Taoist, is particularly careful to avoid the "five sharps"—onions, leeks, etc.); but most poisonous of all are pulse and cereals, in other words, the Five Grains. This is because they are *artificial*, the result of crossing and selection of strains. They "induce thickening and hardening of the muscles and arteries and . . . premature Old Age." The only foods that are relatively harmless are berries and fruits (just as they were for the Six Dynasties Taoist adept), but even Frugivorianism is only a stage on the way to the ultimate goal—living on Air.

Air, according to the Breatharians, is the "Spiritual Essence of the Universe," like *ch'i* for the Taoists. It is absorbed into the body through the Five Sinuses, or "Spiritual Chambers," which sound somewhat like the Nine Compartments of the Upper Field of Cinnabar in the head. These Chambers are "The Temple of God," while the body of man is itself a Microcosm, "a miniature Universe; all things contained in the Macrocosm are also contained in the Microcosm in character if not in degree." The parallel to the interior Gods in the bodily microcosm of the Taoist is not complete, but it is suggestive.

What can the Breatharian expect to accomplish by his conversion to a diet of Cosmic Rays and Pure Air? First of all, like a Realized Man, he will be "impervious to heat, cold, hunger, and fatigue." Second, he will be able to live for hundreds of years; and third—if he is really successful—he will become Immortal. Voluminous evidence is given us, like the case of the woman who, as of May 3, 1936, had neither eaten nor drunk for 56 years and "at the age of 68 years acted and looked like a child." Then there are the people in the Himalayas among whom "ages well beyond 250 years are common." Evidence of immortality itself I cannot quote because I have not purchased the next set of lessons, entitled *Immortalism*.

Breatharianism and the Taoist hygiene school have so much in common that it is hard to believe there is no connection. Such, however, is the case. It may be that health cults throughout the world reflect certain archetypal attitudes towards the body. I have tried without success to get a copy of Ludwig Staudenmaier's *Die Magie als Experimentelle Naturwissenschaft* (1912) in which he discusses the coördination of his "partial souls" with certain organs of the body. Some of these souls, which appeared to him in his interior visions as evil goat-like faces, were connected with parts of the lower intestines. See H. Silberer, *Problems of Mysticism and Its Symbolism* (1917), p. 264.

Earthly Immortal or *Ti Hsien*. If he performed 1,200, he soared up to become an Immortal in Heaven. At any time, however, all his credit could be cancelled by a single backward step. Note that he helped the poor and the sick not out of compassion (any more than he avoided meat out of compassion for sentient beings), but solely in order to procure personal immortality.

The Interior Gods hygiene school drew its materials from many currents of Taoism: not from P'eng-lai, but from a development of P'eng-lai, the cult of *hsien;* its texts quote Lao Tzu, but misinterpret him; it acknowledges the efficacy of alchemy, from which it has borrowed some of its terms, but does not seem to have been much interested in preparing the elixir; it owes some of its gods to the Early Han magicians and many of its practices to older schools of hygiene. But, on the whole, it was an original development. Its hallmark was the abstention from wine. All other early schools of Taoism, I believe, were wine-drinkers. The Taoist church used wine in its rites: Chi K'ang, the poet, used to pass the evenings getting drunk at Mr. Huang's tavern; Ko Hsüan, the alchemist, often spent a whole day, when very drunk, at the bottom of the pond. Chuang Tzu and Lieh Tzu both praised wine. Hence, when we come across a Taoist who rejects wine, it is probably that he is doing so to avoid offending the Interior Gods and belongs to the school to which I have given that name.

There is one other influence to be mentioned in connection with the school: that of Buddhism. One of the nine compartments which composed the Field of Cinnabar in the head was called the Palace of Ni Huan. This is the term (meaningless in Chinese) used to transliterate the Sanscrit "Nirvana." It cannot antedate the introduction of Buddhism in the first century A.D. Buddhist influence is also suggested by the abstention from wine and meat, and by the good works, though the Taoists' different justification of these practices may argue against it. Fasting, on the other hand, is an ancient Chinese custom, and precedents for charity can be found in Mo Tzu and Sung Tzu. I think the question of the extent of Buddhist influence must be left open, although the fact that some, at least, existed, assures us that the school in its fully developed form belongs to the Christian era.

Though the Interior Gods hygiene school made permanent contributions to Taoism (its theories of three vital centers, circulation of breath, and rigorous diet are followed, with some modification, even today), it declined as the Interior Gods were forced off the stage by gods that could be worshipped collectively. Not physical immortality, but mere longevity was gradually to become the objective of hygiene. This happened, I think, because of the spread of Buddhism, which played a clearer role in the decline of the school than it played in its origin. Buddhism introduced the concept of a soul.

Buddha himself did not believe in a soul. His doctrine of *anatta* reduced man to five "heaps"—the body, feelings, perceptions, emotions, and acts of consciousness. This is like the Chinese view during the period in which Taoism developed. The Chinese considered that man's personality was a composite. When he died, one part of it, the *hun*, rose up to join his ancestors in Heaven; another part, the *p'o*, lingered by the grave until it weakened, sank down in the earth to the Yellow Springs, and gradually expired; both these parts were animated by the *ch'i* or "life-breath," which simply dispersed at death. If a man's descendants nourished the *hun* with offerings of food, then it would intervene on their behalf in heaven. If they neglected these offerings, it would not, while if offerings to the *p'o* were neglected, it might become malevolent and dangerous.

Neither *hun*, *p'o*, or *ch'i*, taken singly, constituted a soul. Once they had left the corpse, they could not be reassembled, especially since according to some accounts there were three *hun* and seven *p'o*. For the Chinese of this period,[12] therefore, immortality had to be physical.

The schools of Buddhism, however, which became most popular in China, taught the immortality of the soul, and the existence of paradise and hell. Both concepts were gradually accepted by the Taoists. Physical immortality lost its peculiar significance. Instead of concern for how to survive at all, they came to feel concern for how to survive in heaven rather than hell. The role of hygiene changed accordingly. But these developments came centuries after the Han dynasty, to which we must now return and take up the foundation of the Taoist Church.

[12] H. G. Creel points out that of the bronze inscriptions from the Western Chou period (1122-771 B.C.) only eight per cent contain prayers for the prolongation of the physical life span. For the Eastern Chou (771-255 B.C.) the figure rose to fifty per cent. (*Birth of China*, p. 333.)

4. The Taoist Church

Practically everybody connected with the early history of the Taoist church seems to have borne the surname Chang, and these various Changs belonged to at least three separate families. To prevent confusion I shall begin by giving their genealogical charts.

WESTERN TAOISTS

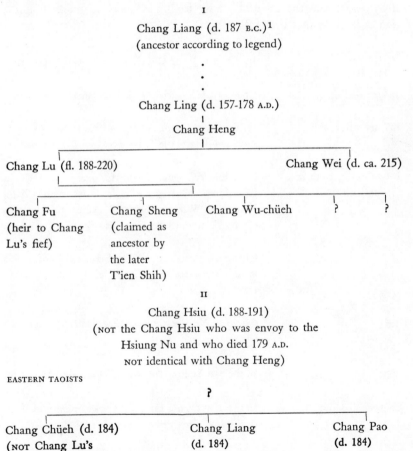

I

Chang Liang (d. 187 B.C.)[1]
(ancestor according to legend)

.
.
.

Chang Ling (d. 157-178 A.D.)

Chang Heng

Chang Lu (fl. 188-220)   Chang Wei (d. ca. 215)

Chang Fu   Chang Sheng   Chang Wu-chüeh   ?   ?
(heir to Chang   (claimed as
Lu's fief)   ancestor by
                    the later
                    T'ien Shih)

II

Chang Hsiu (d. 188-191)
(NOT the Chang Hsiu who was envoy to the
Hsiung Nu and who died 179 A.D.
NOT identical with Chang Heng)

EASTERN TAOISTS

?

Chang Chüeh (d. 184)   Chang Liang   Chang Pao
(NOT Chang Lu's   (d. 184)   (d. 184)
brother)

[1] See p. 101.

In histories of the Taoist church one often meets the phrase "the Three Chang." It is used by Maspero to refer to the three brothers (Chüeh, Liang, and Pao) but by others to refer to the three generations (Ling, Heng, Lu). Furthermore, Chang Heng has been identified with Chang Hsiu, and Chang Lu has been called the brother of Chang Chüeh—erroneously, I think, in both cases.

Not only the Changs, but the events in which they participated have been confused. Therefore I offer next a chronological table (and my apologies to the general reader for introducing so many Chinese names in the pages that follow).

ca. 175 A.D.	In the east Chang Chüeh sends out eight apostles.
184, second month	Chang Chüeh starts the Yellow Turban rebellion.
184, seventh month	In the west Chang Hsiu, the "Wizard Shaman," (*yao wu*) starts the "Five Pecks of Rice" rebellion.
between 188, sixth month and 191	Gov. Liu Yen sends Chang Lu against Shu Ku in Han-chung. Chang Lu collaborates with Chang Hsiu, the "Wizard Shaman." Afterwards he kills Chang Hsiu and takes over his cult.
	Chang Lu then bars the Hsieh Ku road and rebels against the jurisdiction of the Han central government.
194	Gov. Liu Yen dies and is succeeded by his son Liu Chang.
205	In the east Yellow Turbans kill the king of Chi-nan.
between 205 and 211	In the west Chang Lu has rapprochement with Han dynasty, is given titles and sends tribute.
	Liu Chang executes the family of Chang Lu's mother.

211, first month	Chang Lu rebels against Liu Chang. He assumes independent control of Han-chung.
	Liu Chang tries unsuccessfully to subdue Chang Lu.
215	Ts'ao Ts'ao attacks: Chang Lu surrenders.

Now to arrange these tables into a readable narrative, let us go back to Chang Ling. In Szechwan[2] towards the middle of the second century A.D., this first of the Changs started a health cult. He healed the sick, who thereafter, either as payment for their cure or as dues of the cult, paid him five pecks of rice a year. This earned him the name of "rice-thief" and gave his cult the name of "the Way of the Five Pecks of Rice" (*wu-tou-mi-tao*). The title he chose for himself as head of the cult was Celestial Master (T'ien Shih). He expounded his doctrines in a book, though neither the book nor the doctrines can be identified today. Besides this we have many legends and few facts.

Chang Ling's son, Chang Heng, succeeded him as head of the cult but seems to have contributed little to its development. Chang Heng's wife had mysterious influence with Liu Yen, the Governor of I Chou. Thanks to this influence, the scion of the third generation, Chang Lu, was given an army and between 188 and 191 A.D. was sent off to the north to attack Shu Ku, one of the Governor's enemies, who held Han-chung in southwest Shensi. In that campaign Chang Lu received the help of a general named Chang Hsiu.

This Chang Hsiu had had an interesting career. Besides being a successful warlord, he had been running a health cult of his own and had acquired the title of "wizard-shaman." He too collected five pecks of rice a year from the families of those he had cured. Part of his cure was imprisoning patients to think over their sins, on the premise[3] that they would not be sick unless they were sinful. Final expiation was accomplished by writing the sins and penances on three pieces of paper, one of which was exposed on a mountain top for Heaven, one buried for Earth, and one cast in a river for Water—these being the Three Rulers, San Kuan. To minister to the faithful, Chang Hsiu organized an elaborate hierarchy in which the role of parish priest was played by Libationers (*chi-chiu*). One of their duties was to see to it that the

---

[2] The richest province of western China, cut off from the rest of the country by mountains.

[3] A premise also accepted by Jesus (see, for example, *Mat.* 9:2-6).

Tao Te Ching "was observed and practised everywhere," although, as we shall see, their interpretation of the book was bizarre. It is important to realize that this was a military as well as a religious hierarchy. The priests were officers. New converts were called "demon soldiers" (*kuei tsu*). Conversion was recruitment.

Chang Hsiu had originally rebelled in 184 A.D. and seized sections of the province of Pa (in southern Szechwan). However, we may suppose that he came to terms with Liu Yen after the latter became Governor of I Chou (to the south and west of Pa). At any rate, he received the title of Pieh-pu Marshal.

Together he and Chang Lu defeated the recalcitrant governor of Han-chung (far to the north) and occupied that mountainous prefecture. At this point Chang Lu seems to have decided that his new friend's health cult represented an improvement on his own, for he proceeded to take it over. He had Chang Hsiu executed. Then, having disposed of his comrade-in-arms, he began teaching the people new doctrines, which included "honesty and trustworthiness." Soon he felt strong enough to "bar the passes" and set up a theocratic state. He kept his own family title of "Celestial Master." Adding to the institutions of the two health cults he had amalgamated, he set up *i she,* wayside inns for travellers at no charge. Not only did he imprison the sick, as Chang Hsiu had done, but he let criminals go free until their fourth offense. Even then, if their crime was venial, he gave them only a hundred paces of road to repair. He forbad killing of animals in spring and summer[4] and the use of fermented liquor.

Chang Lu ruled his border domain for thirty years, playing the central and provincial governments off against each other. In 215 A.D. he decided to surrender to Ts'ao Ts'ao,[5] who rewarded him with high honors and a princely fief.

Not so fortunate was the third Taoist theocracy. Its origins can be traced to a man whose name, surprisingly enough, was not Chang. This was Yü Chi, a shadowy figure who began to preach and heal in the east (Shantung) about the same time that Chang Ling began his

---

[4] In accordance with the *Yüeh Ling* section of the *Li Chi,* one of the late Confucian classics.

[5] An able, but ruthless Prime Minister who made the last Han Emperor his puppet.

mission in the west (Szechwan). Yü Chi was well-versed in the Five Elements, *wu* sorcery, and medicine. To cure the sick, he used holy water and incense. Sometime before 145 A.D. he incorporated his doctrines in a lost scripture, the *T'ai P'ing Ch'ing Ling Shu,* which might be roughly translated as "The Book of Grand Peace and Purity."

Yü Chi pursued his career, latterly in southern Kiangsu, until he ran afoul of Sun Ts'e, the Marquis of Wu. The latter, jealous of the faith healer's popularity, had him cut in two about 197 A.D. and his head exhibited in the marketplace—though even such an incontrovertible demise did not discourage his followers from believing that he had obtained physical immortality through "Liberation from the Corpse." Long before he died, however, his book had furnished the title of a vast new movement with which Yü Chi himself may have had little personal connection.

This new movement was the T'ai P'ing Tao, or Way of Grand Peace. Its leader was a certain Chang Chüeh, who came from Kü-lu in north China. Beginning in about 175 A.D., Chang Chüeh sent out missionaries to convert the people of the central and eastern provinces of China. His doctrines were evidently an elaboration of Yü Chi's, with many similarities to those of the Five Pecks of Rice in the west. He healed the sick by confession of sins in dramatic public ceremonies which we shall describe below. He organized a church hierarchy which, though parallel to the western hierarchy, had different titles. He himself eventually took the title of "Celestial General"—as opposed to the Celestial Master in the west; the role of priests (Libationers in the west) was taken by "Leaders" (*ch'ü shuai*). With such parallels in organization and the many similarities in doctrine and practice, it is hard to believe that the eastern and western churches arose independently of one another. Certainly all the churches drew inspiration from the same currents of Taoism and I suppose that the church leaders in one region may have heard what those in another region were doing and copied it; but there appears to be no evidence of any direct organizational connections among the several hierarchies.

Now just at the time Chang Chüeh sent out his disciples, the Han dynasty was entering its final decline. Taxes were steadily rising to support the swarm of eunuchs and bureaucrats in the capital and to pay for the luxury with which they corrupted the Emperor. There were repeated famines and epidemics. This may explain why the Taoist faith spread with such explosive speed. The sick and homeless flocked to its great rites of salvation in hundreds and then in hundreds of thousands. Religious fervour, of which some Westerners have considered the Chinese incapable, grew as wild as in the cult of Mithras or in the revivalism of nineteenth-century America. This was not merely because of the troubled times, but also, as Maspero points out, was due to the long unsatisfied yearning for something more personal than the atony of state Confucianism. By 184 A.D. eight whole provinces—most of the country except for Szechwan and the area near the capital—had been converted to the Tao of Grand Peace. If the infiltration had continued unchecked for a few months longer, all China might have fallen to the church and the course of history would have been considerably changed. Early in 184, however, the central government decided to take countermeasures. The Taoists were warned in advance. 360,000 of them put yellow kerchiefs on their heads and rose "with one accord on the same day." This was the origin of the sect's other name, the "Yellow Turbans." [6] It took many years to suppress the rebellion. Chang Chüeh and his brothers were caught and executed in 184, but in 191 and as late as 205 the Yellow Turbans were still a military problem for the government. By the time Chang Lu surrendered in Han-chung (215 A.D.), it seems probable that the Yellow Turbans had lost their military potential, but these uprisings had permanently weakened the hold of the dynasty on the west and south and contributed to the partition of China that was to last nearly four hundred years. Neither of the church hierarchies went out of existence; they continued to minister to the faithful. The Libationers and Leaders became hereditary *tao shih*[7] and the practices of the several sects continued to coalesce.

Such is the history of the origin of the Taoist church. How it fits into the Taoist movement as a whole is another problem. What, for instance, was the source of the idea of collective worship under a church hierarchy? Nothing like it had ever existed in China before. One source was probably Buddhism, which had reached China as

---

[6] Maspero and others apply this name to the western Taoists as well (quite erroneously, I think).

[7] "Gentlemen of the Tao"—the standard term for Taoist priests by the fourth century A.D.

early as 2 B.C. By 65 A.D. we know there was a small group of converts in eastern China, patronized by the Emperor's brother. It was not until three-quarters of a century after this that Chang Ling and Yü Chi started to gather their disciples—ample time for the idea of collective worship to spread. Many of the early Buddhists were also admirers of Lao Tzu. Indeed, there was little distinction—and the most intimate connections—between early Buddhism and Taoism. That may explain why Chang Lu forbade his people to tell lies, to steal, to debauch, and to drink fermented beverages—prohibitions which happen to coincide with four of Buddha's five commandments. (The ban on alcohol was temporary: wine came to be liberally consumed at parish feasts.) Finally, we may see Buddhist influence in the wayside resthouses, in the penance of good works, and in the burning of incense, which appears to have been unknown until the introduction of Buddhism.

As to the question of where the Taoists found inspiration for a church hierarchy, we should note that neither the eastern nor western churches started with a hierarchical apparatus. In either case a faith healer simply began collecting dues from common people he had cured. As success enlarged his area of operations, he appointed disciples who healed and collected dues on his behalf. Then, in the same era when the western cult was taken over by a general, the eastern cult was forced to organize for military action against imperial reprisals. Each of the cults became a government administering its territories through a bureaucracy of priests. The hierarchical apparatus was the result of events, not an imitation of some earlier Chinese model. It is unnecessary to seek for its source.

Sources can, however, be found for other features of the Taoist church. Yü Chi, as we noted, was versed in the Five Elements while his follower in the east, Chang Chüeh, was a votary of Huang-Lao. In the west, the Libationers who taught the *Tao Te Ching* to their parishes, had to know it by heart. It is essential to realize, however, that in both east and west the *Tao Te Ching* was not understood as we understand it today. For example, on its first line their commentary said: " 'The Tao that can be Tao'd,' this is to eat good things in the morning: 'the Tao that is not eternal,' this is to have a bowel movement in the evening." [8]

[8] For Mr. Waley's translation of the first line, see p. 55.

The faithful learned to practice hygiene as well as to recite Lao Tzu. Maspero mentions four grades of honorary titles that were given for prowess in Embryonic Respiration. I think that hygiene was, however, always peripheral in church Taoism. Its goal of physical immortality may have been seriously pursued by the priest, but probably not by the average layman, who simply could not spare the time. The Changs, like Jesus, got their start by healing, and healing, not physical immortality, was at the root and center of the early Taoist church. Furthermore, we know that certain of its rites purported to recall the souls of the dead from hell and give them new bodies in heaven. It is not the same thing to recall the dead as to keep them alive in the first place, and the very fact that the soul has survived makes physical immortality unnecessary. It is true that these rites may belong to a slightly later period and reflect the Taoists increasing effort to compete with Buddhism. But even in the early period I do not believe that hygiene was more than a sideline.

Though physical immortality was not the objective of the church, health was, and immortality is no more than an extension of health. That may be why the church was drawn to the lore and authority of the Taoist movement, why it adopted the *Tao Te Ching* as a scripture, Huang-Lao Chün as a god, the Five Elements as a science, and breath control as an avocation.

The church's unique contribution was to dramatize healing. It taught that through ecstatic repentance at a great public ceremony the believer could expiate sin and be cured of disease. These public ceremonies have been vividly described by Henri Maspero. Some were mass meetings. In others, termed "Fasts," a limited number of participants (between six and thirty-eight) performed elaborate rituals in which they had already received instruction from the priest. Some ceremonies were held as needed; others on fixed days of the year. On every equinox, for instance, there was sacrifice to the Sun God and to T'ai I (the Grand Unity). At the new or full moon certain parishes celebrated the Union of Breaths (Ho Ch'i), a collective sexual orgy which scandalized the Buddhists and Confucians, for in it men and women had intercourse "like animals" without regard to family ties or social status.

We do not know the origin of the Union of Breaths, although it was eventually attributed to the Three Changs.[9] We do know, however, of what it consisted. After joining in a square dance called "the coiling of the Dragon (*yang*) and playing of the Tiger (*yin*)," the participants retired to have intercourse in adjoining cubicles, with frequent changes of partners in a kind of sexual version of "musical chairs." The logic behind this was as follows: semen is the essence of *yang;* the man who nourishes his *yang* will live long[10] and have male children; *yang* is most effectively nourished by the female orgasm (*yin*). Hence it is desirable for a man to have intercourse with a succession of female partners, inducing an orgasm in each, but postponing his own until the last. This is the way to achieve the maximal production and minimal loss of semen. But if loss of semen is harmful, why, we might ask, have an orgasm at all? The answer is that complete continence would lead to "stoppage sickness." What a man can do, however, is to "return the semen to repair the brain." This means that at the moment of ejaculation the adept, heaving a great breath and "grinding his teeth," presses the urethra with the two middle fingers of the left hand at a point between the scrotum and the anus. This forces semen up the spinal column to the Field of Cinnabar in the head, and is immensely restorative. (In reality, of course, the semen is simply forced into the bladder for later excretion.) Such are the secrets which permitted the legendary Yellow Emperor to have intercourse with 1,200 concubines at once without injury to his health. They continued to be practiced in private at least through the nineteenth century.[11]

The Union of Breaths, because its purpose was to fortify health rather than to avert disease, is not altogether typical of the early church ceremonies of "ecstatic repentance" to which I have alluded. For an example of the latter, let us turn to the Fast of Mud and Soot. Maspero's description of it is worth repeating, although it probably does not apply until somewhat after the days of the Yellow Turbans.

[9] See pp. 114, 143. Presumably the Three Changs are here the three brothers in the east: otherwise it is difficult to explain the favourable mention of Chang Ling in the statement quoted on p. 143.

[10] Conversely, exhaustion of semen was regarded as a cause of disease and, when complete, of death. This idea became generally accepted in China.

[11] The most complete information on early Taoist sex practices will be found in Maspero's article in the *Journal Asiatique* (1937, especially pp. 379-413), entitled "Les procédés de 'nourrir le principe vital' dans la religion Taoiste ancienne."

Like all fasts, this one took place on an outdoor altar twenty-four feet square, raised and roped off from the area surrounding. On the first morning we may picture the thirty-eight participants entering in single file, holding each other by the hand. Their hair hangs loose and their faces are blackened with soot to symbolize guilt and misery. Some go to stand by the scrolls of holy writ, some to tend the incense-burners. Drums resound. The priest begins with a stentorian roll call of the various divinities who are expected to be present. A hymn is sung, and all salute the four cardinal points. Then, accompanied by music, the priest leads the congregation in the responsive reading of a long list of sins. This recitation suggests to each of the participants the sins that he has himself committed and the consequences in disease and early death. The air grows thicker with incense, the music quickens, and there is rising fear and exaltation. Finally one of the congregation throws himself on the ground in the center of the sacred square. He thrashes this way and that, smearing his face with handfuls of mud and raising the wildest lamentation. Soon another follows suit, and then the rest. Onlookers who have been standing quietly outside the sacred square begin to tear off their caps and combs and roll on the ground themselves. The hubbub is deafening. At its highest pitch the priest stops it. All rise and stand, breathing heavily, while he announces to the gods the participants' names and stations. After some further ritual they recite the twelve vows of repentance. They knock their foreheads on the ground and beg plenary indulgences for their ancestors and, for themselves, health and long life. Prayers and a hymn complete this first service. But it is repeated at noon and at night. Three times a day it continues for three, four, five, up to *nine* days. The congregation are allowed but one daily meal. With each service they become more dazed by hunger, fatigue, incense, and noise. The effect is cumulative and at the end the exaltation is complete. There has been a psychological break-through.

The fervour of such rites was in perfect contrast to the serenity of philosophical Taoism and to the solitary pursuit of immortality carried on by hygienists and alchemists. As Maspero points out, "one does not gather together thirty-eight persons so that each can pray separately to his own interior gods." [12] The church must have been aware of the alchemists and the various kinds of hygienists, with whom it

[12] *Le taoisme*, p. 173.

shared not only the common goal of immortality, but the common scriptural authority of Lao Tzu and Chuang Tzu. But a clear distinction, I think, existed between the church and other schools of Taoism. By this I mean that not in many cases was the same individual both a Yellow Turban and an alchemist, or a "Five Pecks of Rice" Taoist and a full-time adept in hygiene. The distinction is particularly clear with reference to the philosophical Taoists, whom we shall next consider.

I have spoken of a renascence of philosophical Taoism. This is because I suspect that the school which "loved the words of Huang-Lao" had by now been largely absorbed into church Taoism and that the philosophical Taoism of the third century A.D. was a new departure, made by free-thinking scholars whose interest in Taoism had begun with the study of the *Tao Te Ching* and the *Chuang Tzu*. This new departure is called "Pure Conversation" or "Neo-Taoism."

5. The School of "Pure Conversation"

The term *ch'ing t'an,* or "pure conversation," implies philosophy for its own sake. It was "pure" in the same sense that certain government offices were called "pure" towards the end of the Han dynasty, when Confucian scholars formed a faction opposed to corruption and even to jobs involving the opportunity for corruption. The *ch'ing t'an* Taoists, on somewhat different grounds than these Confucians, also turned their backs on impurity, that is, on worldly advantage.

Some members of the school were scholars. Wang Pi (225-249), who is usually considered with Ho Yen to be its founder, wrote commentaries on the *Book of Changes* and the *Tao Te Ching*. Hsiang Hsiu (221-ca. 300), wrote the commentary on the *Chuang Tzu* which we have, somewhat expanded, over the signature of Kuo Hsiang. Chi K'ang (223-262) was both scholar and poet: he wrote essays on the lute and on "life-nurture."

Wang Pi, Hsiang Hsiu, and Kuo Hsiang maintained the curious thesis that Confucius was a greater Taoist than Lao Tzu and Chuang Tzu. While these two had merely talked about Non-Being, Confucius had reached it—which was why he never talked about it, just as he never talked about eliminating desire because in his own spiritual development he had even eliminated the desire to eliminate desire. Wang, Hsiang, and Kuo amplified on the old Taoist themes of following nature, determinism, and relativity. But they attacked the idea of the Sage as a hermit.[1] Fung Yu-lan believes that they wished to make Taoism into a philosophy better adapted to participants in worldly life. And, in fact, some of them did enter government service. They seem to represent a more purely philosophical, more Confucian wing of the *ch'ing t'an school.*

Other members of the school refused office. They seem to represent a more Taoist, more lyrical wing. Their lyricism is often termed *feng liu* ("wandering from convention").[2] *Feng liu* is best exemplified in the activities of a group known as the Seven Sages of the Bamboo Grove. Not far from Chi K'ang's luxurious estate in Honan was a grove of bamboo[3] where he and certain Taoist friends used to walk in the heat of the afternoon, making up poetry, drinking a little wine, and playing the lute. Here, too, they indulged themselves in "pure conversation" which would end, as Fung Yu-lan puts it, when they reached the Unnameable and then "stopped talking and silently understood each other with a smile." Their strolls invariably wound up at the local tavern. There they would turn to serious drinking. By the end of the evening they would be in a stupor of glorious indifference to the world and intimacy with Tao. Such were the Seven Sages of the Bamboo Grove—the most illustrious literary pleiad of early China. They figured in many of the pungent anecdotes that were intended to exemplify philosophical Taoism in practice and were collected in a work of the fifth century, the *Shih Shuo Hsin Yü.*

Two of the Sages, for example, were Juan Chi (210-263) and his nephew Juan Hsien. Like Chi K'ang, they were poets and accomplished musicians. They were also devoted to the bottle. Indeed, Juan Chi scandalized the Confucians by drinking heavily through his mother's mourning. Since the Juans considered cups an unnatural sophistication, they used to set a monstrous bowl of wine on the ground and sit around it sipping its contents directly. Sometimes the pigs trotted over for a taste. No matter! There was room for all to drink together.

The most celebrated drinker among the Seven Sages was Liu Ling (221-300). His eulogy of wine is still preserved. He used to have

---

[1] Just as I have done in my interpretation of the *Tao Te Ching.* See pp. 79-82.

[2] Literally, it meant "wind-floating." Today it means licentiously bohemian.

[3] According to R. H. van Gulik it was a place *named* "Bamboo Grove."

a servant follow him about with a flask in one hand and a shovel in the other—the first in case he wanted a drink, the second for digging his grave wherever he fell. Liu Ling is also the person who liked to go about his house naked. Once he was interrupted by some stuffy Confucian visitors. They expressed surprise at the absence of trousers. Liu replied: "The whole universe is my house and this room is my trousers. What are you doing here inside my trousers?

The Seven Sages believed in following every impulse. When Juan Hsien's aunt was living at his house, he took up with her maid. One day, while he was giving a party, he looked out on the street to see aunt, maid, and baggage leaving town. Good manners required, of course, that he attend to his guests, but he could not bear the thought of losing such an attractive mistress. One of the visitors' horses was handy. Without a word of apology to anyone, he mounted and galloped off in pursuit. After he returned with the girl on the saddle, the party continued.

This idea that one's integrity depended on following every impulse did not expire with the Seven Sages. Wang Hui-chih, who lived a century later, awoke one night to find that it had snowed. Getting out of bed, he began to pace up and down his room, and to recite poems about paying visits to hermits. This reminded him of Tai K'uei. He dressed, took a boat, and started down the shore. Tai K'uei lived far off and it was not until dawn that he reached his house. But just as he was about to knock on his door, he turned and went home. Someone who found out what had happened asked him why. Wang Hui-chih said: "I came on the impulse, and when the impulse ended, I returned. Why had I to see Tai?"

Not merely impulsiveness, but sensitivity characterized *feng liu*—in particular, sensitivity to the beauty of nature. When one of the school gazed out from a mountain top in Shantung, he wept and said of himself: "Wang Po-yu of Lang-ya must in the end die of his emotions." [4]

There is little in the writings of the Pure Conversationalists to connect them with other currents of the Taoist movement. Philosophical Taoism, which they exemplified, was a stream apart, as I have indicated. Obviously they did not belong to the Interior Gods hygiene

---

[4] For this and much of the other material in section 5, I am indebted to Fung Yu-lan's *Short History of Chinese Philosophy.*

school since they believed that wine, far from offending interior gods, brought one closer to Tao. To my knowledge none of them joined the Taoist church. It is true that Chi K'ang is sometimes called an alchemist. In later sources there are stories of his searching the forest for dietary herbs and apprenticing himself to mysterious hermits. But to me, at least, serious hygiene simply does not jibe with the impulsiveness and the lyrical acceptance of nature that distinguishes the Seven Sages from their other Taoist contemporaries. They are the heirs of —and in a sense our guarantee of—the original purity of Lao Tzu and Chuang Tzu.

6. Ko Hung

The Taoist movement was always a mixture. Every element in that mixture had something in common with every other element, but nothing in common with all the other elements. Alchemy, hygiene, philosophical Taoism, and the Taoist church—these were now the elements. The pursuit of immortality, the use of the *Tao Te Ching* as a fundamental text, the Taoist pantheon, and an individualistic revolt against the demands of society—these were the features they most often had in common. But the Taoist movement was never unified. The mixture never became a compound.

The closest approach to unification was made by the eclectics of the Six Dynasties. Among them Ko Hung is perhaps the most important. He dabbled in almost every school of Taoism. Primarily, however, he is thought of as an alchemist. Before discussing his activities we must therefore retrace our steps a little and see what had happened to alchemy since we left it in 56 B.C.[1]

Our best source is the *Ts'an T'ung Ch'i,* a book compiled about 140 A.D. by one Wei Po-yang. It is the oldest surviving text on alchemy in East or West.[2] In cryptic terms it tells how to prepare the elixir called "returned cinnabar" (*huan tan*) by heating the Dragon (lead) and Tiger (mercury) through twelve cycles. It recommends eating metallic gold on the basis that gold is incorruptible and those who eat it will become so too. It mentions an elixir which, when swallowed,

---

[1] See p. 105.

[2] Unless, as Mr. Waley has suggested, its alchemical passages were all added towards the middle of the fourth century A.D.

"spreads foggily like wind-driven rain. Vaporizing and permeating, it reaches the four limbs. Thereupon the complexion becomes rejuvenated, hoary hair regains its blackness, and new teeth grow where fallen ones used to be. . . . Such transformations make one immune from worldly miseries and one who is so transformed is called by the name of Realized Man." [3]

Besides formulas for the elixir the *Ts'an T'ung Ch'i* offers a curious mixture of philosophical Taoism and hygiene. It refers to the study of Huang-Lao as the foundation of the alchemist's art. Much of its phraseology echoes the *Tao Te Ching*. It recommends trance meditation and circulation of breath "from head to toe." It promises not only immortality, but magic powers to anyone who eats the elixir: he will become a *hsien,* immune to fire and water, able to appear and disappear at will, happy forever. When his time comes, T'ai I will raise him up to become a heavenly official.

What a pity that Wei Po-yang makes his recipes so cryptic! He tells us himself we must read them ten thousand times to see what he is driving at—an odd avowal from an author who has said a few paragraphs above that he wrote his book because he was grieved by the officials, farmers, and merchants who had abandoned their work and ruined their lives trying to figure out old discourses on alchemy.

Now we return to Ko Hung, the Six Dynasties eclectic.

In 317 A.D., about two centuries after the composition of the *Ts'an T'ung Ch'i,* he finished his monumental work, the *Pao P'u Tzu.* This was a kind of encyclopaedia on the art of becoming a *hsien,* in which he cited all the texts and incorporated all the ideas he could lay his hands on. That may explain why it is so full of contradictions. For example, in one passage he denies that the worship of gods is effective in the pursuit of immortality. But in other passages he says that sacrifices to T'ai I, Lao Tzu, the Great Dipper, the God of the Stove, etc., are essential for the successful preparation of the elixir, and he gives a recipe for getting Ssu-ming, the Director of Destiny, to remove one's name from the book of death. Contradictions like this one make it hard to say what Ko Hung's attitude was towards the various schools in which he dabbled. He gives several formulas for killing the Three Worms who, according to the Interior Gods hygiene school, resided in the body's vital centers. He recommends avoiding garlic, mustard,

[3] *Ts'an T'ung Ch'i,* XXVII (see Bibliography).

and so forth for one hundred days before an alchemical experiment. He considers sexual hygiene essential to the quest of immortality. "The most important thing is to return the semen to repair the brain." [4] All this might lead us to suppose that Ko Hung had accepted the doctrine of pleasing the Interior Gods. But as to avoiding cereal foods—one of the first ways to please them—he is equivocal. In one passage he seems to say that eating the five grains actually promotes longevity. In another passage he pooh-poohs grain avoidance as something that does not confer longevity, but merely cuts down on the cost of food. His teacher, Chang, ate the five grains like an ordinary man. As to abstinence from wine, not only did his teacher drink it, but his teacher's teacher, Ko Hsüan, is the man who, when very drunk or in the summer heat, used to spend the day at the bottom of a pond.

Ko Hung seems to be aware of church Taoism, which was just then developing the doctrines of the Ling-Pao gods,[5] for he states that one powerful drug, the "stone mushroom," can only be found by those who carry the five Ling-Pao charms for entering a mountain. Before setting out they must pray together at a *chiao* in which wine and dried meat are sacrificed to the mushroom. On the other hand, Ko Hung is very suspicious of priests or *tao shih,* who often pretend to be *hsien* when they are not and who victimize the public with false teachings.

Ko Hung divides *hsien* into three classes, depending on which elixir they take and what regime they have followed. The highest class are those who have taken elixirs like gold or jade and done twelve hundred good deeds: thereupon they mount to Heaven in broad daylight. Rather than mounting at once, however, such a man may prefer to stay in the world teaching Confucianism (*sic*) to the ordinary folk and alchemy to initiates. In contrast to him, a second class *hsien* has not the talent to save both others and himself: he must disregard human affairs and devote himself only to hygiene. Ko Hung himself, far from being a hermit, held important military and civil posts both while he was writing the *Pao P'u Tzu* and afterwards. So both in his teachings and his life he followed the line of Wang Pi and Kuo Hsiang, the Neo-Taoists who wanted to make Taoism a philosophy for men of affairs.

[4] *Pao P'u Tzu,* VIII (66, see Bibliography).
[5] See pp. 136-137.

It is interesting that Ko Hung, like these Neo-Taoists, preferred Confucius to Lao Tzu and Chuang Tzu. Confucius, at least, had taken no stand on immortality, whereas Lao Tzu and Chuang Tzu had positively rejected the idea, the one by implication, the other outright. That is why Ko Hung considered the *Tao Te Ching* too vague and said that Chuang Tzu, because he "equalized life and death," was "millions of miles away from *hsien*ship." [6]

Ko Hung was even called "famous for his Confucian learning." It is a sad comment on the state of Confucianism in the Six Dynasties that this was said of a man who believed that almost anything could be accomplished by taking a pill. The *Pao P'u Tzu* not only asserts that elixirs are the one avenue to immortality—in contrast to herbs, breathing, gymnastics, and sexual hygiene, which merely prolong life[7]—but also that eating them confers a whole new set of fascinating magic powers.

Besides the old-fashioned powers, like being immune to fire and water, able to disappear at will, assume any shape one desires, and ride the clouds, Ko Hung has a recipe for walking on water; another for raising the dead (if they have not been dead more than three days); another for attracting the company of spirits and Jade Maidens. Then there are pills which outrun the imagination of even the most sanguine enthusiast for our modern science of chemistry. One such is for the use of army officers: as soon as they eat it, the enemy's troops set to fighting amongst themselves. Another pill enables the lowly bureaucrat to get any civil service rank he desires. Another (oh, that Western students of Chinese could lay hold of a few!) makes it possible to read 10,000 characters in a day and remember them all. And there is a pill by *carrying* which one waterproofs one's clothes. The odd thing is that with all these marvelous powers in prospect, those who were training to become *hsien* had to be very careful of themselves. Ko Hung advises them "not to run rapidly, to put on clothes before they feel cold . . . and not to expose themselves to . . . thick mist." [8]

Ko Hung says that he was never able to prepare the elixir himself. He could not scrape together enough money to buy the necessary raw

---

[6] Pao P'u Tzu VIII (69). Here is evidence of the continuing breach between philosophical Taoism and the cult of *hsien*.

[7] Sometimes he says that these practices are necessary adjuncts to the elixir; sometimes that the elixir alone is enough.

[8] *Pao P'u Tzu,* XIII (175).

materials. It is rather consoling, therefore, to learn that at eighty-one he achieved "Liberation from the Corpse" and became a *hsien* (third-class). Thus he capped a career which, as the reader can see, was marked by catholicity even at the expense of consistency.

7. After the Fourth Century: Alchemy and Hygiene

From the beginnings of the Taoist movement in the fourth century B.C. to the death of Ko Hung in the fourth century A.D., we have covered a period of seven hundred years. It is nearly twice as long from Ko Hung's death until today. If we continued our account in the same detail, I am afraid it would be interminable. Let us therefore restrict it from this point on to the salient developments. We shall consider them under four headings: alchemy and hygiene; the pantheon; the church; and philosophical Taoism.

In hygiene the school of Interior Gods declined. By the end of the Six Dynasties collective worship and a change in the character of the Taoist pantheon, which we shall discuss below, had exteriorized the gods. It became unnatural to imagine them in residence inside the body. Soon afterwards there was another shift. About the middle of the T'ang, the practice of circulating the "exterior breath" (the air we breathe) gave way to the circulation of the "interior breath" (*nei ch'i*). The latter was a kind of vital energy drawn from the ether as air is drawn from the atmosphere. To fill the Lower Field of Cinnabar with *nei ch'i,* to circulate it through the body, and to stop it from leaking out became the aim of the adept. He continued to strive for regularity of respiration, but not to hold his breath for such extended periods. The development is easy to understand. Over the preceding centuries too many Taoists attempting to hold their breath for one to three hours must have come closer to Immortality than they expected. The new practice involved neither the difficulties nor the hazards of the old.[1] It is still in use.

There were parallel developments in alchemy. No one could expect even of the devout that they would continue to abstain from meat, bread, and rice in favour of a diet of metallic poisons. As early as the writings of Hui Ssu (515-577) we find mention of the "interior elixir"

---

[1] Though it did involve the effort of constantly wiggling one's toes while walking in order to "make the breath descend below."

(*nei tan*). By the end of the eleventh century the idea was widely accepted. One of its chief proponents was Chang Po-tuan (983-1082), who seems to have been as much of a Ch'an Buddhist as a Taoist. In 1078 A.D. he completed his *Wu Chen P'ien,* or *Essay on Awakening to the Truth.*[2] Its meaning is hidden in luxuriant and exasperating symbolism. This much, however, is clear. The "interior elixir" is not to be prepared in a clay furnace with charcoal and bellows, but inside the alchemist's body. The ingredients are to be "true lead" and "true mercury," not the "vulgar" materials. True lead means the essence of *yang,* and true mercury the essence of *yin. Yin* is to be captured and wholly absorbed by *yang;* this is their "marriage." But what are the essences of *yin* and *yang?* One commentary says that *yang* is the real and *yin* the unreal. Lying on his couch just after midnight and/or just after the winter solstice, the alchemist marries these essences in his stomach under the influence of *ch'i* and gives birth to an embryo. Next morning the embryo or "mysterious pearl" is visible and it grows as the *yang* grows. Eventually the alchemist becomes a *hsien,* immune to tiger and rhinoceros, fire and sword.

I am not sure what this is all about. Evidently the embryo is the embryo of a new self, which is actually one's original self. This new self is not *physically* immortal (in I, 2; 11, 51, 62, 64 we see that Chang puts little stock in physical immortality). Rather, it is immortal because it is Enlightened, because it sees no distinction between subject and object, between the individual and God. Thus the text says that the elixir enables the alchemist to "return to the origin (I, 9) . . . Returning to the origin . . . means imperishable" (II, 51). One commentator remarks that the elixir "makes all things fuse into one and return to T'ai Chi (the Grand Ultimate)." This non-physical approach to immortality is in line with Chang's admiration for Lao Tzu and his belittling of conventional hygiene. "Even if you practice breathing for years," he asks, "how can you make the golden crow (*yang*) capture the rabbit (*yin*)?" (II, 40: and cf. I, 9, 15).

It was many centuries before this meditative alchemy wholly displaced the alchemy of pots and pills. Su Tung-p'o, the great poet and painter, who lived from 1036 to 1101 and was hence a contemporary of Chang Po-tuan, practiced *both* kinds of alchemy, as well as Taoist

[2] There is a rather unsatisfactory English translation by Chao Yün-ts'ung, in the *Proceedings of the American Academy of Arts and Sciences,* Vol. 73, No. 5 (July, 1939).

hygiene. He controlled his breathing, swallowed his saliva and concentrated on the tip of his nose. He had a furnace set up in his lodgings for experiments with cinnabar. At the same time he wrote books on interior alchemy. He considered the heart *yang* and the genitals *yin*. Just as lead must capture mercury, so the fire of the purer emotions in the heart must overcome the waters of venery below. In this way both essences are conserved. As Mr. Waley puts it, alchemy gradually became "a system of mental and physical re-education." [3]

Because the new hygiene of "interior breath" and the new alchemy of the "interior elixir" were both adopted by the same schools of Taoism, the two disciplines tended to coalesce. The result was literature like *The Secret of the Golden Flower*,[4] which Jung has brought to the attention of Western readers, and which represents the union of alchemy, hygiene, and Ch'an Buddhism.

Today in China hygiene is still practiced. There is many an educated person who regularly lies on his side in a darkened room, eyes closed, and concentrates on a point one inch below his navel (where the Lower Field of Cinnabar was located some two thousand years ago). He slackens the tempo of respiration. By keeping his tongue arched back against the roof of his mouth he stimulates the flow of saliva which, along with some breath, he swallows. Gradually he becomes aware of a feeling of warmth at the center of concentration. He shifts this center, first in a small circle between the heart and the genitalia, then in a large circle between the feet and head. This may lead to a climax, a sense of intense euphoria which comes without warning and leaves the same way. Some hygienists avoid wine, meat, and vegetables of the onion family.

These practises are thought to increase a man's resistance to disease and to retard old age. They are not regarded as necessarily or specifically Taoist, although there can be little doubt as to their roots.

A Chinese friend of mine has parents in their seventies, both of whom take up hygiene sporadically. When they leave off, their hair turns gray: when they resume, it turns black again. My friend, who was trained as a physicist, tells me he has seen this himself. I would like to see it too.

[3] "Notes on Chinese Alchemy," *Bulletin of the School of Oriental Studies* (1930).
[4] Translated by R. Wilhelm with an introduction by C. J. Jung. The book is attributed to Lü Tung-pin, a T'ang Immortal, but was more probably composed in the eighteenth century.

Let me repeat that these are not practices of the illiterate masses, but of scholars and officials. Another person I know learned them some years ago from the President of Nanking University, who was eager to proselytize the students. Therefore we should not be surprised by a recent report to the effect that the Communist Chinese government has approved instruction in Taoist hygiene at a new institute in Peking. Perhaps it is part of the campaign to revitalize traditional Chinese medicine.

This is an appropriate point to take note of two tangential features of the Taoist movement: medicine and *feng shui*. *Feng shui* ("wind-water") is geomancy, the science of selecting auspicious sites. Until the end of the nineteenth century few Chinese would think of constructing a building or a grave until they had gotten the opinion of an expert in *feng shui*. The expert would try to find a site that sloped to the south while it was protected from the north, with a hill on the east (wood) larger than one on the west (metal), so that the Green Dragon of Spring might prevail against the White Tiger of Autumn. Valleys were *yin,* but so were rounded hills—in contrast to the *yang* of precipitous heights. The west and north were *yin.* The east and south were *yang.* The perfect site was three-fifths *yang* and two-fifths *yin.* It was dangerous to have high structures in the immediate vicinity (Western telegraph poles were one of the causes of the Boxer Rebellion). Nearby there should be a watercourse to carry off the "earthly breaths" and leave the site bathed in the "breaths of heaven." One objective of the hygienist was to replace the earthly breaths, of which his body was composed, with the heavenly breaths that would make him immortal. Thus *feng shui* is a mixture of Yin-yang, the Five Elements, Taoist hygiene and other ideas. Books on geomancy are mentioned in the bibliographical section of the Former Han History by Pan Ku (32-92 A.D.). The founder of *feng shui* proper, however, is traditionally considered to have been Kuo P'o, a Taoist who attained Immortality about 324.

In Chinese medicine there have also been connections with Taoism. After all, what if not doctors were the early masters of hygiene and the later faith healers who established the Taoist church? It seems fairly probable that some Chinese medical discoveries were made by those Taoists who put less emphasis on sin as the cause of disease and more emphasis on diet, gymnastics, and respiration as the cause of health. Chinese doctors stressed the importance of *ch'i*. The earliest surviving medical book, the *Nei Ching,* which is ascribed to the Yellow Emperor (2697-2597 B.C.), but which was probably written in the second or third century B.C., speaks of an "evil breath" as the origin of all disease. One reason it recommends acupuncture was to release this breath from the interior of the body. Hua T'o (died 220 A.D.) recommended gymnastics for the same purpose. He was a famous surgeon and the first to use anaesthesia. Like some of his colleagues he appears to have been a Taoist.[5] Chinese medicine accepted much of the bizarre anatomy to which I have alluded above.[6] In 1106 A.D. when the second[7] reported autopsy of Chinese history failed to reveal interior organs that corresponded to the Yellow Emperor's description, it was pointed out that he had been describing the organs of a Realized Man (*chen jen*) whereas they had dissected a bandit chief. Yet Taoism made continuing contributions to medicine, and it is easy to see why. Dietary restrictions sent hungry hygienists combing the forest for roots and herbs. Hope of discovering the elixir prompted the alchemist to grind up and eat every new variety of rock that came to his attention. A thousand years of this resulted in a simply enormous pharmacopoeia.[8] We probably have a lot to learn from it.

By now the reader may see why the Taoist movement has sometimes been called the Chinese counterpart of Western science. Hygiene, alchemy, *feng shui,* medicine, and philosophical Taoism—but not the church—sought to explain the operation of nature in terms of impersonal law rather than to explain it in terms of a personal god (like the Christians) or simply to ignore it (like the Confucians). To a large extent the Taoists practiced experimental science. They were reluctant to alter their premises in the light of logic and experimentation, but they did at least experiment. They were ultimately responsible for the development of dyes, alloys, porcelains, medicines, the compass, and gunpowder. They would have developed much more if the best minds in

---

[5] I do not mean to imply that at any time were all doctors Taoists or vice versa. Since before the Han dynasty, the sick have had a choice. They could consult a physician who, whether he was a Taoist or not, would treat them with medication and other physical methods. Or they could consult a *wu* or a *tao shih* who would use charms and spells (to drive away demons) or ceremonies (to effect a remission of sins).

[6] Pp. 106-109.

[7] The first had been in 16 A.D.

[8] The *Pen Ts'ao Kang Mu* (sixteenth century A.D.) fills fifty-two volumes.

China had not been pre-empted by Confucian orthodoxy, which, especially after the Sung Dynasty, looked down on spatulas and herb picking as menial work unsuitable for the scholar. Confucius was once ridiculed for having practical accomplishments.[9] His followers never got over it.

8. The Development of the Taoist Pantheon

As I have already pointed out, Taoism was constantly changing its celestial personnel. The earliest gods had been personifications (1) of natural forces or (2) of metaphysical concepts. T'ai I had been the latter: he represented underlying unity; the San I (Three Ones) were T'ai I plus the natural forces called Heaven and Earth; Ssu-ming was Fate. Around these gods there had gradually developed a hierarchy of immortals or *hsien,* that is, of human beings who had won divinity through hygiene. With the introduction of Buddhism in the first century A.D., this pantheon found itself face to face with serious competition.

The original Buddhist ideal had been the arhat, who sought salvation (nirvana) for himself alone. In the forms of Buddhism which reached China, the arhat had been largely displaced by the bodhisattva. The bodhisattva (or Buddha-to-be) was a man, who, by heroic accumulation of merit through many incarnations, reached the very threshold of Enlightenment and then paused, refusing to cross it until all mankind had crossed before him. As the ordinary man could not or would not aspire to Enlightenment itself (which seemed to mean simple extinction), the role of the bodhisattva was gradually deflected. He became a being who would help people not only towards Enlightenment, but towards satisfying their desires and avoiding dangers, as well as towards rebirth on a higher plane of existence. This was possible because of the enormous fund of merit which the bodhisattva had accumulated in previous incarnations and which he could assign to the benefit of any sentient being. In other words, he became a god of mercy.

The first reaction of the Taoists was to make the Immortals into Instructors, who taught the adept how to follow in their footsteps.

[9] *Analects IX,* 6.

Next they borrowed the idea of reincarnation and asserted that some Instructor-Immortals, like Lao Tzu, had repeatedly descended to the Earth to instruct the Sages. But they went even further than the Buddhists, for instead of saying that Lao Tzu had *begun* as a man (like a bodhisattva), they placed his birth before Heaven and Earth. His departure from Chaos was the cause of Creation. In his incarnations he was, in fact, Tao made flesh. Hence, he received the title of Tao Chün (Lord Tao). Huang-Lao Chün was now merely another name for Lao Tzu in his eternal aspect.

Still, the Taoists did not feel able to compete with Buddhism. Whereas Huang-Lao Chün and the lesser Instructor-Immortals were ready to help the solitary adept in his pursuit of immortality through hygiene, they were not comparable to the gods of mercy who answered the prayers of the masses of the common people for protection and success in a time of troubles. Therefore Huang-Lao Chün was replaced by a new kind of divinity, the T'ien Tsun, or "Celestial Honoured [Being]."

The T'ien Tsun were altogether above the human sphere. They did not begin their careers as men like a bodhisattva, nor did their avatars ever descend to earth like Huang-Lao Chün. The greatest of them, whose name was Yuan Shih T'ien Tsun or T'ai Shih T'ien Tsun ("Celestial Honoured [Being] of the Original Beginning" or "of the Grand Beginning") formed himself spontaneously from the original Breaths before the world began. He created and now rules Heaven and Earth. Herein he resembles Huang-Lao Chün.[1] He is constantly occupied with salvation of *all* men. Herein he resembles a bodhisattva. At the beginning of each Kalpa[2] he dictates the scriptures of the Ling-Pao (Sacred Jewel) to the other gods, some of whom are spontaneously formed like himself and some of whom are men who have attained immortality. They in turn transmit the Ling-Pao scriptures to mankind. These books deal with the structure of the divine hierarchy and the rites by which the layman can invoke its aid on earth and enter it himself in Heaven. The rites include those which

---

[1] See p. 107. Though the *concept* of T'ien Tsun was new, the *title* was not. Huang-Lao Chün had been called T'ien Tsun, perhaps in imitation of Buddha, one of whose epithets, "Bhagavad," was first translated as T'ien Tsun in Chinese.

[2] A Buddhist term for the period of 1,344,000 to 1,280,000,000 years between the cyclical destructions of the universe. Yüan Shih T'ien Tsun and the Ling-Pao scriptures survive such destructions.

celebrate birth and death, release one's ancestors from hell, outfit them with immortal bodies in heaven, and "remove the difficulties" confronting one in day-to-day life. Ling-Pao ceremonies were evidently somewhat calmer in character than those of the Yellow Turbans and their revivalist contemporaries.

We do not know when the transition to the Ling-Pao·pantheon was either begun or completed. In 165 A.D. Lao Tzu was already being worshipped as the creator of the world. Ko Hung mentions "Ling-Pao charms" in the *Pao P'u Tzu* (317 A.D.). The new pantheon was codified by the Taoist physician and hygienist T'ao Hung-ching not very long after 489 A.D. and it was made authoritative by the monk Sung Wen-ming who, in the middle sixth century, wrote commentaries on the Ling-Pao scriptures. These scriptures had allegedly been received from the gods by Chang Ling[3] in purple characters on gold tablets. Maspero guesses they were actually written in the fourth and fifth centuries.

At each stage the pantheon had been capped by a triad. First there were the Three Ones, headed by T'ai I; then the Supreme Triad, headed by Huang-Lao Chün; and now there were the Three Pure Ones headed by Yüan Shih T'ien Tsun. The identity of the other members of this last group is given differently in different sources.[4] But one version came to be that the other two were the "Jade Emperor" (Yü Huang) and the "Celestial Honoured [Being] of Jade Dawn and the Golden Gate" (Chin Ch'üeh Yü Ch'en T'ien Tsun). The Jade Emperor became the deputy of Yüan Shih T'ien Tsun in administering the celestial bureaucracy and governing the world. Then it was asserted that Yüan Shih T'ien Tsun, like a Sage King, had abdicated in favour of the Jade Emperor and that in due time the Jade Emperor would abdicate in favour of the last of the Three Pure Ones.[5]

It is uncertain when this transition took place. Steles were erected to the Jade Emperor during the Six Dynasties.[6] We do know that in 1012 A.D. the Emperor Chen Tsung announced he had received an im-

---

[3] The founder of the western church. See p. 115.

[4] Some include Lao Tzu.

[5] Who thereby became the counterpart of Maitreya, the Buddha of the future.

[6] According to Maspero, *Le taoisme*, p. 134. According to H. H. Dubs in *China* (see Bibliography) he was first mentioned in the ninth century.

portant letter from the Jade Emperor and that in 1115 Hui Tsung honoured him with a temple and the title of Shang Ti.[7] Confucian his-
torians have asserted that these Sung rulers simply invented a new
divinity to divert public attention from their difficulties with the
northern barbarians. Invention or not, the Jade Emperor became the
supreme deity of the common people. His predecessor, Yüan Shih
T'ien Tsun, left the spotlight as T'ai I and Huang-Lao Chün had done
before him. This did not mean that people ceased to believe in their
existence. Taoism, just as it accepted everything, discarded nothing.
But one paid attention only to those divinities who could be helpful.

One sought help, for instance, from the God of T'ai Shan. He
was the Jade Emperor's regent for the earth—and should be distinguished from another God of T'ai Shan who governed the seventh
of the ten hells. Then there were the City Gods (or Gods of Moats
and Walls), to whom the Jade Emperor entrusted the administration
of a particular region and who were more susceptible to prayer than
the "higher-ups," just as a Congressman is more likely to do us a favour
than the President. Even the individual household had its divinities,
the most important being our old friend, the God of the Hearth (or
Stove). He kept the ledger of the good and bad deeds committed by
every member of the family for monthly transmittal to the Gods of
Moats and Walls and annual submission to the Jade Emperor. And
this is only a small part of the vast celestial bureaucracy, which ran
the gamut from deities in charge of the sun and moon to those in
charge of the privy.

Once a year all the gods came to the Jade Emperor's court to pay
homage and hand in accounts of their administration for the preceding
twelve months. They were promoted or punished accordingly. For
the gods were not so much individuals as offices. Those who filled the
lower offices were usually historical human beings. If they did a poor
job, they had to make room for others. Though in theory it was the
Jade Emperor who promoted or punished the office-holder, in practice
it was more often the Chinese government. Presumably they worked
in concert. If, for instance, a rain god had refused to send rain, the
appropriate government official would first read him a stiff lecture. He
might point out, as Po Chü-i once did, that the god was "not divine on

[7] The most ancient and exalted word for god in Chinese.

his own account, it was his worshippers that made him so"; that if the drought continued, people would begin to doubt his powers, and he would "lose face"; that he too would go hungry in case of a famine, for it would be necessary to curtail the sacrifices at his temple; and so forth. If such reasonable arguments failed, the god would be threatened with loss of rank. Finally, an Imperial Decree would be issued, breaking him, let us say, from Duke to Marquis. The ceremonies necessary to solemnize such changes, especially the installation of a new god, were nearly always performed by Taoist priests who, like their Roman Catholic counterparts in the West, had a kind of monopoly on deification.

Hell too had its bureaucracy, and some of the rites of the Taoist church were designed to secure a good position there for the deceased. Hell was divided into ten departments, most of which specialized in punishing a certain type of sinner. After at least twenty-eight months in residence sinners returned to the upper world in the incarnations they deserved.

Besides Heaven and Hell there were special regions like Mt. K'un-lun, which were inhabited by the lower ranks of *hsien*. Eight of the latter—the *Pa hsien*—have beeen favourite subjects for painting and sculpture. Their identity varies. Over the *hsien* at Mt. K'un-lun reigns Hsi Wang Mu, an ancient goddess of the plague, who was adopted by the Taoists early in the Christian era as giver of long life and grower of the Peaches of Immortality.

Such has been the theology of Taoism from the Sung Dynasty until today. In this last phase it has become almost indistinguishable from popular Buddhist theology, except in nomenclature and minor details, and indeed it has shared with the Buddhists a whole assortment of deities, from Kuan Yin, the Goddess of Mercy, to Kuan Ti, the God of War. This has resulted in what W. T. Chan calls "the religion of the masses." Few Chinese are exclusively Buddhist or Taoist. Most of them patronize the institutions of both religions, which offer much the same thing.

The religion of the masses had its moral as well as its theological aspect. This is well illustrated by two short books usually called Taoist: the *T'ai Shang Kan Ying P'ien,* or the "Tractate on Actions and Retributions," and the *Yin Chih Wen,* or "Text on Determining [to do good deeds] in Secret." [8] Probably composed in the eleventh century A.D., these came to be widely distributed by monasteries and by charitable societies—like Gideon Bibles in the United States. In fact, the first was described by F. H. Balfour, a nineteenth-century Sinologist, as "the most popular religious work in China." Let us examine it briefly.

The *Kan Ying P'ien* begins by pointing out that a man's sins are regularly reported to Heaven, not only by the God of the Hearth, but by the Three Worms. (These are the malevolent creatures who figured in the Interior Gods school of hygiene[9] and who reported their host's sins because they wanted to shorten his life and so escape from his body.) According to the *Kan Ying P'ien,* man's life is shortened by twelve years for every major sin and a hundred days for every minor sin. Those who want to live long must therefore exemplify certain virtues and avoid certain vices. If they can go so far as to perform 1,300 good deeds, they will become Celestial Immortals; for 300, only Terrestrial Immortals.[10]

All this, as we can see, represents ancient Taoist traditions. But when we turn to the catalogue of virtues and vices that follows it, we find little that is specifically Taoist. Rather, there is a bland and repetitious mixture of Buddhism, Taoism, and Confucianism. Most of it could be inserted in a Christian Sunday sermon without attracting the least attention. The reader is told not to be dishonest, cruel, slanderous, boastful, or hypocritical, not to take bribes, or use short measures, or covet his neighbour's wife, or waste food, or show disrespect for elders, or damage other people's houses with fire and water, etc., etc. The Buddhist touches—not to kill animals, overturn nests, break eggs—must come as a surprise to those Westerners who have remarked on Chinese inhumanity to animals. The conclusion of the book is Confucian: if anyone dies through misfortune, disease, or early death before he has expiated the sins in his ledger, then the balance is carried forward not to the account of his own future incarnations, but to that of his descendants. Some of the book's 212 injunctions arise more from superstition than morality: one should never urinate, for instance, facing north;

---

[8] One translation of the first is by James Legge in *Texts of Taoism* (Sacred Books of the East, XL). The second has been translated by P. Carus and D. T. Suzuki under the title *Yin Chih Wen, The Tract of the Quiet Way,* Open Court Publishing Co., 1906.

[9] See p. 108.

[10] Ko Hung gives the figures as 1,200 and 300.

nor should one spit at a shooting star. As in most such lists, the vices outnumber the virtues (here by more than ten to one).

The other book, the *Yin Chih Wen*, is even less specifically Taoist. It urges that the reader "impartially observe the Three Doctrines" (Buddhism, Taoism, and Confucianism). Its list of virtues and vices reads like little more than an extract from the *Kan Ying P'ien*: compassion for orphans, care not to walk on worms and ants, avoidance of improper language, and so on. If we strive to do these things in secret and for no reward, either we or our posterity will be benefited. I suppose that those who have observed the Chinese care of orphans in recent decades and listened to the language of the streets would say that these two books had had very little effect. But the same might be said of the Christian Bible during the Thirty Years' War. In any case it was books like these—not the *Tao Te Ching* or the more esoteric volumes of the Taoist canon—which were the Taoist reading of the masses.

9. Taoist Church Organization

When we turn to ecclesiastical organization, we find that over the last seventeen centuries it had one salient feature: there was no permanent central authority to which all church Taoists submitted. Each parish and monastery had its hierachy. In some cases a group of monasteries might submit to the leader of their particular sect of Taoism (for there have been many sects in the church), but usually the pyramid of command terminated at the Abbot. The reason for this lies in early history. At the end of the Han Dynasty, when the Chinese government suppressed the rebellions of the Yellow Turbans and their counterparts in the west, it lopped off the tops of their hierarchies. They were never restored. At various times there was a nominal or partial restoration, but so far as I know it never affected parishes or monasteries throughout China. The Taoist church, like the Buddhist, was atomistic.

During most of the Six Dynasties the hierarchy of the individual parish was headed by the *tao shih*, or priest, whose office was hereditary. Under him was a small council of elders who helped him in performing ceremonies and collecting tithes. In some cases it appears the *tao shih* lived in the village; in others, he lived in a nearby monastery (*kuan*), where, unlike his Buddhist counterpart, he could have a wife and children. Still other *tao shih* wandered about the countryside with small bands of disciples. Whether they celebrated the rites of the church as itinerant priests or mainly practiced alchemy, hygiene, or magic, I do not know. During the Six Dynasties it would seem that monastic life became increasingly the rule. This was not only in imitation of the Buddhists, but also because if one lived in a monastery it was easier to undertake regular fasting and meditation, which, as we shall see, was re-emphasized in the middle of the fifth century.

The income of the early *tao shih* came from two sources. One was the "banquet" (*ch'u*), which the families of the parish served in his honour. Each was attended by a fixed number of families and was the occasion for presenting the priest with a fixed amount of gifts. Besides an annual "banquet," others were held on the occasion of a birth or a death in the family or to seek the priest's help in getting children, money, promotion, and cures.

His second source of income was the "Celestial Rice Tax." Every year every family had to pay five pecks of rice on the seventh day of the seventh month or lose merit according to a fixed schedule. Since loss of merit meant a reduction of the life span in this world and a chance of hell in the next, there were presumably not many tax delinquents. To evade taxes by getting off the register was even riskier. When a parishioner died, an extract from the register was placed in his coffin. This would identify him to Ssu-ming and the other celestial or infernal officials, who, knowing he was a Taoist in good standing, would give him important advantages. It all sounds very Chinese.

The rice tax goes back to the very beginnings of the Taoist church. As we may recall, Chang Ling required that the families of those he had healed should pay him five pecks of rice thereafter. Now everyone had to pay. I do not know how long the system continued.

It may have changed in the fifth century A.D., when a Taoist named K'ou Ch'ien-chih won the highest favour with the Emperor[1] of the Toba Wei Dynasty, which held north China. He assumed Chang Ling's old title of T'ien Shih, or Celestial Master, and in 444, through his influence, Taoism was proclaimed the official religion of the Empire. Some scholars therefore credit him with the unification and the reform of the church. I would question that.

According to the history of the Wei Dynasty, K'ou Ch'ien-chih

---

[1] N. Wei T'ai Wu Ti (424-452). His predecessor, T'ai Tsu (386-409) had lavishly patronized Taoist alchemy.

began his career as a hygienist. In 415 A.D. he had a vision. A spirit told him that "since T'ien Shih Chang Ling has left the world, the world has lacked sincerity . . . and a master's instruction. . . . I have come to hand over to you the position of T'ien Shih. . . . You will banish the false doctrines of the Three Changs. Rice levies and money taxes and methods for the Union of the Vital Breaths of Male and Female[2]—does the purity and freedom of the great Tao have to do with such things? More particularly you will take the regulations of good behaviour for the chief thing and add to them the regulation of diet and exercise in secret." [3] K'ou Ch'ien-chih's mandate appears, then, to have been to cleanse the church of sexual irregularity, to make it less mercenary, and to put new emphasis on the importance of good works and hygiene. However, we know that the orgiastic Union of Vital Breaths was still being openly celebrated in the sixth century, and as to taxes, the Taoists were still known in the T'ang dynasty as the "Religion of the Five Pecks of Rice." [4] It is my opinion, therefore, that the reforms initiated by K'ou Ch'ien-chih were temporary and that his unifying influence did not extend far beyond the area of the Toba Wei capital at Ta-t'ung. It certainly did not extend to southern China.

The next salient development in ecclesiastical history took place in the sixth century. Those priests who lived in monasteries became celibate. Convents were established for women. This was in imitation of the Buddhist monastic rule and was popularized by Sung Wen-ming.[5] With the re-unification of China under the Sui and the T'ang, the laxity of the Six Dynasties was interrupted. This no less than the spread of celibacy was doubtless responsible for the fact that about now the orgiastic Union of Breaths was forced underground, where at some monasteries it continued to be celebrated in secret.

Taoist, like Buddhist, monasteries now began to issue certificates. These attested that the holder was a monk and had reached a stated level of proficiency in the study of the doctrines. To have such a certificate was an important advantage: monks were exempt from military

[2] See p. 121. According to *Pao P'u Tzu* VIII "some *tao shih* devote themselves only to the art of sexual intercourse." One *tao shih* who was noted for leading his parish in the Union of Breaths was Sun En, who led a rebellion in Kwei-ki (not far from Dragon and Tiger Mountain) and died in 402, only thirteen years before K'ou Ch'ien-chih's vision.

[3] Tr. James R. Ware "Wei Shu and Sui Shu on Taoism" (see Bibliography).

[4] It is clear, however, that by the T'ang many Taoist monasteries got their income from landholdings.

[5] Who popularized the Ling-Pao gods. See p. 137.

service, the *corvée,* and most forms of taxation. There was no central accrediting agency: monasteries and even individual masters could train novices and confer certificates, each in their own fashion.

Because of the abuses that developed, the government assumed control of ordination early in the eighth century. Only certificates issued at ordination ceremonies which the government had sponsored were valid. Soon these controls broke down. After the An Lu-shan rebellion (755-757) not only were certificates being issued privately again, but the government and individual officials were selling them to raise money. It is easy to imagine the kind of "clergy" that resulted. Even the established monasteries were becoming corrupt. They had been given large tracts of land by the emperor and by rich parishioners. In other cases they acquired real estate from tax evaders who wanted to use the monastic exemption as a "front." They operated mills and pawnshops. Individual monks, despite legal restrictions on property-holding, grew rich. The monastic life was becoming luxurious.

As I have indicated, there was no episcopal organization which connected all these monasteries. Again, however, we hear of a Celestial Master, or T'ien Shih, and this time the title was reverted to a member of the Chang family. In 748 a certain Chang Kao was addressed as "T'ien Shih" by the Emperor Hsüan Tsung.

In 1016 we hear of another T'ien Shih. That year the Emperor Chen Tsung summoned to court one Chang Cheng-sui and then invested him with a large tract of land near Dragon and Tiger Mountain (Lung Hu Shan) twenty-five kilometers southwest of Kwei-ki in Kiangsi. Chang Cheng-sui was allegedly a descendant of Chang Kao and through him of Chang Ling. The story went, in fact, that the Chang family had been living at Dragon and Tiger Mountain ever since the time Chang Sheng, the great grandson of Chang Ling, had moved there in the third century. This story, like the genealogy that accompanied it, was probably an invention, but it served to justify a long episcopal dynasty. The Changs continued to maintain a vast establishment near Dragon and Tiger Mountain right down to 1949.[6]

This brings us to the question of Taoist sects. Since as many as eighty-six can be enumerated and since the statements that have been made about them are even more contradictory than is usually the case

---

[6] See pp. 147–148. In most dynasties the title *officially* recognized was not Celestial Master, but Realized Man, or Master of Chaste Stillness, etc.

in Taoism, it is a question that I would be happy to ignore—as, I think, would the reader. But there they are, those eighty-six sects, and we have to get them out of the way before we can proceed. Fortunately just three are important: the Northern School; and the two Southern Schools, one in the Sung and one later.

The Northern School was founded by an eccentric individual named Wang Che (1112-1170), a native of the northwesterly province of Shensi. Although we are told that the doctrines of his sects were imparted to him by two strangers, there is also a tradition that he was a disciple of Lü Tung-pin, one of the Eight Immortals of the T'ang. Since Lü Tung-pin had presumably ascended to Heaven some three centuries before, he must have instructed his disciple either in a vision, or, more prosaically, through his books. (We shall shortly find other disciples who were separated from their masters by long periods of time.) In any case, because one of Lü Tung-pin's epithets was "Ch'un Yang," or "Pure Yang," this became a name for Wang Che's new sect. Another name was Chin Lien, or "Golden Lotus," after the hall in which Wang preached when he moved to Ninghai on the Shantung peninsula. The third and commonest name for the sect, however, was Ch'üan Chen, or "Perfect Realization," which is what we shall call it hereafter.

"Perfect Realization" was one of several sects[7] that arose soon after the Chin Tartars overran the northern half of China. A modern Chinese scholar, Ch'en Yüan, has suggested that their purpose was to mobilize non-cooperation with the foreign invaders. This may have been one reason why Wang Che preached an ascetic withdrawal from the affairs of the world. But surely the main reason was religious rather than political: he wanted to restore man's nature to its original purity.

The asceticism required for "Perfect Realization" was fanatical. First of all, the disciple was to avoid everything that pleased the eye, ear, palate, or any other bodily sense. This entailed perfect continence and sobriety. Second, he was to nurture the *yang* (Heaven) and suppress the *yin* (Earth). This was connected with the old idea of replacing Earthly Breaths with Heavenly Breaths.[8] Third, he was to

---

[7] Two others were the "Grand Unity" sect, founded by Hsiao Pao-chen about 1140 and the "True Great Way" sect founded by Liu Te-jen in the same period.

[8] See p. 133. Contrast the earlier view that *yang* and *yin* are not good and evil, but necessary complements.

give up sleep. Perpetual wakefulness was called "smelting away the dark demon." Some members of the sect did not lie down for a decade. Finally, he was to practice all-out meditation. Wang Che once buried himself ten feet deep for two years.

Wang was by no means exclusively a Taoist. He acknowledged "the Three Doctrines," i.e., the Confucian Doctrine of the Mean; the Ch'an Buddhism of Bodhidharma; and the Taoism of Lao Tzu. His successor, Ch'ang Ch'un, considered Lao Tzu's doctrine the original one, but disdained chemical elixirs (his was internal alchemy), and rejected the magical concept of the Immortal, or *hsien*. Once he wrote a hymn which read:

> Sweep, sweep, sweep!
> Sweep clear the heart until there is nothing left.
> He with a heart that is clean swept is called a "good
>   man."
> A "good man" is all that is meant by "holy *hsien*" or
>   "Buddha."

On another occasion, when he performed a rite to avert the ill-effects of a conjunction of stars, he was congratulated on the swift efficacy of his magic. "What is this about magic?" he replied. "Prayer is no new thing. All that is needed is to believe in it. This is what the Ancients meant when they said 'Absolute faith could move heaven and earth.' " [9]

It was natural that as the sect of "Perfect Realization" spread, some of its original ascetic elan was lost. Many of its monks, however, continued to practice gymnastics, breath-control, and meditation. Like their Buddhist counterparts they were celibate and abstained from wine and meat. Indeed the Taoist monastic system became so similar to the Buddhist that in recent times Taoist monks were welcome to stay at Buddhist monasteries and vice-versa. The seat of the Perfect Realization sect, the White Cloud Monastery [10] in Peking, where

[9] Probably alluding to Confucius' alleged comment on the story of Shang Ch'iu-kai. See *Lieh Tzu*, II, F. These two quotations of Ch'ang Ch'un are from Arthur Waley's *Travels of a Chinese Alchemist* (p. 140), which is the best English source on his life and school.

[10] I.e., the Po Yün Kuan, situated just outside the Hsi Pien Gate on the west wall of the Outer City. It is to be distinguished from the Pi Yün Ssu, or "Azure Cloud Temple," a Buddhist institution built by the notorious eunuch Wei Chung-hsien during

Ch'ang Ch'un took up residence in 1224, kept its role as *primus inter pares*. It was from there in 1923 that the Commercial Press secured one of the two remaining copies of the Taoist canon for re-publication.

But we are getting ahead of ourselves. The sect of "Perfect Realization" came to be divided into a northern and a southern school, the former so called because Wang Che and Ch'ang Ch'un had been born in the north and had carried on their teaching there. Both the White Cloud Monastery and most of the adherents of this school were in the north. It is less obvious how the Southern School was named. Its founder, Liu Hai-ch'an, was a northerner from Shensi. Some of his successors came from the south (like Chang Po-tuan,[11] from Chekiang) and some from the north (like Hsüeh Tao-kuang, from Shensi). The primary concern of the school was "interior alchemy." Compared to the Northern School it appears to have been smaller and more loosely organized. Its members did not have to become monks. The distinction that is usually made between the Northern and Southern Schools is that the former "cultivated life" (*ming*), while the latter "cultivated nature" (*hsing*). The first meant seeking for physi-

---

the Ming dynasty. The latter is in the Western Hills some miles from Peking and is a popular picnic spot.

[11] See p. 131. Succession in the Southern School presents a twofold chronological problem. Liu Hai-ch'an was minister to the King of Yen in 911-913. It was not until 1070, however, that Chang Po-tuan became his disciple in Chengtu. Furthermore, there is a theory that Liu Hai-ch'an himself was, like Wang Che, a disciple of Lü Tung-pin (fl. ca. 800). This theory connects the Northern and Southern Schools by deriving them from the same source. But if that is so, Liu Hai-ch'an must have lived some 270 years, a ripe old age even among Taoists. I would take all this as further evidence that the disciple could adopt his master posthumously, either through books or visions.

Here is one version of the succession in the Northern and Southern Schools:

Chung Li-ch'üan

Lü Tung-pin

Wang Che	Liu Hai-ch'an
Ch'iu Ch'ang-ch'un	Chang Po-tuan
Li Chih-ch'ang	Shih Hsing-lin
Chang Chih-ch'ing	Hsüeh Tao-kuang

cal immortality through *exterior* means (like drugs or incantations): hence it was called the "other-power" school. The second meant seeking the realization of one's original nature by *interior* means (like hygiene and meditation): hence it was called the "self-power" school. Frankly I cannot understand the application of these terms to the two schools in question. It seems to me that although Ch'ang Ch'un may have put a little more stock in "other-power" techniques than Chang Po-tuan, both were primarily concerned with "cultivating nature" and neither were much interested in physical immortality. As for the classification into North and South, I suspect that it was not based on geography, but arose by analogy with Ch'an Buddhism. The Southern School of Ch'an advocated sudden rather than gradual enlightenment. It is significant that Chang Po-tuan claimed to have acquired "the highest degree" from Hui Neng, the Sixth Patriarch[12] of the Southern school of Ch'an.

We come now to the *second* Southern School, which has no connection whatever with the *first* Southern School. It is, in fact, none other than the sect of the Chang family, the Celestial Masters of Dragon and Tiger Mountain. Towards the end of the thirteenth century the Changs were given jurisdiction over all the Taoists in Kiangnan[13] and began to call themselves Cheng I Chen Jen, or "Realized Men of the Right Unity." From this the sect got the name it still bears, "Right Unity."

In contrast to both the schools we have been discussing, the interests of "Right Unity" clearly included "life" (*ming*), and the methods by which "life" was to be cultivated were clearly "other power." Realization of one's original nature (*hsing*) was a secondary concern, if it existed at all. Priests of this sect marry and hand down their arts hereditarily. They do not live in monasteries, do not wear Taoist robes "off-duty," and do not restrict themselves to a vegetable diet, although they fast on occasion. Living by the family hearth, they are called "fire dwellers" (*huo-chü shih*). People come to them to purchase talismans that protect the holder from malevolent ghosts, sorcery, disease, drought, floods, cuts, burns, and bad luck in general. People also engage them to perform various rites, not only for protection from all the dangers just named, but also to summon the soul of a dying

---

[12] Another example of chronological separation between master and disciple.
[13] I.e., Kiangsi, Anhwei, and the part of Kiangsu that lies south of the Yangtze.

man back into his body or, after death, to summon it to ceremonies designed to help it get safely through hell. Some Taoist priests offer more varied services, such as using a planchette to communicate with spirits, telling fortunes by physiognomy, astrology, and hexograms, and even displays of magic like fire walking.

The relationship of these priests to the Celestial Master has been tenuous. During the Republican period (1911–1950) about one percent of them used to apply for his diplomas, which he issued in nine grades, certifying to the degree of religious competence. But he was not the head of a sect with effective powers to appoint or discipline priests or to pass on the validity of doctrine. It is erroneous (though convenient) to call him the "Taoist Pope." He was nothing more than the leading repository of one tradition in Taoism. As such, his talismans (also issued in nine grades) were presumably more effective than those of ordinary priests. Recipients of diplomas and talismans expressed their gratitude with donations to his treasury, and he received similar donations for the performance of Taoist rites. His largest item of revenue was the rent from the 250 acres of rice fields that he owned, tax-exempt. He was able to maintain a staff of about eighty secretaries and servants, who occupied a large complex of offices and temples just to the east of the town of Shang-ch'ing several miles away from Dragon and Tiger Mountain itself. At these headquarters he kept the Precious Sword, handed down from Chang Ling, with which he could slay demons at ten thousand miles. There were also rows of sealed jars, apparently empty, but actually imprisoning demons that had been subdued by his ancestors.

The last half century has treated the Chang Celestial Masters with wavering respect. In the anti-religious tide released by the 1911 revolution, the governor of Kiangsi abolished their titles and confiscated their property. Fortunately for them, they had a friend in Chang Hsün, the arch-conservative and Manchu loyalist. In 1914 Chang Hsün persuaded President Yüan Shih-k'ai that both property and titles should be restored. Thereafter the Celestial Master (the sixty-second of his line) showed his enterprise by travelling to Peking (in order to bless the President's attempt to make himself Emperor) and to Loyang and Nanking, where he performed rites at the invitation of prominent war lords, Wu P'ei-fu and Sun Ch'uan-fang. In 1920 he became head of the Federation of the Five Sects of Taoism.[14]

---

[14] This appears to have been the first attempt at a national Taoist organization.

On his death in 1924 the title passed to his eldest son, Chang En-p'u, who was not so fortunate as his father. In April 1927, he happened to be in the provincial capital of Nanchang when it was occupied by a band of Communist guerrillas.[15] He was briefly imprisoned. In 1931 a Communist army [16] took over the whole area around Dragon and Tiger Mountain, looted his headquarters, and executed his brother as an "advocate of superstition." He himself escaped to Shanghai, where he stayed quietly, but comfortably in the French Concession. In 1936, after Kiangsi had been cleared of Communists, he returned to live amidst the remains of ancient pomp until April 28th, 1949. Seven days before the Communists crossed the Yangtse, he left home for the last time.

He made his way through Macao and Hong Kong to Taiwan, where he was still alive in 1965. Under his aegis various Taoist organizations were set up there and the Taoist Canon was reprinted. But since one of his sons was dead and the other was in the hands of Communists, it seemed likely that the sixty-third generation of the Celestial Masters would be the last.[17]

This concludes our discussion of Taoist sects. They are a complicated phenomenon and resist generalization. Nonetheless it is probably safe to say that after the thirteenth century most celibate monks belonged to the "Perfect Realization" sect, while most married priests (who were greater in number) belonged to the "Right Unity" sect.

We should note that the Taoist monastery, like its Buddhist counterpart, has had a broader function than the Christian church. It has been a place to go for an outing or to entertain friends in attractive surroundings; a hostel for travellers; a sanatorium for the tired urbanite; and a service center for coping with all kinds of worries — from worry about the fate of parents after death to worry about the cooling ardour of one's lover.[18] Since there has never been a hierarchy to en-

---

[15] Led by the Communist martyr Fang Chih-min.

[16] Led by P'eng Te-huai, later Chinese Communist Minister of Defense.

[17] For a fuller discussion of the recent history of the Celestial Masters see Holmes Welch, "The Chang T'ien Shih and Taoism in China," *Journal of Oriental Studies,* 4.1–2:188–212 (Hong Kong, 1957–1958).

[18] Peter Goullart tells how a certain Taoist monastery used to cater to the Shanghai demi-monde who came to recover from dissipation or to rekindle the flagging interest of rich patrons. See *The Monastery of the Jade Mountain,* London, 1961, pp. 191–199. This is a fascinating book with many firsthand observations of modern Taoist activities, written by an enthusiast who, as he told me once, is less interested in the accuracy of his historical facts than in the validity of his metaphysical conclusions.

force standards, the character of monasteries has varied. At some one could find dirt and degeneracy, at others beauty and peace. The character of their personnel varied too — from pimps and gangsters to men of spiritual power.

In general it was not the role of Taoist monks or priests to provide moral leadership. The layman called on them more often to get him out of supernatural trouble than to dissuade him from committing the sin that would get him into it. Their spells and talismans were considered effective regardless of their morals. Whereas Buddhist monks through their pure lives accumulated merit that they could discharge for the benefit of those who patronized them, the Taoists drew their power less from merit than from professional expertise in hygiene and magic. This is not to depreciate their role. They were often useful members of the community, who solved many problems that resisted solution otherwise. Who else could help people overcome their fear of ghosts or regain their self-confidence when it had been sapped by a run of bad luck? In appraising the alleged degeneracy of religious Taoism, we must remember that our picture of it has been drawn largely by Christian missionaries and their Chinese converts.[19]

10. The Taoist Church in Politics

In politics for some eight centuries the church Taoists had one overriding objective: to win the Emperor's favour and turn him against the Buddhists. They engineered two of the three great persecutions of Buddhism: those of 446 and 845. Though it is to the credit of the Chinese people and their system that little blood was shed in the course of this long feud, no one can deny that there was lots of dirty work.

It began when K'ou Ch'ien-chih[1] conspired with a reactionary Confucian named Ts'ui Hao to persuade the Northern Wei Emperor that Buddhism menaced the security of the state. K'ou Ch'ien-chih evidently wanted to eliminate the competition of Buddhist gods and ceremonies. Ts'ui Hao, on the other hand, wanted to establish a Confucian New Jerusalem, based on the classics of the Chou Dynasty. The difference in objectives did not prevent collaboration. Under their influence the Emperor issued decrees restricting Buddhist ordination to men over 50 (in 438 A.D.), abolishing unlicensed temples (in 441), for-

---

[19] The Buddhist clergy has been the target for similar indiscriminate denigration.
[1] See pp. 142-143.

bidding monks to travel (444), executing all the monks in the capital (445) and, finally, executing all the monks in the realm.[2] K'ou Ch'ien-chih, the Taoist, opposed the bloodier measures, including the last, whereas Ts'ui Hao, the Confucian, was all for "killing the bad to help on the good." The persecution was relaxed in 450 and over in 452, when a new emperor succeeded. Buddhism continued to improve its competitive position.

The next skirmish—really a whole series of skirmishes—occurred during the sixth century, again in north China. These took the form of debates among Confucians, Taoists, and Buddhists on the merits of their respective creeds. Starting as early as 520 A.D., they were held in the presence of the Emperor, who determined the "winner" and sometimes ordered the losers to accept the winner's religion. This made them a serious business. One of the Taoists' favourite arguments was that Lao Tzu had gone to India after his westward departure from China, and had converted—or become—the Buddha. Buddhism then was only a somewhat distorted offshoot of Taoism. To support this telling thesis the Taoists about 300 A.D. forged an account of Lao Tzu's missionary activities, the *Hua Hu Ching,* or *Classic on Converting the Barbarians.* In reply, the Buddhists pushed back Buddha's birth date from the sixth to the eleventh century B.C.: Lao Tzu could not possibly have converted anyone who lived four hundred years before him. And so it went.

In 555 the Taoist debaters lost. They were ordered to shave their heads and be converted. In 573 the Taoists edged ahead of the Buddhists, though behind the Confucians. This so piqued the Buddhists that the next year they went on from criticizing the Taoists as impure to criticizing the Emperor himself. That was simply not done. Next day both religions were proscribed. Forty thousand temples were demolished, including the images and scriptures therein and three *million* monks and retainers were returned to lay life—an interesting indication of the place of religion in China, since the whole population, north and south, was then only about forty-six million.[3] Soon the proscription was withdrawn and the monastic life resumed.

---

[2] The realm of the Toba Wei did not include South China, where there was no religious persecution during the Six Dynasties. Even within the realm these anti-Buddhist decrees were not everywhere strictly enforced.

[3] Chinese population statistics are notoriously unreliable.

In 618 Li Shih-min founded the T'ang Dynasty. Lao Tzu's surname had also been Li. In a flash the Taoists knew that the new emperor must be his descendant. Though Li Shih-min accepted the honour, his personal inclination was to Buddhism. He merely gave the Taoists precedence at court. Many of his successors, however, were ardent patrons of Taoism. His son, Kao Tsung, worshipped at Lao Tzu's temple and honoured him with the title of "Most High Emperor of the Mystic Origin." Hsüan Tsung (712–756) conferred further dignities on Lao Tzu, ordered that a Taoist temple be built in every city of the Empire, and that every noble family should have a copy of the *Tao Te Ching* in their home. In 721 Hsüan Tsung himself accepted a Taoist lay diploma (showing not that he was a monk but that he was proficient in Taoist doctrine). Later in his reign (741) the works of Lao Tzu, Chuang Tzu, and Lieh Tzu were officially recognized as classics. One could now choose the Taoist rather than the Confucian classics as one's field of study for the civil service examinations. This was a radical, and temporary, change. Hsüan Tsung must be ranked as one of the two or three outstanding imperial patrons of Taoism in Chinese history.

Patronage of Taoism was not always a safe pastime. The Emperor Hsien Tsung took a liking to one Liu Pi, a Taoist alchemist. In 820, after he ate a "longevity pill" which the latter had prepared for him, he died.

It was inevitable, I suppose, that the Taoists should renew their struggle with Buddhism. In 840 Wu Tsung came to the throne. He was a mentally unstable young man of twenty-six whose sympathies had been shifting from Buddhism to Taoism. He surrounded himself with Taoist priests and alchemists and dabbled in fasts and elixirs. His Taoism became so fanatical in the end that he is said to have forbidden the use of wheelbarrows. Wheelbarrows broke "the middle of the road," which in Chinese can also mean "the heart of the Tao." Like most emperors in the latter part of a dynasty, Wu Tsung spent more than he collected in taxes. It was probably this fiscal embarrassment as much as his fanaticism that made him receptive to the sinister proposals of his Taoist advisers. In 842 he began to issue a series of anti-Buddhist decrees, which reached their climax in 845. That year 260,000 monks and nuns were ordered to become laymen, subject to taxation. The gold, silver, and bronze images from 4,600 temples and even from the homes of Buddhist families were to be melted down and handed in to the Board of Revenue. Finally the proscription was extended to all "foreign" religions, including the Nestorian Christians, and the Zoroastrians. These did not make as full a recovery as did the Buddhists when, in 846, the persecution abated.[4]

In the Sung Dynasty, two Emperors were particularly ardent Taoists: Chen Tsung (998-1022) and Hui Tsung (1101-1126). We have already noted their respective roles in popularizing the Jade Emperor and enfeoffing the Chang Celestial Master at Dragon and Tiger Mountain. We need only add that both of them patronized the compilation of the Taoist canon, which was catalogued in the tenth century and first printed in 1019.

The Sung was succeeded by the dynasty of the Mongol invaders, or the Yüan. The Yüan saw the zenith of Taoist political fortunes. In 1219 Chingiz Khan, who was at that time in the west, summoned the Taoist monk Ch'ang Ch'un to come and preach to him. Ch'ang Ch'un had succeeded Wang Che as head of the Northern School[5] in 1170; he was now seventy-one years old. Four years later, after a tremendous journey across Central Asia, he reached Imperial headquarters in Afghanistan. When he arrived, he lectured Chingiz on the art of nourishing the vital spirit. "To take medicine for a thousand years," he said, "does less good than to be alone for a single night." Such forthright injunctions to subdue the flesh pleased the great conqueror, who wrote Ch'ang Ch'un after his return to China, asking that he "recite scriptures on my behalf and pray for my longevity." In 1227 Chingiz decreed that all priests and persons of religion in his empire[6] were to be under Ch'ang Ch'un's control and that his jurisdiction over the Taoist community was to be absolute. On paper, at least, no Taoist before or since has ever had such power. It did not last long, for both Chingiz and Ch'ang died that same year (1227).

Ch'ang Ch'un was succeeded as head of the Northern School by Li Chih-ch'ang (1193-1278),[7] who proceeded to throw away all the

---

[4] This episode of Chinese history is well described in E. O. Reischauer's *Ennin's Travels in T'ang China.*

[5] See pp. 146-147.

[6] Which still included only a small part of China. The Mongol conquest was not completed until 1278.

[7] Li Chih-ch'ang wrote the excellent account of Ch'ang Ch'un's journey to the west, which Arthur Waley has translated in *Travels of a Chinese Alchemist.*

political advantage that his master had won. He did not at once lose favour. In 1253 Mongka Khan confirmed him as head of the Taoist church and decreed that all persons taking their vows as Taoist monks and nuns must get their certificates stamped by him.[8] But in 1255, soon after the Mongols had enthusiastically taken up Buddhism in its Tibetan form, Li Chih-ch'ang decided to renew the old feud. He sent emissaries to the capital at Karakorum who began distributing the *Classic on Converting the Barbarians*.[9] This led to three debates (in 1255, 1256, and 1258) in each of which the Taoists were shown to be guilty of calumny, circulating forged texts, and appropriating Buddhist temples and images. The Mongol rulers, who presided, ordered them to make restitution and desist. Finally in 1281, after the Taoists had set fire to one of their own temples in order to cast blame on the Buddhists, Khubilai Khan ordered that all Taoist scriptures except the *Tao Te Ching* be burned. Though this book burning was not completely effective,[10] it did mark the end of the Buddhist-Taoist feud.

We might suppose that it also ended imperial favour towards the Taoists. But the very next year (or if not then, in 1289) who should Khubilai receive at Court but Chang Tsung-yen. He was the Celestial Master then in office at Dragon and Tiger Mountain: he claimed to be thirty-sixth in line from Chang Ling. In a previous imperial audience (1277) Khubilai had already confirmed his title and given him jurisdiction over all the Taoists in Kiangnan.[11] Now he summoned him again and asked that he bring along the Jade Seal and Precious Sword that had been in the family since the Han Dynasty (so the story went). Over these regalia the Emperor sighed a long time, saying: "Dynasties have changed I don't know how often, but the Sword and Seal of the Celestial Master, handed on to son as to grandson, have come down to today. Must not this outcome have had the help of the gods?" The title and ecclesiastical jurisdiction of the Changs was made hereditary for future generations. The old Southern School had faded away: the new Southern School was now launched. As Fu Ch'in-chia points out, this was really the beginning of the Chang family's importance.

[8] Since the Mongols by now held all north and west China, this meant a wider jurisdiction over the Taoist clergy than that held by Ch'ang Ch'un.

[9] See p. 152.

[10] It was effective enough to reduce the size of the Taoist canon from 4565 volumes in its Sung edition to 1120 volumes in its Ming edition.

[11] See p. 148, note 13.

It is significant, I think, that Khubilai showed such favour to the Celestial Masters after having wholly lost patience with the Taoists in the North. It indicates that he saw no connection between the two schools.

Once having gained imperial favour the Celestial Masters were eager to keep it. In 1368, as soon as the first Ming Emperor had driven out the Mongols, Chang Cheng-ch'ang hastened to Court. He was confirmed in the title of "Realized Man." It was not so grand a title as "Celestial Master," but in the new Taoist Control Office that the Ming set up in 1383, he was accorded the second of the nine official ranks. This Control Office, the Tao Lu Szu, supervised the activities of Taoist priests throughout the Empire. Its non-salaried bureaucracy extended down to the level of the *hsien,* or township. Such tight supervision was characteristic of the Ming. It also reflects an increasing tendency on the part of the government to view the Taoist clergy as a single group, often rascally and potentially seditious. The Control Office classified them into two categories: "Right Unity" and "Perfect Realization." This confirms the idea that during this period most of the clergy belonged to one of these two schools.

The long reign of Ming Shih Tsung (1522-1567) was probably the last in Chinese history which saw the Taoists in high imperial favour. Shih Tsung's enthusiasm for Taoist fasts and diplomas are said to have distracted him from the tasks of government. A priest from Dragon and Tiger Mountain, one Shao Yüan-chieh, was given high honours and made general head of the Taoist religion. Another Taoist became Tutor to the Heir Apparent.

All this was, as I say, for the last time. In the Ch'ing dynasty (1644-1911), the Celestial Master was demoted from the second to the fifth rank. He was forbidden to issue diplomas. Only two emperors, Yung Cheng and Chia Ch'ing, showed any interest or favour towards Taoism. This did not reflect any sudden change in the status of Taoism. Rather, it signalized the end of a decline in its political fortunes that had begun in the Sung dynasty and to which reigns like that of Ming Shih Tsung had been merely exceptions.

The primary reason for this decline was, I think, the rise of Neo-Confucianism. The latter, which was a synthesis of Confucianism, Taoism, and Buddhism, had begun to draw the literati away from Taoism and Buddhism proper during the Sung Dynasty. In 1237 the government made it orthodox and it remained so until 1905.[12] Religious Taoism was completely abandoned by the upper classes. Gone were the times when a great scholar like Su Tung-p'o would look with equal favour on Buddhist philosophy, Taoist elixirs, and Confucian ethics. Today, after centuries of decay, the church has reached the end of the road. The sixty-third Celestial Master will probably be the last. The White Cloud Temple and a few others may be preserved as cultural monuments with a handful of priests as caretakers, but their religious function is over. This is not merely because the Communist government disapproves of religion, but because Western technology has shown the people more reliable ways of coping with practical difficulties than the purchase of amulets.

Today the most vital element in Taoism, aside from the philosophy of Lao Tzu, is the lay societies and sects. Often secret, they have flourished in China since the days of the Red Eyebrows, who overthrew Wang Mang in 25 A.D. They might be compared to the Continental — in contrast to the Anglo-Saxon — Freemasons. One of their goals has been to foster charity and asceticism on the part of their members: another has been to organize opposition against "too much government." Their secrets include everything from passwords to charms and spirit-writing. Thus, although their function is partly secular, they owe many of their ideas to Buddhism and especially to Taoism. Since the beginning of the Ming Dynasty such groups have led at least eight rebellions against the central government, in two of which they probably came as close to conquering China as the Yellow Turbans did in 184 A.D.[13]

Because they represent a two-thousand-year tradition of individualism and of revolt against tyranny, they have been vigorously suppressed since the Communists came to power. But they have proved a tougher nut to crack than the Celestial Master. The I Kuan Tao ("Way of Pervading Unity") is a case in point. Its origins are very obscure: perhaps it was started by remnants of the Boxers (themselves a society with Taoist roots). It accepts all the major religions—Confucianism, Taoism, Buddhism, Christianity, and Islam. It worships the images of their respective gods and prophets. Behind and above these, however,

[12] With an interruption in the early Yüan Dynasty. Yüan Jen-Tsung re-established it in 1313.

[13] The White Lotus rebellion (1356-1369) and the T'ai P'ing rebellion (1854-1867).

it honours the Mother of No-Birth, who created the world. Like other such groups it encourages abstinence from meat, alcohol, and tobacco; reduction of desires and control of the mind. Its members use the planchette (for automatic writing), talismans, and incantations. The Communist campaign against the I Kuan Tao and similar groups started in 1951. At the end of 1953 it was announced that "four million duped members had withdrawn from these reactionary sects." [14] But reports of their activities continued to appear frequently in the mainland press through the year 1958.

11. Later Philosophical Taoism

Finally, we come to philosophical Taoism. What was its role in Chinese life after the third century A.D.?

Its role is difficult to describe, not because it was slight, but because it was so large. The ideas of Lao Tzu and Chuang Tzu, instead of remaining the special property of a group like the Pure Conversationalists, slowly permeated Chinese society. "In office a Confucian, in retirement a Taoist," became the tag of the scholar-official and even his Confucianism, after the thirteenth century, was to a large extent philosophical Taoism in disguise. This Neo-Confucianism, as it was called, developed because Confucius had never formulated a metaphysics and the lack of it put his later followers at a disadvantage in their rivalry with the complete philosophical systems of Taoism and Buddhism. Hence the Neo-Confucians borrowed the Taoist concept of an underlying unity, which does nothing, but accomplishes everything. They called it T'ai Chi or the Grand Ultimate. They took the old Confucian concept of the Rites, li, and extended it to include the laws of nature as well as of man. T'ai Chi and li were thus equivalent to the Unnameable and Nameable aspects of Tao.[1] The Neo-Confucians further adopted the Taoist goals of minimizing desires, returning to the purity of one's original nature, identification of the individual with the universe, and even the self-expressionism of feng liu. As Fung Yu-lan says, the Neo-Confucians were "more Taoistic than the Taoists and more Buddhistic than the Buddhists." [2] And, as he also points

---

[14] See Richard Walker, *China under Communism*, p. 189.

[1] See p. 55 ff. *Li*, the Rites, is not written with the same character as *li*, the laws of man and nature, or Reason.

[2] *A Short History of Chinese Philosophy*, p. 318.

out, the brand of Buddhism that influenced them the most was Ch'an which, in turn, was the brand most heavily influenced by Taoism. Neo-Confucianism, which thus received a double infusion of Taoism, was orthodox in China from 1237 to 1905. Every Chinese official had to master Chu Hsi's commentaries on the classics or fail in his examinations.

I have just mentioned the Taoist influence on Ch'an Buddhism. This school, which appealed particularly to intellectuals, flourished in China from the T'ang through the Sung dynasties and in Japan from the time of the Sung until today. The Japanese—and most Westerners—call it Zen. We have only the space to note that its roots in Lao Tzu are clear. Zen rejects verbal teaching, disregards logic, "discards morality," and regards Heaven and Earth as "unkind." It sees no value in "good deeds." The only way to be saved is to do nothing about it. Zen believes that salvation, in fact, is a return to our original nature; that no one else can do it for us; and that doing it makes us into the most ordinary and wonderful people. The residents of Lao Tzu's utopia (Chapter 80) might join the Zen monk in saying

"Here is a miracle of Tao!
I draw water, I chop wood."

What Zen asserts and Lao Tzu did not was that this return to our original nature could, after certain preparation, occur irreversibly in the twinkling of an eye. Hence it was called the School of Sudden Enlightenment.

Zen Buddhism and Neo-Confucianism illustrate only two aspects of the Taoist permeation of Chinese society to which I alluded above. Another aspect was in the field of art. Philosophical Taoism, first on its own account and then through Zen Buddhism as well, exercised an important influence on Chinese painting, poetry, music, and sculpture. It is no coincidence that the reign of Hsüan Tsung, the great imperial patron of Taoism, was probably the most creative period in Chinese cultural history. In Lao Tzu and Chuang Tzu Chinese artists have found purpose, method, and themes. As an example, let us consider landscape painting. In China the *purpose* of landscape painting has been to express the identification of the painter with nature.[3] To use

---

[3] Kuo Hsi, the great Sung painter, said this explicitly: "The artist should identify himself with the landscape."

Lao Tzu's words, the painter, like the sage, must "clasp the Primal Unity" (22W). His *method,* once his novitiate is passed, is to reject rules (like the wheelwright in *Chuang Tzu* XIII, 10), to "discard knowledge" (19W). He must "see without looking" (47W) so that he comes to know his subject from the inside, like the carver in *Chuang Tzu* III, 2. Only in this way can his brush catch the *ch'i,* or vital breath, of what he is painting. The first of the Six Canons of Hsieh Ho (ca. 500 A.D.), which became the basis for the Chinese theory of art, was *ch'i yün shen tung,* that is, "[through being in] harmony [with] the vital breath [of the subject, portray its] living movement." The *ch'i* must be caught even at the expense of inaccuracy or distortion, for if the artist misses it, he has missed the essence, the spark of Tao. The *theme* in landscape painting is the natural world. We dive with the artist into the luminous water where fishes take their pleasure, as in *Chuang Tzu* XVII, 13. Or we may think of *Chuang Tzu* I, 2 when we see a cicada as tall as a man and the grass bending over our heads as high as the tree tops. In landscapes proper the artist leads us from busy villages up a mountain path past pines as twisted as the tree in *Chuang Tzu* I, 7 until we reach a precipitous niche, suitable for quiet and meditation. There he confronts us with the Void. The mountains melt into mist and the mist into nothingness. We think of what was "formlessly fashioned, that existed before Heaven and Earth, without sound, without substance, dependent on nothing, unchanging, all pervading, unfailing" (25W). We remember that if we "push far enough toward the Void, hold fast enough to Quietness, all the ten Thousand Things can be worked on by us" (16).

This does not mean that the philosophy of Lao Tzu and Chuang Tzu was the only kind of Taoism that influenced the artist. Taoist hagiography, with its fantastic legends and innumerable Immortals, was rich in themes for the artist. The earliest essay on landscape painting by the first great Chinese painter was *How to Paint the Cloud Mountain Terrace* by Ku K'ai-chih (344-406). In it he discusses the way to depict an episode in the life of Chang Ling, the first Celestial Master.

Much that I have said about landscape painting could be applied to poetry. Some of the themes of the Chinese poet are personal emotions, like homesickness and love. Others stem from the Confucian view of art—that its purpose is to edify. But more characteristic than any of these is the theme of communion with nature. The poet no less than the painter loved mist and silence. He was fascinated by the ideal of the hermit who practiced inaction far from cities and had found serenity and perhaps immortality in his mountain hut. Chia Tao (777-841) writes of a visit to such a hermit:

> Under a pine
> I found his boy. He told me,
> "Master's off to gather roots and herbs.
> But where he is
> Upon this mountain in the depth of cloud
> I cannot tell."

Creative art is not so rigidly compartmentalized in China as in the West. Painting is a branch of calligraphy.[4] Poetry is both calligraphic and musical. The artist does not confine himself to a single medium. Some of the greatest poets, like Wang Wei or Su Tung-p'o, were equally great painters. Underlying creation in all media, even by artists of a Confucian outlook, there was a basically Taoist concept: spontaneity. If the creative work reflected the "original nature" of the artist, it would be fresh and perfect.

This is as far as we shall carry the history of philosophical Taoism. I hope it is far enough to suggest that Lao Tzu, in the long run, succeeded remarkably well. He believed in anonymity and his greatest success has been under labels other than his own. Yet the *Tao Te Ching* itself has continued to be one of the most widely read and highly prized of Chinese books, as necessary a complement to the Confucian classics as *yin* is to *yang*. We find it not only in the hands of those who announce themselves as philosophical Taoists: we find it everywhere—in the imperial palace, in the family bookshelf, in the artist's studio, in the alchemist's laboratory, at the elbow of the poet, by the hermit's pillow, in the library of the Taoist temple, in the lodge-room of the secret sect. Everyone has interpreted it after his own fashion, just as everyone does today. But we must not assume that it was wholly misinterpreted—even in the temple. Lao Tzu's ideas penetrated downwards into every branch of Taoism until they were blocked by that branch's peculiar preoccupations. The Taoist clergy, for instance, could

---

[4] The greatest Chinese calligrapher, Wang Hsi-chih (321-379), was a "Five Pecks of Rice" Taoist.

hardly accept the idea that "riches and honour breed insolence that brings ruin in its train" (9)—though they found it to be true enough at times. They could, however, preach "serenity and calm." Taoist books like the *Kuan Yin Tzu* (T'ang dynasty) contained a strong element of philosophical Taoism along with alchemy and hygiene. Li Po, whom many consider the greatest Chinese poet, was deeply interested in alchemy, took a Taoist lay diploma, and seriously considered himself a "Banished Immortal," that is, a *hsien* who had been sent down to earth for committing a misdemeanor in Heaven. None of this, I think, would have appealed to Lao Tzu. And yet Li Po exemplified as well as any of his contemporaries the philosophical tradition of devotion to Nature and spontaneity at all costs. Like many others he only took a part of Lao Tzu—the part that he needed—and in so doing he added another chapter to the history of the parting of the Way.

But there were certain centripetal forces acting on the Taoist movement. One was the Buddhist-Taoist feud, which must have tended to throw all Taoists together. Another was the T'ang dynasty's acceptance of Lao Tzu as imperial ancestor, which must have encouraged the various branches of Taoism to claim him as their common founder.

A third was the Taoist control office inaugurated by the Ming. A fourth was the recurrent compilation of the Taoist canon, which included everything from Lao Tzu and Chuang Tzu through the *Pao P'u Tzu* and works on the pantheon to the travels of Ch'ang Ch'un and the *Kan Ying P'ien*. The fact that all these books were included in a single compilation implied that all were connected. One of the things that connected most of them was a common reverence for the name of Lao Tzu. Thus he continued to be the patron saint of men who differed as much in tastes and goals as the Mississippi Senator differs from the Harlem Congressman, though both belong to the same party.

For the Taoist movement was essentially heterogeneous, despite the centripetal forces I have mentioned. Indeed, its vastness and variety leave one a little dazed, wishing there were some simple way of summing it all up. I am afraid there is not. We can only say that it has been immensely important. Half the soul of China is Taoist. Anyone who attempts to understand or to cope with China without understanding this iceberg of thought patterns, so little of which shows on the surface of the modern Chinese mind, can have only partial success.

The Chinese themselves sum up Taoism by dividing it into *Tao chia* and *Tao chiao*—the "Taoist school" and "Taoist sect." The first category they restrict to partisans of the philosophy of Lao Tzu and Chuang Tzu. In the second they include all those groups that have taken immortality as their goal—alchemists, hygienists, magicians, eclectics, and, in particular, the members of the Taoist church. This is a rough division, but it is a helpful one. Immortality was the issue that marked off Chuang Tzu from the *fang shih;* Liu Ling from the alchemists; and that today marks off the Taoists whom we in the West might listen to and those whom we can only regard as representatives of quaint, but moribund superstition.

What will happen to Lao Tzu in the new China? I do not know. His book is still in print. He can, of course, be made into something of a Marxist. The first line of Chapter 17 has been translated: "In highest antiquity [the people] did not know private property"; versus Mr. Waley's "Of the highest, the people merely know that such a one exists." In the same way the summons to trance in Chapter 56 [5] becomes a plea to "dissolve the feudal class-distinctions." Joseph Needham, following Hou Wai-lu, develops such interpretations at length in the second volume of his monumental *Science and Civilization in China.* [6] At his hands Lao Tzu the individualist becomes Lao Tzu the collectivist. Lao Tzu's opposition to all property becomes opposition to *private* property. His opposition to all government becomes opposition to *feudal-bureaucratic* government. Perhaps Mr. Needham is right about Lao Tzu: or perhaps he is falling into what he calls "the practice of making the ambiguities of Lao Tzu serve one's own purposes." [7] But I do not see how even the most judicious re-interpretation can make Lao Tzu into an advocate of the police state. I think there is hope in the fact that, just as his book was spared by the First Emperor in 213 B.C. and then inspired the gentle reigns of the Early Han, so it is being spared today.

[5] See p. 70 for Mr. Waley's translation.
[6] Vol. II, pp. 107-115.
[7] *Ibid.,* Vol. II, p. 432.

Part Four: TAO TODAY

GONZALO: I' th' commonwealth I would by contraries
Execute all things; for no kind of traffic
Would I admit; no name of magistrate;
Letters should not be known; riches, poverty,
And use of service, none; contract, succession,
Bourn, bound of land, tilth, vineyard, none;
No use of metal, corn, or wine, or oil;
No occupation; all men idle, all;
And women too, but innocent and pure;
No sovereignty,—

    SEBASTIAN: Yet he would be king on 't.

    ANTONIO: The latter end of his commonwealth forgets the beginning.

    GONZALO: All things in common nature should produce
Without sweat or endeavour: treason, felony,
Sword, pike, knife, gun, or need of any engine,
Would I not have; but nature should bring forth,
Of it own kind, all foison, all abundance,
To feed my innocent people.

    SEBASTIAN: No marrying 'mong his subjects?

    ANTONIO: None, man! All idle—whores and knaves.

    GONZALO: I would with such perfection govern, sir,
T' excel the golden age.

                             —*The Tempest*, II, i, 147-168

Utopias always have a certain fascination, but seldom much practical use. How many of Lao Tzu's ideas, for example, would be useful to twentieth-century Americans?

On the face of it, it is a silly question. We believe—or most of us do—that it is good to be vigorous, progressive, and forward-looking. Lao Tzu believes it is good to be weak and to look inwards and backwards. We believe that what America needs is dynamic, aggressive leadership. He prefers leadership that is listless and passive. We believe in keen competition. He believes in dull indifference. We believe in education. He considers it dangerous. We believe that a man or a business or a nation can never stand still, that they must either go forward or backward. He teaches that to stand still is the most effective way of dealing with almost every problem and of finding spiritual contentment. We want to be high. He wants to be low. The *Tao Te Ching* might—with apologies to Dr. Peale—be called *The Power of Negative Thinking*. Lao Tzu is not the kind of thinker to whom twentieth-century Americans would turn for advice.

Furthermore, it is likely that if Lao Tzu were here today and we applied to him for advice on the problems facing us, he would answer not a word. To tell others what to do would be most unsagemanlike. And if—heaven knows how—we forced him to speak, he would probably tell us to "do nothing, leave great problems to solve themselves, each of you attend to his own affairs."

If this answer left us still unsatisfied and we managed to press him further, asking that he tell us if not how to mend our troubles, at least how they originate, I think he would begin as follows.

"America's greatest troubles come from the advertising business. Do not smile. That business is harmful and dangerous—oh! very harmful and very dangerous. It makes people want to buy things that they would not otherwise want to buy. It fills their minds with desire for ingenious devices and with ambition to have more than their neighbours. How, confused by ingenuity, can their characters become simple? How, being full of ambition, can they ever turn inwards and grow quiet? On the contrary, they must be always excessively active to earn the money to buy what has been produced by the excessive activity of others. But this is not the worst. Advertising agencies are Press Gangs in the warfare between manufacturers where one pits his brand against the others. Here is a poor citizen minding his own business. See how the advertisers advance upon him and persuade him to choose a brand and be loyal to it! He becomes a soldier; he learns that because the brand he uses is superior, he is superior; and soon he enjoys the battle, for he learns that by having a Cadillac, he can crush the neighbour who has a Chevrolet. This cannot help but damage his character.

"The advertising business supports newspapers, magazines, television, and radio. Without advertising most of these would pine away. That would be very good, oh! very good. Then people would not know what was happening in the world and soon they would not care. After they ceased to care, they would become quiet. After they became quiet, they would be ready for understanding. The best thing any American could do would be to make a big pile in his back yard of all books and

radios and anything else that talks all the time, and set it on fire. To
be always talking is against nature. Clever people are so busy supplying
demand for talk and the rest of the people are so busy keeping the
supply consumed that everybody knows everything, but understands
nothing.

"Then there is the practice of 'public relations.' Public relations
are not only harmful, but foolish. To deafen the country with clamour
about the good deeds of a man or company is to risk their goodness,
while to say that the bad is good will be one's own undoing. Why does
clamour about good deeds risk their goodness? Because it makes
everyone ask himself questions. Those who have benefited from a
good deed ask if it has not made them debtors and dependents. Those
who have not benefited ask why others have. And everyone asks why
the good deed had to be publicized at all: was it because it was not in
fact good and therefore must be made to appear so? Was it because the
deed was done only in order to create the occasion for publicity? These
questions are the reason why clamour is a risk and why it is foolish.
But it is more than foolish. It damages character. It teaches the greedy
to talk of morality and righteousness. It turns some people into mon-
keys who do not care what they are so long as everyone knows it. It
turns other people into peacocks who do not care what they are so long
as everyone admires it. And it spreads like a plague, damaging the character of all the Hundred Families. Soon in your country there will be
no one left who does not think it is right to call attention to what he
does. There will be no one for whom mention in a newspaper or
appearance on television is not a cause for rejoicing, whereas actually it
is a calamity.

"What is needed by each of your great men and great companies is
not an advertising program, not a public relations program, but an
anonymity program. Each company then would have a Vice-President
in charge of Anonymity, who would do what he could to keep people
from learning about its good products and good works. Then the
good works would be wholly successful and the good products would
be bought only by those who needed them. Bad products, being the
only ones advertised, would not be bought at all. Thus business activity would be greatly reduced; producers and consumers would cease
to spend their time in large cities cultivating diseases of the heart and
stomach, and instead become quiet. You of all peoples are in a po-

sition to be quiet because you have found how one man in a month can produce the necessities of life for a year. But you are not quiet. Behold the result of ingenious devices!

"The next of your great troubles is education. Those who want young men to go to college are like a lot of bandits preying on the land. Your American college is a school of struggle. Examinations are struggle, athletics are struggle, fraternities are struggle. Instead of teaching a boy to unlearn all the vicious competitive ways he has acquired from childhood, it reinforces them. Instead of turning his mind inwards, it fills him with ambition. Instead of making him quiet and opening his ears to intuitive understanding, it disturbs him and stifles his inner powers. The factual subject matter of college courses is harmless enough, but the perversion of character by college life is terrible indeed!

"What else could be expected? The teachers—the very ones who should be healing young minds sick with struggle—are sick themselves. Their first concern is not wisdom, but survival in a jousting match. Like creaking champions they have to be ever padding themselves with heavier degrees and the production of thicker books, straining their ears for faculty rumour, sharpening their tongues for cleverness and reprisal. Are these the perfected men who should be the teachers of the unperfected?

"I have just spoken of the danger of college sports. *All* sports are dangerous. Could anything destroy character more surely? Sometimes you call sport a 'harmless substitute' for warfare. Sometimes you make it a part of military training. Sometimes the individual participates with his own body and sometimes by watching others. But always, the result is the same. He learns to expect success by force. He learns to think of himself habitually as part of one group *against* another group. He tastes the fruits of victory and the weeds of defeat—more dangerous than opium.

"Defeat and victory: these are the terms in which you Americans think of almost everything you do, and so it is impossible for you to do anything without it recoiling upon you. What is there that you have not made into a struggle? Your political elections are a struggle between two parties: your careers are a struggle to get ahead of fellow workers. Consider the Social Register, the Critics' Awards, the Miss America Contest, the Kentucky Derby, the National Spelling Bee—

everywhere I see struggle. But all this makes you beam with pleasure and knock your heads three times in homage to the 'fair, free competition' which, you say, has made America succeed. I say to you, your success is failure and your competition drives half your people mad with praise while it drives the other half mad with blame. You justify this by calling it the way to produce the greatest quantity and highest quality of goods and services—as though any goods and services were more important than the people to whom they are supposed to give a happy life, but do not!

"I say to you there is no disaster greater than never having enough. Let efficiency slide and productivity slip: strike not for higher, but for lower pay and longer hours at a lazier tempo; abandon the vicarious struggle of the baseball park and the $100,000 Question. Resolutely turn your back on all this 'fair, free competition' that has made each great city of your land into a torture house, furnished with a hundred contrivances by which man, as both executioner and victim, can spend his life putting himself to death."

It is true that we asked Lao Tzu to comment on our troubles, not on our blessings. Even so, I think most of us would say that his picture of American life is negative. He, on the other hand, would say that it was positive. Before we go any further, let us clear up once and for all this quibble about "negative" and "positive."

It is an important quibble. It is difficult to understand the *Tao Te Ching* unless we realize that our "positive" is to a large extent his "negative." To Lao Tzu, for instance, *wu wei* is the highest ethical good: it means no struggle, no hostility, no aggression, and is therefore negative. In our eyes the equivalent good is "peace" and, whether we mean world peace or peace of mind, we would certainly not call it negative. In order to achieve it we have to make a very positive struggle—"Exactly why you do *not* achieve it," Lao Tzu would say. One corollary of *wu wei* is non-interference, either by the government in the affairs of the individual, or by one individual in the affairs of others—in a word, the absence of oppression. We call this "freedom," but far from thinking of it as the absence of anything, we consider it the presence of something—something positive and almost palpable, for we like to breathe "the air of freedom." Similarly, tolerance is for us a positive approach to other people's opinions, while for Lao Tzu it was doubly negative: it meant to have no decided opinions of one's own and therefore to conduct no warfare against the opinions of others. And so forth. There may be as much to be said for his semantics as ours.

I think that one reason for his semantics may be found in the evolution of his philosophy. Early in our study of Lao Tzu we considered the possibility that his philosophy may have been a product of his times—those times of the Fighting States when duke vied with duke, treasuries and torture chambers were full, and villages were empty. If, in fact, Lao Tzu's thinking began when he looked about himself and asked the question "Can this ever be stopped?" he evidently decided that stopping it would require a radical operation on human nature. Human nature would have to be emasculated, to be made incapable of that emotional polarization which leads to violence. Therefore in the *Tao Te Ching* he performs a series of excisions. First he cuts out desire for superfluous material goods (they only keep their owner awake at night), then desire for praise and fear of blame (both drive men mad), then desire for power (the only successful ruler is one who suffers as his kingdom suffers). But this is not enough. Morality is frequently used to justify violence. Morality must go. Violence frequently starts with a fixed difference of opinion. Fixed opinion must go. But without desire, morality, and opinion, what is left for a man to occupy his time? The best things of all: physical enjoyment and cultivation of the inner life. Once a man knows these, success in competition will seem a poor reward for living. Thus Lao Tzu completes his negative operation on human nature—though not wholly negative, since he has implanted a new motivation to replace the old.

But let us turn to Lao Tzu again and ask him to tell us more. He has only covered the domestic field. What about our difficulties abroad? Here is what I think he would say.

"Your foreign troubles are grave indeed. Soon they will be graver. That is because your statesmen want America to play the role of the male. They would have America, like the stag, rush forward through danger, expecting that because it is strong and handsome all the other nations will follow. But nations are not a herd of deer, and leadership is not won by physique alone.

"Thus in crisis after crisis you have tried to exercise 'leadership': again and again the result has been to make the crisis worse and yourselves suspected by everyone. Why is this, do you suppose?

It is because you have continually opposed Tao. Tao cannot be opposed, as those who try are forever learning to their sorrow. Tao ordains that only when you relinquish the role of world leadership will you be able to assume it: only by pursuing a policy of isolationism will you be able to help other nations without danger to yourselves.

"What does this mean to 'relinquish the role of world leadership'? It means to place America last, not first, among nations; to resign your lofty place on the Security Council; to cease propaganda activities abroad; to renounce all foreign policy objectives that affect other peoples more directly than they affect you.

"What does it mean 'to pursue a policy of isolationism'? It means to call back the soldiers in foreign countries and give away no more produce, factories, and devices of war. What madness it is to vote your foreign aid on the open basis of 'self-interest,' then in the next breath to call it 'making friends' and congratulate yourselves on your generosity! He who boasts is not given credit. If you have anything to spare, whether it is economic or military or educational or technical, put it at the disposal of all the nations together. It is only from this unity—the United Nations—that you should not be isolated.

"This is the way in which you, the larger country, can play the female role and get underneath the smaller countries, for the smaller countries together will see that they are larger than you are. Then they will no longer resent your leadership and your interference. Rather they will be attracted to you and to the objectives that your leadership and interference have so far hindered you from accomplishing. Train your ambassadors to droop a little, drift a little, appear a little stupid, miss opportunities to promote your interest, and give other peoples a chance to laugh at your expense. Then your ambassadors will find their work easy. For superiority is the form of aggression which is hardest to forgive because it is hardest to requite. Simply to let your superiority be known is challenge enough, but to flaunt it by assisting peoples or proselytizing them to your way of life—this brings ruin in its train. Leave such things to the leaders of enemy nations. They are digging their own graves. Why must you interfere?

"In a word, let your ambassadors be men who understand Tao. True, to understand Tao is not easy, especially when it is the Tao of nations. A nation is not a man. A nation has no heart. Only its citizens have hearts.

"Now inaction cannot succeed except by its call on the heart. Therefore, as a technique for handling nations it is full of risks. Under certain conditions it succeeds and under others it does not. Truly the Tao of nations is difficult indeed!

"Gandhi used inaction successfully because he was allowed to reach the hearts of the people of England and they have power over their rulers. Gandhi is a good example of how an attitude can become effective as knowledge of it seeps through society. But if Gandhi had practiced non-violence in the German Volga Republic to save it from annihilation after your last war or if he had practiced it to save Merv seven hundred years ago when it fell to Tuli, youngest son of Chingiz Khan, he would have perished as ineffectually as a candle in a blast furnace.

"That is why force is sometimes necessary. For inaction can only be relied on in relations between individual human beings who regard one another as human beings. But force is effective only to the extent that it is regretful. Let your generals cut their nails before they go out to the front, as though they were on their way to a funeral. Slowly, slowly, yes! like water softly dripping on rock, regret and passivity can wear away the granite of enemy ambition."

Lao Tzu's views seem so basically un-American that I would not care to be called on to justify them to a Congressional committee. For the American instinct is to play the role of the male. Even if we acknowledge that there is some theoretical truth in the paradox of action, most of us will continue to prefer that our country act, no matter how frustrating the process becomes.

Is there, then, any part of Lao Tzu's teaching that we *can* use? Though his theories turn out to be too radical when applied to domestic and foreign affairs, are we able to find any problems in the life of the individual for which his solutions are congenial or in any way satisfactory? Perhaps, but there are certain obstacles.

The biggest obstacle is probably the element of mysticism. Most of us take an Apollonian view of the mystic. At best we feel that he needs psychiatric attention and at worst we consider him a charlatan. We—and this includes not only most readers, but myself—have never practiced contemplation, any more than we have practiced scapulimancy or phrenology. So, while many of Lao Tzu's theories are not at all mystical and one can make a good case for them by common sense, still it is difficult today not to be suspicious of a teacher who makes so many dubious statements about yoga, trance, secret essences, and mysterious females.

True, Lao Tzu does not claim to have ridden the wind or walked through a mountain. But his references to Non-Being, which is after all a cornerstone of his philosophy, often sound like little better than a play on words. Non-Being or *wu yu* has usefulness, for "if you mold clay into a vessel, from its non-being (hollowness) arises the utility of the vessel" (11). We would rather say, I think, that it is not the space in the middle of the vessel that gives it utility but the walls which contain whatever fills this space. Again, "Being comes from Non-Being" (40). Now, to the extent that this refers to the creation of the universe, we can accept it, for it is as good as any cosmogonical explanation. But it also refers to the relativity of opposites (2). Brilliance is only brilliance against a dark background. What does this "not-being-brilliant" have in common with the "non-being" from which the universe came? There is a much more serious question: What does it have in common with the Non-Being whose secret essences Lao Tzu implies he has seen in trance? And how is it possible to see the secret essences of Non-Being? If Non-Being is what-is-not, then to see any part of it means simply not to see. And in trance Lao Tzu does *see,* however little his seeing resembles ordinary seeing and however little what he sees resembles what can ordinarily be seen.

In short, we feel that he is using the word "Non-Being" to indulge in a kind of verbal nonsense. Whatever he may be talking about, in some way it *is:* ineffable as he may have found it, he has no right to denote it with a word that means it *is not.* If it *is not,* then it is not the source of anything, it cannot be useful, and it cannot be seen.

I think this is a little unfair to Lao Tzu. There is no question that his metaphysics are verbal nonsense. But at a non-verbal level, they may not be nonsense at all. He is endeavouring to tell us about something that leaves him at a loss for words. One after the other he tries out everything available as public, common property of human minds and finds that it does not give an inkling of this something. It is neither light nor sound nor mass nor motion nor form nor anything else that is. So, rather naturally, he refers to it as what is not. So far as we have any conception of Being, this something is Non-Being. So far as we have any conception of anything, this something is nothing.

Nevertheless we can know it, each of us, directly. When we do we will understand in what way it is useful, perceptible, and a first cause. In the meantime we have only Lao Tzu's word to go on. This is because there is no way to validate objectively the wholly subjective experience. The Tao whose Secret Essences Lao Tzu sees in trance may be Mind-at-Large, or a physical substratum, or a product of self-hypnosis. It may be an intuitive abstraction of the order of the universe (like a sub-verbal Unified Field Theorem); or a hazy glimpse of the Christian God which mystics like St. Teresa have seen in clear focus; or an alteration of consciousness caused by some natural bodily secretion like adrenachrome. We cannot know. The only thing we can know is that neither the materialists who dismiss trance as auto-suggestion nor the enthusiasts who accept it as a valid experience of God can prove their case.

Lao Tzu himself, I think, would not have been troubled by this problem. He considered that each human being inhabits his autonomous private world, and that these many worlds are very different. The point is not hard to grasp. Consider how the world of the Hindu peasant differs from the world of the Point Four technician working at his side; how the mental patient's differs from his guard's; how the Republican's differs from the Democrat's; how your world differs from mine. So many different worlds, in every one of which nothing can exist unless its inhabitant has accepted it! No one else can accept it for him. He may not accept *them,* and if he does, he can understand them only in his own terms. He cannot see with the eyes of another or feel with their feelings or take a word as they mean it. He is the king and the prisoner of his own experience.

This autonomy of consciousness is, I think, the final secret that Lao Tzu had in mind when he urged us to believe the truthful man and the liar. It permits the Sage to have complete respect for his fellow man. In fact, one might go so far as to say that *only* by recognizing the autonomy of the consciousness can he have complete respect for his fellow man, just as *only* thus can he be certain that he deserves theirs in return—though he understands why often he does not get it. That is why the Sage is a person who "has room in him for everything" (16W), who has faith in his own world, but is never going to use a weapon in defense of his faith or in an attack upon anyone else's. He is a peaceful person. He will not be disturbed to find that the Pope is infallible in matters of faith and morals or that Comrade Beria had been working for the Germans since 1917 or, for that matter, that his eccentric neighbour aboard a train thinks he is sitting on a fried egg. Perhaps he is. If so, it is no less real than the one the Sage himself had for breakfast. To find a logical connection between eggs in his own world and eggs in this particular neighbour's may or may not be possible. If it is possible, it is only in his own world that it will necessarily be logical. He will nonetheless be interested to hear his neighbour talk about eggs. He will lend him a handkerchief in case of an accident, though he may sit in a different car the next day.

This attitude may seem more sophistical than sophisticated, and it is undoubtedly one that requires mental agility. To have it means to keep many things in separate compartments, to be capable of inconsistency. Just as the Sage does not tell the lie himself which he accepts as truth from others, so he has one compartment for his own point of view and a separate compartment for the point of view of every man into whose place he must put himself if he is to understand him and feel compassion for him. In this way he is able to pity others in the fear and suffering of death, but regard his own death impersonally. In this way he approves the thug no less than the Jain. If we have such an attitude, the result is courtesy and civil peace. We do not inquire of a man, "Can you prove what you say?" We are interested rather in whether or not he really believes it. And we may have one further question: Is there any part of his belief that is acceptable?

This is the question which we have yet to answer in the case of Lao Tzu. Are any of his beliefs acceptable to us? What would be the consequences of putting them into practice? The answer to *that* question will scarcely brighten the *Tao Te Ching* in our eyes. For I think the consequences of practicing it on a world scale would be a world of lotus eaters—or such, at least, they would seem to the normal American. Can nothing better be salvaged from the *Tao Te Ching*? No, I do not think so. "Lotus-eating" connotes the slipshod, the ignoble, and what we would call spiritual bankruptcy, but, with a few qualifications, the term covers pretty well the way of life that Lao Tzu recommends. Few of us could accept it.

That is a pity, because it has two obvious advantages. In America today competitive life is becoming unbearable — at least it is for some of us, and may be for more of us than are aware of it. Like Sisyphus no one can get his stone to the crest of the hill. Each year's production must be higher than last. If we are a foreman now, we must become a superintendent. If we are Chairman of the Board, we must retire and start a new business. Or if we do not win promotion, still we must strike for higher wages. Our standard of living must always go up. It can never get to the top. If only it could get to the top! If only we did not have to buy a Buick next year because we bought a Pontiac last! To such subconscious protests Lao Tzu answers: You need not.

Lao Tzu turns upside down the pyramid of values and offers us the material for a comedy. Failure becomes success. The common labourer, the swillman, and the tramp turn out to be more successful than the Chairman of the Board. Since there are more common labourers than Chairmen of the Board, this yields a net gain to the success of the community. But the Chairman benefits by the inversion of values. If he accepts Lao Tzu's teaching that it is good to be low, he has something to look forward to again. Conversely, the swillman benefits less than we might think. He is already on his way to being a Sage or he would not be content to be a swillman.

But this is not as comic as it may appear. It is a serious answer to serious problems. Because *te* is independent of social success, Lao Tzu does not *necessarily* accord the unsuccessful man a greater *te* than his successful neighbour. *Probably* he would, since today's success is difficult to achieve except by those aggressive traits which he considers contrary to *te*. Therefore the bank clerk who has never gotten out of the General Settlement Department, the unpublished poet who for some twenty years has had to make his living as a bus boy, the widow who can find nothing better than housework when her friends are earning high wages in factories, the girl who is still at home long after her sisters have married, the man who lives on First Avenue and feels crushed by a walk down Fifth, the racial outcast, the misfit, the pervert, and the recluse — for all these people Lao Tzu has an important message. He does not tell them that they have an immortal soul which an infinitely just God may one day reward with millennial splendour for their present obscurity. Rather, he tells them that they are wise to be obscure; that there is a standard by which here and now they are better than most of the successful people who seem so far above them; that this unbearable stone which they have thought they must push to the top of the hill may be discarded. He urges that they observe the order of life and see the suffering to which aggression and excessive activity have led the men of success. He offers them the comfort of an esoteric discipline which some, at least, are capable of accepting. Thus I think Lao Tzu goes to the core of their pain. He makes it possible for them once more to think well of themselves.

The second advantage to the general acceptance of lotus-eating would be to solve the problem of man's survival. Usually those who discuss this problem conclude that man can survive only if his character is brought up to date with his technology. His character must be improved. Possibly Lao Tzu has a better idea than we do of what improvement means.

For him improvement of character means better suiting man to not fighting wars. A noble man can fight wars: a brave man can fight them: a strong man can fight them. Our ideals of character resemble those by which primitive societies raised their children to be hunters, warriors, and kings. In raising our children to become warriors and kings at school, in the factory, on the political platform, and in the bomber cockpit, we teach them strength and courage. We excite their ambition, giving them—if we can—an indomitable will to get to the top. We show them that they must always be ready to sacrifice themselves or others for the good of the tribe, for a moral principle, or for a difference of opinion. The result is inevitable. They cannot leave one another at peace. Kings will have kingdoms and warriors wars.

Today such an education may be unnecessary for man's survival. Wild animals do not threaten us. Nature delivers more than we need. Lao Tzu was foolish, perhaps, to suggest that his Chinese contemporaries abandon competition in favour of lotus-eating. Their technology would hardly have provided lotus-eaters with food enough—even considering the elimination of the waste that war was bringing to China. But human beings today could still furnish themselves with food and shelter if they became very listless and very weak. No one in the world needs be strong enough now to get food and shelter by plunder. Against whose plundering then—if this were universally recognized—would anyone have to make himself strong?

Lao Tzu tries to tell us, I think, that humanity, if it does perish, must perish for its nobility. To perish for our nobility is a noble thought. Or is it better to be ignoble than extinct? So here we stand, fretted with golden fire, unable to reconcile ourselves to a quieter role on the earth.

What Lao Tzu had in mind, perhaps, was that nations could grow quiet gradually and contagiously. A contagion of quietism could steal across national boundaries that do not yield to propaganda or force. Any human being, even the Eskimo or you or I, could be a carrier of this contagion. In no instance of human contact would we not have an opportunity to pass it on. Like the Black Death, its most effective carrier would be the one who was unrecognized. But it would take a very long time. Those who were first infected would have to be capable of that odd kind of courage which, according to the *Tao Te Ching,* makes it possible to defend oneself without giving offense.

"He whose braveness lies in daring, slays.

He whose braveness lies in not daring [to slay], gives life" (73W).

"Only he that pities is truly able to be brave" (67W).

It is possible to imagine such a quieting of human society, even a conversion to the lotus, but is it very likely to happen? Not from exposure to theoretical knowledge, whether of Taoism or any other philosophy or religion.

Evolution—and I include in this term the development of attitudes as well as physiology—is commonly thought of as the process of survival of the fittest. Fittest for what? Fittest for survival. That bulk and strength do not best fit a species for survival was indicated by the fate of the dinosaurs. That wits and nobility do not best fit a species for survival may soon be indicated by the fate of man—in particular, those men who are noble or clever. Here is an interesting feature of nuclear attack. It begins so suddenly that those who had wits enough to prepare retreats in the country will not be in them; while those who are noble enough to be at their posts in the factory or airfield will be at their posts; and the majority of survivors will be peasants and savages: an unforgettable instance of natural selection, no less than of Tao.

Some events—indeed, all events—give lessons to the species they overtake. The glacier gave the rabbit a lesson in the need for changing the colour of its fur in winter. Similarly, the next war may give mankind a lesson in the need for being negative. Mankind may take the low road whether it wants to or not.

It is reasonable to suppose that *some* clever people will survive the next war. From a Taoist point of view, therefore, the only hope can be that all other surviving human beings will be so confirmed in their stupidity that cleverness cannot lead them astray. Dolts, bumpkins, and savages, they will dully and persistently refuse to rebuild what they have seen to be a self-destructive way of life. They may even—though it is a dubious hope—teach the clever people to be as stupid as themselves. Then at last Chapter 80 of the *Tao Te Ching* will be realized. Men will "live in small settlements, refusing to use machinery even though it requires ten times, or a hundred times, less labour. They will value their lives and not go far away. There will still be boats and cars, but no one will ride in them. There will still be small arms, but no one will drill with them. They will have no use for any form of writing save knotted cords, will find sweet savour in their food, beauty in their clothes, peace in their homes, and pleasure in their rustic tasks. The next settlement may be so near at hand that they can hear the cocks crowing in it, the dogs barking, but the people will grow old and die without ever having been there."

Appendix I

The Authorship of the *Tao Te Ching*

Many eminent Sinologists have expressed their views on the question of who wrote the *Tao Te Ching* and when. To me the "who" seems more important than the "when" because it raises a dangerous issue: collective authorship. Fung Yu-lan, for instance, maintains that the *Tao Te Ching* is not the work of one man, but a collection of Taoist sayings. If that is all it is, we can no longer expect it to make coherent sense. We cannot decide the meaning of this or that doubtful passage by comparing it with passages that are clear. If two passages may have been written by different authors at different times, one has no necessary bearing on the other. The *Tao Te Ching* then becomes not so much a puzzle as a hodgepodge. Because the book seems to me to expound a coherent system of thought, I resist this idea. I would agree with what Mr. Waley said when he was fresh from translating it: that its author adapts many conflicting elements "subtly weaving them together into a pattern perfectly consistent and harmonious." [1] To support this thesis I would like to offer a few comments.

If the *Tao Te Ching* is a compilation—a mere anthology—how is it that it refers to no persons, places, or events? There is not a proper name in the whole book, which cannot be said, so far as I know, of any other book in early Taoist literature. If some one compiled five thousand words of Taoist maxims at random, surely a few, at least, would have contained proper names, whether of the persons who first said them or of the persons who exemplified their principles. Hence I believe that the *Tao Te Ching* cannot in any case be a *random* compilation. The anthologist must either have excluded any maxims that contained a proper name or edited all proper names from maxims that

[1] *The Way and Its Power*, p. 97. Mr. Waley now inclines to the view of Fung Yu-lan.

he did include. Both alternatives suggest a fixed determination to preserve his anonymity, to deprive the book of "provenance." But would such determination, which might be felt by an author, be felt by an anthologist? A Taoist author might well believe that his book would be more successful if no one knew who wrote it—if, as Lao Tzu says, he did not "take credit for it." A Taoist anthologist, on the other hand, would be likelier to expect the greatest success for his book if it included the names of all the ancient worthies with whom its maxims were connected.

Even if we accept the idea of an anthologist, we are faced with a problem. Why would he limit his editing to the deletion of proper names—a rather peculiar limitation? Why would he not go on to edit out everything that did not conform with his concept of Taoism? And in that case, he was not an anthologist, but an author. One does not need new bricks to build a new house.

Another version of the "collective authorship" theory is that the *Tao Te Ching* was the product of a long process of accretion. This seems to me even less satisfactory. It presupposes an initial textual core to which material was gradually added, and this core must have been large enough so that its lack of proper names struck all those who added to it. Then we are back where we started: who wrote the core? Bamboo strips do not spontaneously assemble themselves into books, and certainly not into books that rhyme like the *Tao Te Ching*.[2]

Finally I cannot help feeling that Chapter 70 is best taken at face value. In it the first person singular is repeatedly used; the writer, whoever he was, protests that a system underlies his sayings, but that people do not recognize the fact. Is it not simpler to suppose that these "sayings" are the book we hold in our hand?

Therefore, though the text is doubtless corrupt and though there are doubtless interpolations, I think that the absence of proper names is evidence that it bears the impress of a single mind—and that is all that matters. Who he was has no bearing on the value of his book.[3]

As to the question of when he wrote it, I do not feel qualified to

---

[2] See Bernhard Karlgren, *The Poetical Parts of the Lao Tsï.*

[3] My own guess is that he was a well-educated ex-official who had seen both court life and the misery of the people; who had participated in military campaigns; who in his middle years was laughed out of government service because of the ideas he had begun to develop on Tao and Te; who retired to a contemplative life during which he wrote the *Tao Te Ching.*

express an opinion. But I do question the reasoning with which some Sinologists have approached the problem. Fung Yu-lan, for instance, says: "Prior to Confucius there was no one writing in a private, non-official capacity; hence the *Lao Tzu* cannot be earlier than the *Lun Yü.*" This amounts to saying that, since the *Tao Te Ching* was written after Confucius, no one prior to Confucius was writing in a private capacity, and hence the *Tao Te Ching* was written after Confucius.

In the opinion of some Sinologists, a good approach to the problem of dating is by the analysis of ideas. If we know what ideas were current at each stage in the development of Chinese thought, we can assign any work to its proper stage by finding where its ideas best fit. In particular, we can find "the opponents with which it deals," as Mr. Waley puts it. Lao Tzu, that is, would not attack Confucian morality unless Confucian morality were already in existence.

This approach is circular. If we were sure when the *Tao Te Ching* was written, we could be much surer about its ideas. If we were sure about its ideas, we could be much surer when it was written. I have the impression that there has been a readiness to interpret the book in terms of the ideas current in a certain period and then to show from its ideas that this was the period to which it belongs.

Then there is the method of dating by quotations. Chapter 6 of the *Tao Te Ching,* for example, quotes from the lost *Book of the Yellow Emperor,* if we take Lieh Tzu's word for it. This should prove that the *Tao Te Ching* came after the *Book of the Yellow Emperor.* On the other hand, it is possible that the *Book of the Yellow Emperor* was quoting from the *Tao Te Ching,* or that both were making use of a common stock of aphorisms. The laymen cannot help noting that in attacking these problems each Sinologist tends to reject as interpolations the passages that conflict with his own thesis.

The only method of dating that I personally find convincing is that based on comparison of grammar and rhyme structure with works of known date. But even here I think we are naïve if we assume that the ancient Chinese author might not have been master of several styles, varying from the colloquial to the archaic, entirely aside from the fact that in this case the author tells us (in Chapter 42) that he has incorporated quotations from diverse sources. Using the reasoning that has been applied to the *Tao Te Ching* we would have to conclude that *The Waste Land,* for instance, was also a "collection."

Is there a way to by-pass the circularity of dating methods? Possibly one way would be to consider the *Tao Te Ching* in a vacuum, without reference to works that may or may not be contemporary, as though it were the only Chinese book we had. Our task would then be to make an interpretation that would be consistent with itself. This assumes, of course, that our concept of consistency is the same as Lao Tzu's. But, making that assumption, the result would be a scheme of ideas not dependent on secondary assumptions about date and text. In a modest way, that is what I have tried to do. It is the reason that in Part II, I avoided comparison with other thinkers of the Chou Dynasty.

The fact is, however, that the date and authorship of the *Tao Te Ching,* as well as its ideas, will remain problematical. One reason for this is that the book presents two classes of problems under one cover. The first class is philological; the second is philosophical. To solve the first requires a thorough grounding in Chinese studies, which make the most crushing demands on memory and patience. If there is any *métier* designed to smother the imagination, it is Sinology. Yet imagination above all else is what is required to solve the second class of problems, the philosophical. Therefore the man who copes successfully with the *Tao Te Ching* will have to be both a formidable pedant and an utterly free spirit. Where is there such a man?

Appendix II

CHRONOLOGICAL CHART

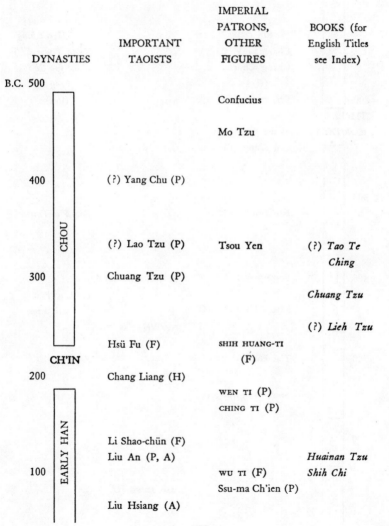

DYNASTIES	IMPORTANT TAOISTS	IMPERIAL PATRONS, OTHER FIGURES	BOOKS (for English Titles see Index)
B.C. 500			
		Confucius	
		Mo Tzu	
400	(?) Yang Chu (P)		
CHOU	(?) Lao Tzu (P)	Tsou Yen	(?) *Tao Te Ching*
300	Chuang Tzu (P)		*Chuang Tzu*
			(?) *Lieh Tzu*
	Hsü Fu (F)	SHIH HUANG-TI (F)	
CH'IN			
200	Chang Liang (H)	WEN TI (P)	
		CHING TI (P)	
EARLY HAN	Li Shao-chün (F)		
	Liu An (P, A)		*Huainan Tzu*
100		WU TI (F)	*Shih Chi*
		Ssu-ma Ch'ien (P)	
	Liu Hsiang (A)		

183

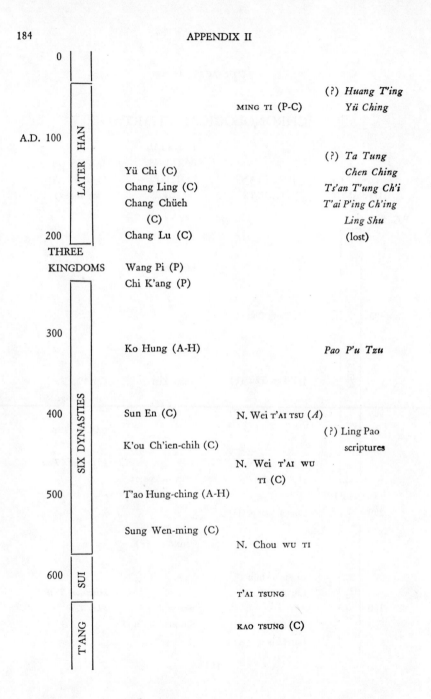

0

A.D. 100

LATER HAN

200
THREE
KINGDOMS

300

SIX DYNASTIES

400

500

600

SUI

T'ANG

MING TI (P-C)

Yü Chi (C)
Chang Ling (C)
Chang Chüeh
       (C)
Chang Lu (C)

Wang Pi (P)
Chi K'ang (P)

Ko Hung (A-H)

Sun En (C)

K'ou Ch'ien-chih (C)

T'ao Hung-ching (A-H)

Sung Wen-ming (C)

N. Wei T'AI TSU (A)

N. Wei T'AI WU
       TI (C)

N. Chou WU TI

T'AI TSUNG

KAO TSUNG (C)

(?) *Huang T'ing*
    Yü Ching

(?) *Ta Tung*
    Chen Ching
Ts'an T'ung Ch'i
T'ai P'ing Ch'ing
    Ling Shu
    (lost)

Pao P'u Tzu

(?) Ling Pao
    scriptures

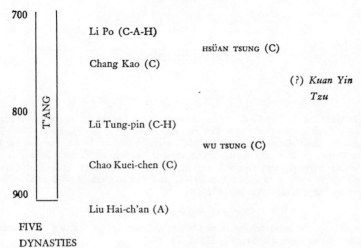

700

Li Po (C-A-H)

HSÜAN TSUNG (C)

Chang Kao (C)

(?) *Kuan Yin Tzu*

T'ANG

800

Lü Tung-pin (C-H)

WU TSUNG (C)

Chao Kuei-chen (C)

900

Liu Hai-ch'an (A)

FIVE
DYNASTIES

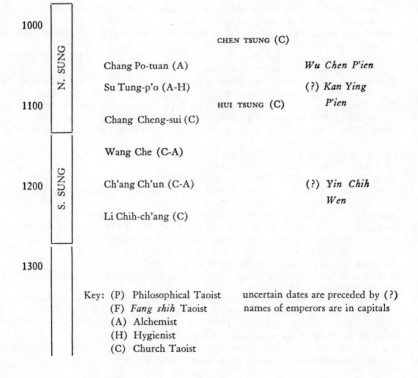

1000

CHEN TSUNG (C)

N. SUNG

Chang Po-tuan (A)   *Wu Chen P'ien*

Su Tung-p'o (A-H)   (?) *Kan Ying*

1100   HUI TSUNG (C)   *P'ien*

Chang Cheng-sui (C)

Wang Che (C-A)

S. SUNG

1200   Ch'ang Ch'un (C-A)   (?) *Yin Chih Wen*

Li Chih-ch'ang (C)

1300

Key: (P) Philosophical Taoist   uncertain dates are preceded by (?)
     (F) *Fang shih* Taoist   names of emperors are in capitals
     (A) Alchemist
     (H) Hygienist
     (C) Church Taoist

Bibliography

For translations of the *Tao Te Ching* the reader is referred to the list on page 4 ff. Translations of *Chuang Tzu* and *Lieh Tzu* are mentioned on page 91, footnote 4. The bibliography that follows does not include general reference books, material in Far Eastern languages, or works with only an indirect bearing on Taoism. I have drawn considerable material from two volumes in the second category: *History of Chinese Taoism*, by Fu Ch'in-chia (Shanghai, 1937); and *Fundamental Studies in the Taoist Religion* by Fukui Kojun (Tokyo, 1952).

Works in Western Languages

Barnes, W. H., "Possible references to Chinese alchemy in the 4th and 3rd centuries B.C.," *China Journal* (Shanghai, 1935), 75-79.

Chan, W. T. *Religious Trends in Modern China* (New York, 1953).

Chao Yün-ts'ung and Davis, T. L., "Chang Po-tuan of T'ien T'ai, His *Wu Chen P'ien*, Essay on the Understanding of the Truth," *Proceedings of the American Academy of Arts and Sciences*, Vol. 73, No. 5 (July, 1939).

Chao Yün-ts'ung and Davis, T. L., "Four Hundred Word Chin Tan of Chang Po-tuan, etc." *ibid.*, Vol. 73, No. 13 (July, 1940).

Chavannes, Eduard, *Les Mémoires Historiques de Se-ma Ts'ien* (Paris, 1895-1905), 5 vols. (a translation of the *Shih Chi*).

Ch'en Kuo-fu, and Davis, T. L., "Inner chapters of *Pao P'u Tzu*," *Proceedings of the American Academy of Arts and Sciences*, Vol. 74, No. 10 (December 1941).

Ch'en Kuo-fu and Davis, T. L., "Shang Yang Tzu, Taoist writer and commentator on alchemy," *Harvard Journal of Asiatic Studies*, VIII (1942-3), p. 126.

Ch'en, K. S., "Buddhist-Taoist mixtures in the *Pa Shih I Hua T'u*," *Harvard Journal of Asiatic Studies*, 9:1 (1945-47).

Chin P'ing Mei, see Egerton, Clement.

Creel, H. G., *Chinese Thought* (Chicago, 1953).

Creel, H. G., *The Birth of China* (New York, 1937).

Creel, H. G., "What is Taoism?" *Journal of the American Oriental Society*, Vol. 76, No. 3, July-Sept., 1956.

Davis, T. L., "Chinese beginnings of alchemy," *Endeavour* (October, 1943).

De Groot, J. J. M., "On the origin of the Taoist church," *Third International Congress for the History of Religion, Transactions* of (Oxford, 1908), 1:138.

De Groot, J. J. M., *The Religious System of China* (Leiden, 1892-1910).

De Groot, J. J. M., *Religion in China* (New York, 1912).

Dore, Henri, *Researches into Chinese Superstitions* (Shanghai, 1931; especially Volume IX translated by D. J. Finn).

Dubs, H. H., "The date and circumstances of Lao-dz," *Journal of American Oriental Society*, 61:215-221 (1941); 62:8-13, 300-304 (1942); 64:24-27 (1944).

Dubs, H. H., "Taoism," in McNair, H. F., ed., *China* (Chicago, 1946).

Dubs, H. H., "Beginnings of alchemy," *Isis*, vol. 38 (November, 1947).

Dubs, H. H., *History of the Former Han Dynasty by Pan Ku, A Critical Translation with Annotations* (Baltimore, 1938, 1944, 1955), 3 vols.

Duyvendak, J. J. L., tr., *The Book of Lord Shang* (London, 1928).

Egerton, Clement, tr., *The Golden Lotus* (London, 1939).

Eichhorn, W., "Zur chinesischen Kulturgeschichte des 3. und 4. Jahrhunderts," *Zeitschrift der Deutschen Morgenlandischen Gesellschaft,* 91.2:451-483 (1937).

Eliade, Mircea, *Le chamanisme et les techniques archaïques de l'extase* (Paris, 1951).

Erkes, Eduard, *Ho-Shang-Kung's Commentary on Lao Tse* (Ascona, 1950).

Feifel, Eugene, tr., *Pao P'u Tzu*, in *Monumenta Serica,* 6:113-121 (1941); 9:1-33 (1944); 11:1-32 (1946).

Fung Yu-lan, *Short History of Chinese Philosophy* (New York, 1948).

Fung Yu-lan, *History of Chinese Philosophy* (Princeton, 1937, 1953).

Giles, Lionel, *A Gallery of Chinese Immortals* (London, 1948).

Granet, Marcel, "Remarques sur le Taoisme ancien," *Asia Major,* 2:146-151.

Van Gulik, R. H., *Hsi K'ang and his Poetical Essay on the Lute* (Tokyo, 1941).

Hodous, L., "Taoism," in E. J. Jurji, ed., *Great Religions of the World* (Princeton, 1946).

Hu Shih, "A Criticism of some recent methods used in dating Lao Tzu," *Harvard Journal of Asiatic Studies,* 3:373-397 (1937).

James, William, *The Varieties of Religious Experience* (New York, 1902).

Johnson, Obed S., *A Study of Chinese Alchemy* (Shanghai, 1928).

Legge, James, *The Religions of China* (New York, 1881).

Legge, James, *The Texts of Taoism* (London, 1891).

Levy, Howard S., "Yellow Turban Religion and Rebellion at the end of the Han," *Journal of the American Oriental Society,* 76:4 (October-December, 1956).

Li Ch'iao-p'ing, *Chemical Arts of Old China* (Easton, Pennsylvania, 1948).

Lin Yutang, *The Gay Genius* (New York, 1947).

Lyall, Leonard E., tr., "Yang Chu chapter of *Lieh Tzu,*" *Tien-hsia Monthly* (September, 1939).

Maspero, Henri, *La Chine Antique* (Paris, 1927).

Maspero, Henri, "The mythology of modern China," in J. Hackin *et al., Asiatique Mythology* (London, 1932), 252-384.

Maspero, Henri, "James R. Ware, 'The *Wei shu* and *Sui shu* on Taoism,'" *Journal Asiatique,* 226:313-317 (1935).

Maspero, Henri, "Les procédés de nourir le principe vital dans la religion Taoiste ancienne," *Journal Asiatique,* 229:177-252, 353-430 (1937).

Maspero, Henri, *Le taoisme* (Paris, 1950).

Masumi, Chikashige, *Alchemy and Other Chemical Achievements of the Ancient Orient* (Tokyo, 1936).

Morgan, Evan, tr., *Tao the Great Luminant; Essays from the* 'Huai Nan Tzu' (Shanghai, 1933).

Mukerjee, R., *The Theory and Art of Mysticism.*

Needham, Joseph, *Science and Civilisation in China,* Vol. II (Cambridge, 1956).

Northrop, F. C. S., *The Meeting of East and West* (New York, 1949).

Pao P'u Tzu, see Ch'en Kuo-fu; Wu, L. C.

Porter, L. C., *Aids to the Study of Chinese Philosophy* (Peiping, 1934).

Reischauer, E. O., *Ennin's Travels in T'ang China* (New York, 1955).

Suzuki, D. T., *Brief History of Early Chinese Philosophy* (1913).

Suzuki, D. T. and Carus, P., *Yin Chih Wen, The Tract of the Quiet Way* (Chicago, 1906).

Ts'an T'ung Ch'i, see Wu, L. C.

Waley, Arthur, "Notes on Chinese alchemy," *Bulletin of the School of Oriental Studies* (1930).

Waley, Arthur, *The Travels of an Alchemist* (London, 1931).

Waley, Arthur, *The Way and Its Power* (London, 1934).

Waley, Arthur, *Three Ways of Thought in Ancient China* (London, 1939).

Waley, Arthur, *The Life and Times of Po Chü-i* (London, 1949).

Waley, Arthur, *The Poetry and Career of Li Po* (London, 1950).

Waley, Arthur, *The Real Tripitika* (London, 1952).

Waley, Arthur, *The Nine Songs* (London, 1955).

Wang, C. H. and Spooner, R. C., "The Divine Nine Turn Tan Sha Method: A Chinese Alchemical Recipe," *Isis*, February, 1948.

Wang Ch'ih-min and Wu Lien-te, *History of Chinese Medicine* (Shanghai, 1936).

Ware, James R., "The *Wei shu* and *Sui shu* on Taoism," *Journal of the American Oriental Society*, vol. 53 (September, 1933), and vol. 54 (September, 1934).

Werner, E. T. C., *Dictionary of Chinese Mythology* (Shanghai, 1932).

Wieger, Leon, *Le Taoisme* (Paris (?), 1911), Vols. I and II.

Wieger, Leon, *A History of the Religious Beliefs and Philosophical Opinions in China* (Shanghai, 1927).

Wilhelm, Richard, tr., *The Secret of the Golden Flower* (London, 1931).

Wu, Lu-ch'iang, and Davis, T. L., "Chinese Alchemy," *Scientific Monthly* (September, 1930).

Wu, L. C., and Davis, T. L., translation of *Ts'an-t'ung-ch'i*, in *Isis*, vol. 18 (October, 1932).

Wu, L. C., and Davis, T. L., translation of Ko Hung's biography in *Lieh-hsien-chuan*, in *Journal of Chemical Education* (1934), 517-520.

Wu, L. C., and Davis, T. L., "Ko Hung on the Gold Medicine and on the Yellow and White," *Proceedings of the American Academy of Arts and Sciences*, vol. 70, no. 6 (December, 1935).

Yetts, Maj. W. Percival, "Taoist tales," *New China Review* (March, 1919).

Index

$$
\begin{array}{r}
7 \\
490 \\
\times\ 18 \\
\hline
39\ 20 \\
49\ 0 \\
\hline
88\ 2\ 0
\end{array}
$$

18
4